4⁰⁰
PS
3114

D0966678

ALSO BY DOUGLAS E. SCHOEN

What Makes You Tick?: How Successful People Do It—and What You Can Learn from Them (with Michael J. Berland)

Threat Closer to Home: Hugo Chávez and the War Against America (with Michael Rowan)

Declaring Independence:
The Beginning of the End of the Two-Party System

The Power of the Vote: Electing Presidents, Overthrowing Dictators, and Promoting Democracy Around the World

On the Campaign Trail:
The Long Road of Presidential Politics, 1860–2004
(Editor)

Pat: A Biography of Daniel Patrick Moynihan

Enoch Powell and the Powellites

THE POLITICAL FIX

THE
POLITICAL
★ ★ ★
FIX

**CHANGING THE GAME OF AMERICAN DEMOCRACY,
FROM THE GRASS ROOTS TO THE WHITE HOUSE**

DOUGLAS E. SCHOEN

TIMES BOOKS   HENRY HOLT AND COMPANY   NEW YORK

Times Books
Henry Holt and Company, LLC
Publishers since 1866
175 Fifth Avenue
New York, New York 10010
www.henryholt.com

Henry Holt® is a registered trademark of
Henry Holt and Company, LLC.

Copyright © 2010 by Douglas E. Schoen
All rights reserved.
Distributed in Canada by H. B. Fenn and Company Ltd.

Library of Congress Cataloging-in-Publication Data

Schoen, Douglas E., 1953–
    The political fix : changing the game of American democracy, from the grass roots to the
White House / Douglas E. Schoen.
        p. cm.
    Includes bibliographical references and index.
    ISBN 978-0-8050-8973-8
    1. Presidents—United States—Election—2008.   2. Elections—United States.   3. United
States, Congress—Reform.   4. Justice, Administration of—Political aspects—United
States.   5. Political participation—United States.   6. United States—Politics and
government—2009.   I. Title.
    JK5262008 S38 2010
    324.973'0931—dc22   2009021113

Henry Holt books are available for special promotions and premiums.
For details contact: Director, Special Markets.

First Edition 2010

Designed by Kelly S. Too

Printed in the United States of America
10   9   8   7   6   5   4   3   2   1

To my dear friend who got me started down this path,
R. W. Johnson, a scholar and political activist in his own right

CONTENTS

THE POLITICAL FIX

INTRODUCTION

A Simple Question and a Straight Answer

> A cocktail of political and technological trends have converged in the last decade that are making it possible for the idiots of all political stripes to overwhelm and paralyze the genius of our system.
>
> —THOMAS FRIEDMAN, 2009

Call it an occupational hazard. After I spent thirty years working at the highest levels of American politics, my clients aren't the only ones who ask for my opinion on current events. Friends, family, my barber, the guy behind the counter at the corner store—after Barack Obama's historic victory in 2008, everyone was asking: "Doug, what do you think? Are politics in America finally going to change?"

This book is my answer.

On election night in Chicago's Grant Park, the president-elect declared, "Tonight, change has come to America." In the midst of two wars and the worst recession in at least a quarter century, America had broken historic barriers and elected the nation's first African American president. Barack Obama is transformation incarnate—racially, generationally, geographically, and demographically—and no one can deny the historic change that his victory represents.

Of course, no one can deny that Obama forever changed the way campaigns are run and organized, as well. His revolutionary use of the Internet and social networking tools were the foundation of a people-powered movement that coalesced around him. Obama's online effort empowered small donors and average voices in a way never before seen—and it neutralized the power of special interests in a way that recent efforts at campaign finance reform had not. Obama's experience as a community organizer served him and his vast staff well, particularly in deploying an astounding five million volunteers that organized one thousand phone bank events in the weeks leading up to the election. In all, it was a groundbreaking campaign effort that enabled Obama to best two of the biggest brand names in American politics—Hillary Clinton and John McCain.

There's no doubt about it: the Obama campaign was innovative and inspiring. It broke conventional wisdom, and it broke new ground. It altered history, and it altered the way campaigns are conducted. But did 2008 fundamentally change our politics?

The answer is, unfortunately, no.

It would be a serious mistake to declare the days of dysfunction over and the political system fixed as a result of Obama's election. As encouraging as the 2008 campaign was, it did not change several long-standing political realities.

First, despite the media hype and expectations of record voter participation in response to Obama's historic candidacy, turnout in 2008 was not much improved from years past. In fact, close to 50 percent of eligible voters stayed home, and some 4.1 million fewer Republicans voted in 2008 than in 2004. Obama's victory was won by modest improvement in the Democratic share of the vote, a slight uptick in new voter registrations, and a small increase in the number of African Americans who came to the polls. In fact, turnout increased three times as much between 2000 and 2004 (17 million votes) than between 2004 and 2008 (6.5 million votes). If anything, given America's growing population, the 2008 election cycle showed a net contraction in participatory democracy.

Second, as in the past, issues took a backseat for most of the campaign. We—the pundits, the politicians, and the voters—spent more time talking about 1960s radical Bill Ayers than any Senate bill Obama sponsored. And there is no getting around the fact that much of the energy in this campaign was driven by personalities instead of policies, and in no small part by the broad, bipartisan animus toward George W. Bush. Indeed, the Obama campaign team played this to its advantage,

talking as much about Obama's style of leadership as about the substance of
his policies. In contrast to Hillary Clinton, whose campaign was plagued
by leaks and internal fighting, Obama's effort was marked by military-
style efficiency when it came to staying on message. Substance was important to the campaign, to be sure, yet it mattered less than appearance.
The campaign weighed every statement and strategy first and foremost
for its "optics"—how it would be seen by the American electorate.

Third, press coverage in 2008 was abysmal, as in elections past. As
Obama's communications director and White House press secretary,
Robert Gibbs, noted with dismay after the campaign, "We were watching hundreds of thousands of people lose their jobs, and [the press was]
debating the meaning of the phrase 'lipstick on a pig.'"[1] The troubling
press coverage during the run-up to Election Day—or lack thereof, to
be precise—predictably continued after the election. The precedent had
been set. In a story that lingered for weeks, the press slobbered over each
detail of the Obama camp's contacts with disgraced Illinois governor
Rod Blagojevich—even while federal prosecutors had repeatedly stated
that no one in the incoming administration was in any way a target of their
investigation. Having the word "scandal" attached to a story about the
president-elect was enough to propel even the most mundane information to the status of headline news. Suffice it to say, journalists let down
the American people in 2008.

Finally, in the end, the 2008 campaign came down to what it always
does: money. Obama raised a record-breaking $650 million in contribu-
tions from more than three million people, many of whom donated
online. He spent an astounding $293 million on television ads between
January 1, 2007, and October 29, 2008, according to TNS Media Intelligence. Meanwhile, Republican contender John McCain spent $132
million, less than half that figure. With the dust now settled, it's clear
that 2008 wasn't the beginning of a new era in politics; in fact, it proved
a political axiom imparted to me more than two decades ago by Senator
Richard Shelby: "Doug, it is just money. It's all money. Everything is
money down here. You have to grow up, wake up, and learn that it is all
about money. That is my life, that's the life of this institution, and if you
do not figure that out, I don't care how good your polling is, it won't
matter." When you look at the numbers—something I've built a career

on as a political pollster—the 2008 election wasn't the drastic departure from previous elections that we had hoped. In fact, it wasn't much of an improvement at all. In reality, it was a relatively average election, which happened to produce a historic outcome.

It's going to take much more than one historic night and a phenomenal campaign to fundamentally alter our politics for the better. Besides, the issues we face go far beyond our presidential elections. From Congress to the courts and beyond, our system has degraded at each and every level. Change may have come to America in 2008—but not the change we need to permanently and meaningfully transform America's political system.

On election night in 2008, I was at Gracie Mansion in New York City with Mayor Michael Bloomberg, a friend and client whom I was proud to help elect in 2001. As much of the nation was celebrating a breakthrough they never thought they would live to see, the mayor and I talked about the issues the new president would face—many of which Bloomberg himself already had on his plate. The financial crisis. Skyrocketing unemployment. The budget shortfall faced by the nation's largest city, and that of cities and states across the nation. There was a certain wistfulness on the mayor's face. He was proud of Barack Obama's election and what it meant for America. But he was clearly concerned about the elephant in the room. *What next?*

The political professional in me could not help but feel a flash of déjà vu as I talked that night with Mayor Bloomberg—who, a pragmatist to his core, left the Republican Party to become an independent in June 2007. Sixteen years before Obama's remarkable victory, America chose another young, brilliant, change-promising figure to lead the country. Bill Clinton promised a "third way" that would transcend the tired, brain-dead partisan debates of the past generation. He called for a new commitment to national service and cooperative governance. His innovative campaign manifesto was "Putting People First," and it included a bold vision for reinventing the federal government from top to bottom. Clinton was so right for the transformational part, in fact, that he actually hailed from a town called Hope.

Then he got to Washington. And by the time he was done, the president who had hoped to construct a new politics had almost been wholly consumed—not to mention constitutionally convicted—by the old broken system he and many others were trying to remake.

Don't get me wrong. Bill Clinton, who was a client of mine, was an ambitious political animal with serious personal limitations. But he came to the White House genuinely intent on doing things differently. He meant to bring a new kind of politics to Washington. And he did—but not the kind he intended.

In short order, the permanent campaign took off and the poisonous partisanship that fueled it exploded to exponentially new levels. Congress deteriorated into the world's greatest dithering body, gridlocked by petty disputes and hocked to special interest groups. The chase for money got so crazed that presidential fund-raisers were being held in Buddhist temples.

The mess was hardly limited to the two ends of Pennsylvania Avenue. The new twenty-four-hour news cycle grew fixated with feeding the beast instead of informing citizens, sowing conflict and selling manufactured and trivialized scandals whenever possible. Independent prosecutors, whirling dervishes of partisanship, were all too happy to perform to the media's new tune, turning the already overpoliticized judicial system into a regular extension of the gotcha game that came to dominate Capitol Hill.

I had a front-row seat for the dysfunction derby of those days. After two decades of working as a pollster and political consultant in New York, I spent most of the Clinton presidency as a senior adviser inside the White House. As I look back, it was somewhat miraculous we were able to get as much done as we did—reforming welfare, passing NAFTA, and putting one hundred thousand new cops on the street. But those accomplishments stand out as exceptions and don't account for the countless opportunities we lost to meet big challenges.

Shortly after the White House hired me in 1995, I found myself in the Oval Office with President Clinton. You could read his deep frustration in the lines on his face, and he told me about the difficulties of getting anything done in what had become an unbearably partisan Washington. He had already endured a showdown with his own party over an economic stimulus package, the implosion of his signature plan for national health care, and disastrous midterm elections that gave birth to the Gingrich era in Congress. Here was the most powerful man in the world—a man who was deeply committed to the issues on which he had campaigned—yet his hands were tied by the politics as usual that he had hoped to change.

What I came to appreciate during this time, in a way I could not from the outside, was that the forces corrupting and corroding our politics went far deeper than any one group of individuals, administration, or party. The problem then wasn't Bill Clinton or the Speaker of the House Newt Gingrich. It was everyone and no one. It was an endemic breakdown.

Indeed, I saw a lot of smart people of goodwill on both sides who got sucked into a sick system and ended up doing things they could have never even contemplated before entering this arena. This helps explain, at least in part, why the change in party control of the White House in 2000, then of Congress in 2002 and 2006, did nothing to change the perverse culture of Washington. Instead, the place has spiraled even further out of control.

Not even the trauma of 9/11 and the unifying reflex it triggered could overcome the powerful partisan pressures that were pulling the country further and further apart. The relations between Congress and the White House and between the parties got even nastier. The Republicans questioned their critics' patriotism. Democrats openly called the president a liar—and some dared attack him as a murderer. And those accusations seemed downright friendly compared to the vitriol that was spewed and spread on the proliferating political blogs on the Internet.

After the Clinton-Gingrich cold war entered a phase of détente, Congress—under the leadership of both parties—continued to run on influence peddling, favor trading, and special interest sellouts. Tom DeLay. Randy "Duke" Cunningham. Jack Abramoff. The corruption reached into the highest levels of the Republican leadership that controlled Capitol Hill. And the partisanship reached new lows. Even John McCain, the great bipartisan crusader for reform, succumbed to the partisan vortex swirling around Washington. Bowing to pressure from lobbyists and hacks, in 2008 McCain was persuaded not to choose his longtime friend and ally Joe Lieberman as his running mate. Instead, he picked the little-known Alaska governor Sarah Palin. An archconservative, Palin helped McCain secure the right-wing base of his party, but he also forfeited his maverick mantle—and many of his deeply held principles—in selecting a predictable conservative like Palin.

But Democrats hardly had clean hands. Congressional Democrats under the leadership of Senate majority leader Harry Reid and Speaker of the House Nancy Pelosi largely failed in the mission that the American people empowered them to accomplish—to remake Congress and the way it does business. Since regaining Congress in 2006 in an ethics-driven voter backlash against the GOP, they have done little to end the gridlock; their earmark reforms have been halfhearted and have largely preserved the age-old tradition of pork barrel spending; and they were fully complicit in enabling the underregulated, overlobbied mortgage industry, whose meltdown precipitated a breathtaking recession. As 2008 came to a close, like that of the Bush administration, Congress's approval rating was among the worst in American history.

Probably the most confidence-crushing low point of the Bush years, though, was the total politicization of the Justice Department. U.S. attorneys fired for not prosecuting partisan opponents. Career government lawyers illegally screened out for their views on abortion and other ideological litmus tests that had nothing to do with their jobs. An attorney general who covered up his underlings' wrongdoing instead of holding them accountable.

Little of substance was accomplished, other than the initiation of one of the most politically destructive wars in America's history and the proliferation of the biggest budget deficit since the Union was founded. At the end of the day, a man of faith who had campaigned on restoring honor and dignity to the White House left office as arguably the most despised and divisive American president ever.

This is the context I was considering at Gracie Mansion on election night. And the obvious parallel between Clinton and Obama raised the questions: Was Barack Obama destined to meet the same fate as his equally promising predecessor? Could he actually and substantially change the game of Washington? Or would the immovable object trump the seemingly irresistible force of Obamamania?

As I've thought about the possible answers, they have me more worried than hopeful as we look at this new era of American politics, because the problems with the American electoral system are not just endemic—they are *structural*. No amount of hope or frustration, and no one leader, is capable of making them disappear. Change is going to take hold and last only if we come together around structural solutions— solutions that transcend a single person and a single party and involve the entire American public and its politics.

So there is danger as well as promise in Obama's presidency: that is, the danger of complacency. Of assuming that Obama's different style and tone of leadership and his genuine commitment to bipartisanship are enough to overcome and dissipate the destructive forces that consumed the last two administrations and the productivity of our national government.

Let's assume for the sake of argument that, in a best-case scenario, Obama lives up to the high expectations he has engendered. That he consistently reaches across the aisle and finds common ground on big issues. That he limits the influence of special interest lobbyists. That he appoints Justice Department officials and judges who are committed to restoring the independence of our judicial system. Despite these potentially (and realistically) positive changes, what happens when he leaves office? Can we expect the next administration will govern in the same way? Can we expect the news media to voluntarily change their ways and refocus on serving the public interest? Can we honestly trust good intentions to prevent the old divisions and powerful pressures from returning?

Even if Obama brings about the change we need, will it be change that lasts?

I highly doubt it. And that's why I believe that charging each branch of government—and of the parts of the political system that are outside the government—to identify and address its dysfunctions is more important than ever. Obama opened a door to new possibilities in our politics. But I am afraid it will slam shut in America's face, and we will lose a once-in-a-lifetime opportunity to truly change the way Washington works, unless we focus on making the permanent, systemic fixes that will save our politics tomorrow.

Which brings me to the real question I wrote this book to answer: Can we fix the American political system? I believe the answer is yes. But only if we have the resolve to buck the powerful minority that has a vested interest in maintaining the status quo. Only if we enact straightforward changes to restore responsiveness and openness in our politics and government. And only if those changes eschew ideology and partisanship and embrace pragmatism and transparency. That is the spirit in which I wrote this book—as a practical guide for reformers, from the grass roots to, I hope, the White House, at a historic opportunity for change. And as such, this volume is a departure from other works that have preceded it.

As a trained political scientist and a practitioner, I've always felt that there was a huge gap between what academics write and what actually happens in the real world. Most of the politicians I've advised are either blissfully unaware of the academic literature or dismiss it out of hand as irrelevant to their daily lives and their life experiences.

This book is different. It is based directly on more than thirty years of participation in and observation of our system, and it is an insider's take on how we can change that system to make a real-world difference. The ideas themselves come from my own experience, my own observations, and what I have concluded can actually improve how America really works. It is also based on a series of conversations with practitioners at the highest levels and reflects their own practical judgments as well.

My concern here is about getting things done, not pointing fingers and laying blame. I'm not interested in partisan bloviating. I'm interested in fixing our politics. And to that end, I'm equally critical of Democrats and Republicans. But my criticism is purposeful, not retributive or doctrinaire. There are lessons to be learned from mistakes that have been made in the past by partisans of every stripe, and these lessons inform the many structural solutions I present throughout the book.

Finally, a note on the architecture of this book, which is also different from others of this sort. More than anything, this is a book of solutions—solutions that are new, solutions that are different, and solutions that are practicable. Each chapter provides important context needed to understand a particular aspect of our political paralysis and then offers a number of fixes to the structural problems we face. My one and only litmus test for the solutions I've included here is whether we can enact these reforms before the next presidential election. In other words, this is not an exercise in terse academic analysis, a regurgitation of tired old ideas, or a litany of pie-in-the-sky reforms. It is an insider's take on long-standing problems and an introduction to new solutions that have broad appeal and the potential to change our politics. Each solution included here is uncomplicated and nonpartisan, universally attractive, and could be put in place within one to three years.

Our founders had faith that we who inherited this democracy would guide it, as they did, through treacherous waters. I believe this moment, in the wake of the historic 2008 election, presents a fresh opportunity to do just that—to build a more perfect union. I'm cautiously optimistic that change can and will come to America. But there's much that must be done—and done quickly—to perfect our union and preserve our democracy. It is my hope that this work will contribute to that effort.

1

SHOW THE MONEY
Financing Democracy

> Politics has got so expensive that it takes
> lots of money to even get beat with.
> —WILL ROGERS, 1931

It all begins, and ends, with money.

Before a potential candidate ever tests the water, the first thing a team of advisers does is formulate a strategy for raising a ton of cash. In order to establish oneself as a front-tier presidential candidate, it is now necessary to raise roughly a hundred million dollars—and that's *before* the first caucus or primary occurs.

Yet it's not the amount of money per se that's the problem; even a billion dollars is a modest amount when a presidential race is viewed as a nationwide marketing campaign. The problem is which people the money comes from, the candidates they tend to favor, and those donors' impact on the way our government functions. It's no coincidence that American politics has recently taken a dynastic, celebrity-friendly turn, and that for a time the junior senator from New York led the Democratic primary race and New York City's former mayor led the Republican contest. Nor is it a coincidence that a charismatic senator from Chicago and a former venture-capitalist-turned-governor from Boston were their primary opponents. Candidates with name recognition and a built-in story for the media are obvious front-runners. But more so, candidates with ready access to the financial centers of

New York, Chicago, and Boston simply have a huge advantage in the money race.

Those politicians who can raise that money—Hillary Clinton, Rudy Giuliani, Barack Obama, the independently wealthy Mitt Romney (estimated net worth: $200 million)—are given the imprimatur of "serious contender" out of the gate. Those who can't, aren't. John McCain raised $24 million during the first six months of 2007, but due to overpaid consultants and careless spending by his advisers he was $300,000 in debt by June. McCain's campaign broke even by the end of the summer, but by the following November it was more than $500,000 in debt and viewed by most to be out of the race. His incredible comeback on relatively low campaign funds is one of the few anomalies to the current standard.

A quick glance at the chart below demonstrates just how difficult this phenomenon is to confront.

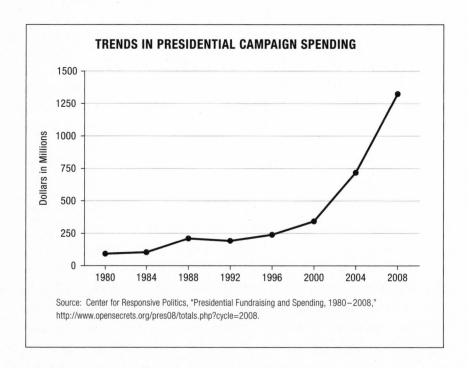

TRENDS IN PRESIDENTIAL CAMPAIGN SPENDING

Source: Center for Responsive Politics, "Presidential Fundraising and Spending, 1980–2008," http://www.opensecrets.org/pres08/totals.php?cycle=2008.

In the last six election cycles alone, the amount spent on the quest for the Oval Office has quadrupled.

How candidates go about raising this kind of money can be dauntingly complex. Despite all the press scrutiny, we still live in a world of murky campaign financing, where politicians coddle various wealthy donors, groups, and organizations. Basically, there are five key constituencies when it comes to raising and spending campaign cash.

- *The big donors:* the ultrawealthy financiers who make their money on Wall Street or in Hollywood, but whose hobby—and indeed life's passion—is political fund-raising. It is almost a sport for them, like collecting art or acquiring other expensive assets. They are wheeler-dealers who run hedge funds and go to the best restaurants. In 2004, this small subset of wealthy Americans provided Senator John Kerry with nearly a quarter of his total receipts and President George W. Bush with some 58 percent of his.
- *The bundlers:* the elites whom both parties' front-runners rely on to assemble the largest packages of legal campaign cash. These wealthy individuals pool a large number of contributions and are able to funnel far more money into campaigns than they could give personally under campaign finance laws. Many campaigns are able to avoid disclosure of their bundlers due to a loophole in Federal Election Commission (FEC) rules. By the time of the Super Tuesday primaries in February 2008, more than 2,500 bundlers had raised almost $600 million for the various presidential candidates.
- *The political action committees (PACs):* the fund-raising juggernauts that raise untold millions for candidates that support their industries' chosen causes. PACs are the slush funds for special interest groups, such as the conservative Club for Growth, which raises money for Republican candidates who pledge to support limited government and lower taxes, and the left-leaning feminist group Emily's List, which works to build a progressive America by electing pro-choice Democratic women. PACs enforce orthodoxy in each party. They have the ability to secretly influence the course of the campaign, because they don't have to disclose the sources of their massive funds.
- *The consultants:* my colleagues, in whom the expertise needed to conduct a national election campaign now largely resides. They have an enormous impact on the way money is raised and spent. My former colleague Mark Penn, for example, drew some of the blame for the way the assets of

Hillary Clinton's presidential campaign were deployed during the early primary season of 2008—$4.3 million of it having been paid through February 2008 for his consulting firm's work.[1] Other consultants direct the operation of Web strategy and fund-raising. Consultants make up a small, powerful, and rather incestuous group of politicos that are indispensable to modern campaigns and elections.

• *Internet and small-dollar donors:* including the more than three million people who contributed to Barack Obama's campaign in 2008, an astounding number that provided him with an unprecedented war chest (and which just about equaled the number of donors to all candidates in 2004 combined). The explosive growth in small donors, the majority of whom donated online to Obama's campaign, has catapulted this collective group to stand as a coequal player in the game of political fund-raising.

If you look at the recent presidential cycle, despite the predictable rancor, the outcome suggests that the system worked rather well. Voters were able to buck the trend of recent years and produce nominees in both parties who were not establishment candidates. McCain's effort was pronounced dead on arrival months before the first vote was cast. Yet he was able to secure the nomination without significant funds or the coalition of right-wing stalwarts who twice put George W. Bush in the White House. Obama captured the imagination—and the campaign contributions—of millions of Democrats, upsetting the most storied name in modern politics. Granted, the party nomination almost went to a floor fight, but Obama wrapped it up by securing enough popular votes, as well as the support of the majority of Democratic Party operatives.

On its face, everything finally worked like it should. An underfunded outsider won the Republican nomination. A relative novice rode a grassroots wave to victory over a powerful political machine. But if you really think the system worked as designed in 2008, you're kidding yourself. In fact, the exceptions of 2008 prove the rule of the past forty years: the system is unfair, undemocratic, and arbitrary, and fundamental fixes are needed to revitalize our presidential elections. After the 2008 election, it's less obvious to the casual observer that we're headed for a disastrous wreck—but that's where we're headed.

First, consider the public financing system for presidential elections.

After McCain's careless spending put him in the red, he needed an infusion of cash to stay in the race. He got it by leveraging the public finance system for presidential elections, established by the Federal Election Campaign Act (FECA), to secure a bank loan.

Public financing allows qualifying candidates to receive funds from the federal government if they agree to a spending cap. Candidates are eligible for public financing during both the primary and general elections. McCain initially opted out of public financing, which allowed him to raise and spend unlimited sums. But when he ran into money trouble, his campaign backtracked.

The campaign had already received a $3 million loan from Maryland-based Fidelity and Trust Bank in November 2007. When the campaign applied for an additional $1 million from Fidelity and Trust in mid-December—weeks before the critical Iowa and New Hampshire primaries—the bank asked for additional collateral. In an unprecedented move, McCain promised that if the campaign was not able to repay the loan on its own, he would reapply for public funds to repay the amount.[2]

However, McCain won New Hampshire, and private donors rewarded his success by restocking his campaign coffers, at which point he opted out of public financing. In doing so, McCain was able to far exceed the spending limits that public financing would have imposed. Democrats cried foul, but the FEC ultimately ruled that McCain's crafty loan was kosher. Regardless, McCain gamed a broken system to his advantage, and in doing so he found a path to the nomination.

Make no mistake: Obama used the broken system to his advantage as well, albeit differently. His campaign message was, in effect, a call to arms to overcome the deficiencies of our current process. In fact, his strategy included a historic end run around the rules that had governed political fund-raising for decades. From the earliest days of his campaign in January 2007, Obama's strategists were plotting how to use the power of the Internet to buck the system that was stacked against his candidacy.

In February 2007, the Obama campaign hired Chris Hughes, a cofounder of Facebook, to start up the campaign's My.BarackObama.com Web site. MyBo, as it came to be known, created a social networking space where campaign supporters could organize. As the *New York Times* noted, "While many candidates reach their supporters through the Web, the social networking features of MyBo allow supporters to reach one another."[3] This gave the Obama team unprecedented organizing and fund-raising abilities. By the end of the primary campaign, in July 2008, the site had nearly a million members, a literal army of volunteers they could communicate with and dispatch easily and effectively. But early on, savvy use of the Web also gave Obama an extraordinary ability to raise small-dollar donations. Obama shocked the political world when he announced that his campaign had raised a staggering $25 million in the first quarter of 2007 from some one hundred thousand donors. This Herculean fund-raising effort was especially surprising because Obama nearly bested Hillary Clinton's haul of $26 million during the same period, which she raised from fifty thousand donors—half the number that gave to Obama.[4]

In 2007, it was unthinkable that a novice first-term senator could be financially competitive in a national presidential contest. But Obama's online efforts allowed him to eclipse Clinton's fund-raising and organizing advantage from early 2007 until his primary victory, some eighteen months later. It also enabled him to become the first candidate in the modern era to reject public financing during the general election. As Silicon Valley mogul and Obama supporter Wade Randlett told the *San Francisco Chronicle*, "In fifty days, Obama went from not having announced [his campaign], and not having an e-mail list—from zero to one hundred thousand [donors]. . . . That is just unprecedented in American politics, and you could never do it without the Internet."[5]

Obama's use of the Internet to solicit small-dollar contributions is reflected in campaign finance data compiled by the Center for Responsive Politics after the election. His bottom-up strategy of courting small donors online is especially apparent in the table below. According to the center, McCain received 34 percent of his campaign funds from donors who contributed $200 or less. Thanks to Obama's bottom-up online fund-raising, his campaign received a whopping 54 percent of its donations from these small-dollar donors. McCain, on the other hand, took a top-down approach. Nearly half of his funds came from donors who gave the maximum allowable contribution of $2,300.[6]

Candidate	Number of $200 or Less Donors	Percentage from Donors of $200 or Less	Number of Donors of $2,300+	Percentage from Donors of $2,300+	Number of "Maxed-Out" Donors ($4,600)	Percentage from "Maxed-Out" Donors ($4,600)
Barack Obama	357,777	54%	63,838	30%	12,574	9%
John McCain	141,597	34%	34,272	48%	6,582	16%

Obama's online campaign was tailored to allow him to break away from the flawed system of campaign finance. His motto "Change we can believe in" was crafted to target these disaffected voters, who flocked to his campaign's promise of a different kind of politics. Early on, volunteers were counseled to guide anyone interested in policy stances to the campaign Web site. It was a brilliant strategic move. Since Obama's positions on real issues were virtually indistinguishable from his Democratic primary rivals, this positioning took aim at politics itself. Running against establishment candidates Hillary Clinton and John Edwards, Obama channeled the sheer frustration voters felt not just at rampant partisanship, but also at the broken machinery of our presidential politics. Even though he eventually received twice the number of "maxed-out" contributions compared to McCain, his campaign was able to credibly tap pent-up frustrations about money buying politicians voiced by regular Americans.

In 2008, America finally witnessed an exciting and competitive presidential campaign, with a historic outcome—not because the system worked, but because it was fundamentally broken.

FALSE ASSUMPTION #1:
"CAMPAIGN SPENDING IS OUT OF CONTROL"

If you want to take the pulse of the nation, go to the heartland. "Ugh," was the literal reaction of the *Topeka Capital-Journal* newspaper in Kansas, to the record spending of the 2008 election cycle. This sentiment, and the paper's editorial, well sums up the way most Americans feel about the cost of our presidential campaigns.

Earlier this week, it was revealed that presidential contenders had spent
just over $200 million on TV ads during the primary season. . . . Just think
of all the ways that money might have been better spent. Take, for example,
an initiative launched by broadcasting tycoon Ted Turner recently to fight
malaria in Africa. The fundraising goal? Exactly $200 million, which, ac-
cording to Turner, would be enough to "practically eliminate" the disease
in Africa, where hundreds of thousands of children under five are dying
annually from malaria. . . . It's an arms race that won't end until lawmakers adopt meaningful campaign spending limits.

Never mind that the Supreme Court has repeatedly struck down
spending caps as unconstitutional, most recently in June 2006, ruling on
a challenge to campaign spending limits imposed by Vermont's legislature. Spending caps are a silly idea, because campaigns *should* cost a lot
of money.

Americans have always had a visceral aversion to money in politics.
Our distaste for the way campaigns are financed and the volume of cash
involved is part of our national DNA. According to Anthony Corrado, a
professor of government at Colby College and a fellow at the Brookings
Institution, it has been this way for as long as anyone can remember.
"Controversy over the role of money in politics did not begin with
Watergate. Nor did it start with the clamor over the high costs of campaigning that accompanied the growth of radio and television broadcasting in post–World War II America," he wrote in a history of campaign
financing laws. "Though public criticism of the campaign finance system has been particularly acute in recent decades, the issues raised, and
the consequent demand for campaign finance reform, can be traced to
before the Civil War."[7]

Most Americans today, like their forebears generations ago, believe
the amount of money spent on campaigns and elections is at best obscene,
and at worst poisoning our political process. This sentiment has grown
in proportion to the cost of running for president, which increases about
40 percent every four years. Al Gore and George W. Bush collectively
spent $343.1 million in 2000. In 2004, John Kerry and Bush spent
$717.9 million. In 2000, candidates, political parties, and issue advocacy
groups spent $770 million on television ads alone. In 2004, this figure

more than doubled to $1.6 billion.[8] When the dust finally settled in 2008, nearly $1.6 billion was raised and spent by Obama and McCain in the primary and general elections—more than $700 million of it on television.[9] And that's not counting the other big-spending candidates for the party nominations.

At first glance, a couple billion dollars seems like an awful lot of money to spend on a presidential election. That is, until you compare that figure to the tens of billions that the country's top brands spend on national marketing campaigns for everything from kitty litter to laundry detergent. In 2007, for instance, Campbell Soup Company spent $670.3 million on advertising condensed soup and other products to American consumers. McDonald's spent $1.15 billion. Anheuser-Busch spent more on advertising beer in 2007—$1.354 billion—than all of the candidates in the 2008 primary elections combined. And the private sector is not the only big spender when it comes to advertising. The federal government, in fact, is one of the top advertisers in the nation. U.S. taxpayers spent $1.12 billion in 2007 on advertising for the military, drug control efforts, and other public-service messaging—more than Walmart, the nation's largest retailer, spent over the same period.[10]

This isn't to say that presidential campaigns should spend wastefully or for the sake of parity with big box retailers. The idea here isn't to enact a law that would give each candidate the same advertising budget as a Big Mac. Rather, my point is that advertising and marketing are fundamentally important, irrespective of their costs. An effective marketing campaign will increase a company's market share and sales. The same is true of an effective political marketing campaign, which raises awareness about candidates and their issues and encourages citizens to vote. Sure, this costs a pretty penny. But democracy, in the end, is well worth the price.

That said, broadcasters have certainly taken advantage of the necessity of political advertising. One reason why campaigns have become so expensive is that they have become a corporate welfare trove for broadcasters.

A huge percentage of campaign funds are spent on TV time in the sixty-day home stretch between Labor Day and Election Day. According to the Television Bureau of Advertising, spending on political ads increased 1,200 percent from 1970 to 2006.[11] During the 2000 cycle, when total receipts for airtime topped $1 billion, broadcasters in the nation's ten largest media markets saw a 46 percent profit on average.[12] In 2004, according to the campaign finance watchdog CQ Money Line, George W. Bush spent 58 percent of his campaign budget on the airwaves, and John Kerry spent 54 percent. From April to November 2008, Obama and McCain spent $125.5 million and $235.9 million, respectively.[13]

Interestingly, while advertising airtime is more expensive than ever, political coverage on the networks has nosedived to a near record low. In 1992, the major networks aired 24.6 minutes per day of political coverage. In 1996, that number plummeted to 12.3 minutes per day and rebounded only slightly to 19.1 minutes in 2004.[14] The amount of airtime devoted to "earned media"—coverage of candidates that they win by "making" news, as opposed to "paid media," the commercial airtime campaigns pay for—is dwindling.

With ever-decreasing political coverage, candidates are forced to increase their advertising. That means raising megabucks any way possible to purchase the airtime needed to increase their name identification and make voters aware of, and interested in, their campaigns (or, at least, disinterested in their rivals' efforts). For decades, political spending has been a wonderfully reliable source of revenue for television stations, and broadcasters take this formula to the bank every election year. With advertisers and consumers turning to the Web, creating a particular hardship for the networks and local affiliates, broadcasters are especially hard-pressed to give up the quadrennial windfall. Still, television stations obtain their broadcast licenses free of change, with the rather minimal promise to serve the public interest and abide by Federal Communications Commission (FCC) regulations. They are also required by campaign finance law to offer political candidates the "lowest unit charge" to air campaign ads. The airwaves are a public trust, and broadcasters are abusing that trust.

The larger point, though, is that running any kind of national campaign is expensive, whether you're selling a politician or a new car. The money spent on political advertising is a fraction of 1 percent of what American companies spend each year on convincing us we need a new kitchen appliance or the latest innovation in lawn care. I cannot imagine that folks in the heartland seriously believe that knowing our choices in adult beverages is more important than knowing our choices for president of the United States. Yet that is precisely the ludicrous argument that proponents of a spending cap are making. We live in one of the most populous nations on earth, and it costs real money to run a national campaign in a country this vast.

The real problem is not so much the amount spent on campaigns, but the time it takes candidates to raise such large sums, the public's ability to see where the money is coming from and going to, and how the funds are spent. Americans simply need to get over the cost of campaigning in and of itself—and move on to other far more important issues.

FALSE ASSUMPTION #2:
"LOBBYIST MONEY IS SWAMPING THE SYSTEM"

Given the increasing cost of seeking the nation's highest office, the public is understandably concerned with the extent to which fund-raising makes a president beholden to certain donors. Polling tells us that a high percentage of voters are concerned with the influence of special interests in presidential politics. And politicians, acting on the advice of pollsters and media consultants, take advantage of this fair-minded concern.

Take Barack Obama's campaign in 2008. In explaining his rationale for opting out of public financing for the general election, Obama told supporters, "If we don't stand together, the broken system we have now, a system where special interests drown out the voices of the American people, will continue to erode our politics and prevent the possibility of real change." In 2004, Vermont governor Howard Dean, who later became chair of the Democratic National Committee (DNC), went on a verbal tirade against John Kerry, following the disclosure by the Center for Responsive Politics that Kerry had received more lobbyist contributions than any other senator over a fifteen-year period. Dean called Kerry "yet another special interest clone."[15]

It is entirely right and proper that voters are worried about the influence of campaign contributors on our elected officials. Indeed, this is an extremely valid concern in congressional elections. Contributions can and do influence the actions of incumbents in Congress, and our system must account for the possibility of quid pro quos and corruption. This is the subject of much of chapter 4.

In a general election campaign for president, however, there is little evidence that traditional special interests—PACs and registered lobbyists—have any influence on, or significant interest in, the candidates. Again, the numbers tell the real story. In 2008, both McCain and Obama raised only a tiny fraction of their total campaign funds from lobbyists or PACs. According to the Center for Responsive Politics, McCain received some $11 million from lawyers and lobbyists, and just over $1.4 million from PACs.[16] Together, these special interest contributions represented a tiny drop in McCain's $368 million bucket. Similarly, Obama's campaign took in $42.7 million from lawyers and lobbyists, and only $1,820 (that's not a typo) from PACs.[17] Of the $751 million raised by Obama in the 2008 cycle, the donations he received from special interests hardly register. Given the stratospheric amounts that candidates raise in modern presidential elections, even a seemingly significant contribution from a lobbyist or PAC is unlikely to buy any special privilege or consideration should their horse win the race.

This doesn't stop pollsters, of course, from advising candidates to take on the special interest straw man. It's a smart political move, given the concerns of the average voter. Attacking special interests has always tested well and has always been a powerful line for candidates to take.

During the 2008 campaign Obama took a predictably hard line against special interests, vowing to exclude them from his administration and enact tough new rules that closed the "revolving door" between government and the private sector. I remember one lobbyist telling me that Obama had said to him laughingly, "We'll let you in the White House through the back door." And while I don't question Obama's sincerity about his pledge, it nonetheless points out the absurdity of the notion that special interests are inherently bad.

Complaining about special interest money in a presidential campaign is disingenuous. Unfortunately, this populist ruse reinforces the assumption that special interests are somehow influencing our presidential elections—an assumption that just isn't borne out by the data.

FALSE ASSUMPTION #3:
"BUNDLING IS A DISTURBING NEW DEVELOPMENT IN POLITICS"

From the media coverage of bundling during the 2008 cycle, the unin-formed voter might have thought this routine fund-raising tactic was somehow a perverse anachronism on the order of pederasty. Press cov-erage routinely led one to believe that bundlers—those wealthy or influ-ential individuals who solicit legal campaign contributions from family, friends, and business associates, and deliver them in bulk to campaigns—must be the worst of the worst.

I remember when I began in politics in the early 1970s, there was no such thing as bundling. There were big donors and megadonors, to be sure. People like venture capitalist and tech industry doyen Max Palevsky gave Senator George McGovern hundreds of thousands of dol-lars for his presidential bid in 1972, a huge donation at that time. In re-turn, Palevsky was treated like a potentate in Democratic circles. What Max wanted, how he wanted his coffee, and how much time he wanted to spend with the candidate were all issues of central concern, simply because one man could give such a disproportionate amount of cam-paign funds.

Ironically, it was the McGovern campaign that first developed grass-roots, direct mail fund-raising, which fundamentally changed the busi-ness and impacted what Barack Obama was able to do some thirty-six years later. That presidential race also spawned the campaign finance reforms of the mid-1970s because of the abuses of Richard Nixon's reelection campaign. With the introduction of limits to fund-raising, first to $1,000 and now up to $2,300, big money was effectively removed from the presidential selection process.

Stated bluntly, someone giving $2,300 for a primary, or $4,600 for the combined primary and general election, simply doesn't have much influence in a multimillion-dollar race. The only way that such a person can have an influence is by bundling, that is, bringing friends together. Yet, even in a presidential race, a bundler really cannot make much of a personal difference. To be sure, candidates want people who can and will raise money from their friends and business associates, but with the $2,300 limit in the primary and in the general election, somebody who gets ten or fifteen business associates to give $4,600 each is still just a drop in the bucket. Imagine that a single bundler had pulled together contributions that totaled 1 percent of Obama's total fund-raising in 2008. To raise that $7.5 million, the bundler would have to know 1,620 people (or, conceivably, 810 couples) who were willing to "max out" their contributions for the bundler's favored candidate. Most likely, someone who knows that many wealthy people is probably also competing against some of their wealthy friends in the bundling race.

The major exception is when industries get together and bundle bundlers, as sometimes happens. If industry representatives, say, hedge fund managers or pharmaceutical industry executives, are able to gather contributions, either formally or informally, and raise hundreds of thousands of dollars, then the candidate necessarily takes notice. But it's much more difficult for bundlers qua bundlers to make a difference.

Indeed, several fund-raisers have been convicted of using bundled contributions to bypass the federal cap on individual contributions. In a sticky, bizarre, and high-profile case in 2007, Hillary Clinton's campaign was forced to return $850,000 in bundled contributions from Norman Hsu, who was charged by federal investigators with illegally reimbursing donors through a complicated investment scheme (among other things).[18] In 2004, John Edwards's campaign received $127,000 in bundled contributions from Geoffrey Fieger, a wealthy trial lawyer and former Democratic gubernatorial nominee in Michigan, who was indicted for reimbursing his employees for their contributions with corporate bonuses.[19]

Despite the increased attention it has received thanks to a few bad apples, bundling has, in fact, been around for at least two decades. Emily's List, the pro-choice PAC that supports Democratic women, began bundling big- and small-donor contributions for congressional campaigns back in 1986. In 2000, George W. Bush raised bundling to an art form, implementing a tracking system and giving these important financiers Lone Star monikers including "Ranger" and "Pioneer." By 2008, bundling had gone mainstream. According to a *Wall Street Journal* analysis, while bundled donations accounted for 7.7 percent of total campaign contributions in 2000, in 2004 this figure more than doubled to 18.2 percent, and by October 2008 bundling accounted for more than 28 percent of total fund-raising.[20]

In light of this surge, many assumed the proliferation of bundling would have disastrous ethical implications, and that bundling was the new back door for special interests. This is hardly the case. Of the more than two thousand bundlers in the 2008 presidential campaign, according to the Center for Responsive Politics, lobbyists accounted for only 3 percent of them.[21] The Honest Leadership and Open Government Act of 2007, passed in the wake of lobbyist Jack Abramoff's indictment for fraudulent campaign contributions and conspiracy to corrupt public officials, now requires both congressional and presidential candidates to disclose the lobbyists that bundle for their campaigns.

Although full disclosure of bundled contributions for presidential candidates has not yet been codified, in 2008 both the McCain and Obama campaigns accepted guidelines for voluntary disclosure. Today, bundlers are no longer operating in relative anonymity. The public has information on who they are, where they live, what they do for a living, and how much money they raise.

So who are the other 97 percent of bundlers? They are largely political hobbyists who, by dint of their relative wealth or power, are able to cobble together checks from like-minded associates. They are corporate executives and Hollywood types, like director Steven Spielberg and record executive David Geffen. They get a kick out of politics (who can blame them for that?), and bundling is how they choose to get involved. With continued disclosure of who they are and what they have raised, bundlers are no more or less harmful than anyone else who gets involved in the full-contact sport of presidential politics.

Granted, we need hard and fast disclosure requirements for presidential bundlers. Today, these don't exist, and they should. For that reason, it's impossible to say exactly *how much* these bundlers raised during 2008, because candidates aren't required to disclose that information. However, as I noted above, during the 2008 cycle, both Obama and McCain released lists of their bundlers, as well as totals that each bundler collected—within a range. For instance, Obama's list noted that Jeffrey Katzenberg of the movie studio DreamWorks SKG bundled at least $500,000 for the Obama campaign. While Katzenberg may have, in fact, bundled more than this amount, the records released by the Obama and McCain campaigns give us approximations from which we are able to make abstractions about bundling during the 2008 cycle.

Based on the figures released by the campaigns, and a subsequent analysis by the Center for Responsive Politics, we know that some 540 bundlers raised at least $63 million for the Obama campaign in 2008. Even if we assume that these numbers are a vast understatement, the amount raised by Obama bundlers is still dwarfed by the amount raised by other means during the presidential contest. Bundlers, as a group, represented just 8 percent of the nearly $751 million raised by the Obama campaign.[22]

The McCain campaign is a slightly different story. Some 561 bundlers raised a minimum of $207 million for the campaign in 2008, which represents at least 56 percent of its $372.5 million haul.[23] While bundlers accounted for a much more significant percentage of McCain's fund-raising, this is hardly a cause for alarm. McCain received public funds during the general election, limiting the amount he could raise, which explains the seemingly large percentage of bundled contributions. More important, McCain simply failed to implement a proactive Internet fund-raising strategy. He relied on traditional fund-raising methods, which the Obama campaign emphatically demonstrated are all but obsolete.

Bundling is certainly a mechanism of campaign finance that needs to be reported and regulated. Like any other component of big-money politics, it's also a way in which elites are able to gain access to candidates. However, bundling is hardly the devious back channel that many political observers make it out to be.

During the 2008 campaign, a prominent bundler asked for my advice in devising a strategy as to how to get the maximum impact for the $160,000 he had raised for McCain. I told him that he should go to the campaign's senior officials and make it very clear that he wanted recognition for his large gift. But I told him that stopping there was a mistake, if he was looking for recognition should McCain win the election. In that case, I said he should find McCain himself at a donor event, take the candidate aside, and literally show him copies of his checks. That would be the surest way to let McCain know that a large sum had been raised by a supporter who wanted to be remembered going forward.

The donor, a respected businessman, said, "Isn't this a bit blunt? A bit extreme? You're telling me to wave copies of checks in his face?" And I honestly told him that the only way he would get that attention in a presidential race is if he did that very thing. Indeed, this is how savvy donors operate, whether directly or indirectly. They let candidates know when they are raising large sums of money, because, absent that, candidates frequently will have no way of knowing.

I heard another story about the 2008 campaign that speaks to the relative lack of influence among bundlers and large donors. In past years, a major donor had given large sums to Illinois Democrat Rahm Emanuel, who was then chairman of the Democratic Congressional Campaign Committee (DCCC). He described Emanuel as one of his close friends and himself as one of Emanuel's biggest supporters. He said, though, that when Emanuel became chief of staff to the newly elected President Obama, he had called Emanuel to congratulate him and Emanuel was a bit standoffish. The donor mentioned that a family member was hoping for an entry-level job or an internship in the administration, but Emanuel wouldn't make any commitments. My response was to say, "Boy, Rahm was completely accessible when he needed your money in the campaign, and now he is suddenly less accessible."

That's not a knock on Emanuel. In fact, it's to the good, because we don't want our elected officials or their top aides to be for sale. In a certain sense, the exchange between the donor and Emanuel should give us comfort that jobs and favors are seldom—if ever—bought and sold in presidential politics.

FALSE ASSUMPTION #4:
"PUBLIC FINANCING IS BETTER THAN PRIVATE FINANCING"

In 2008, nearly every candidate in both parties opted out of public funding for the presidential primary campaign, and Obama became the first candidate since FECA was enacted in 1971 to forgo public funds for the general election. Many called his move the final deathblow for public financing and assumed this was somehow a bad thing. Obama was dragged through the mud by editorial pages and political pundits alike for going back on his word to participate in the public financing system. But in hindsight, his decision was not only smart—it was a first step to fundamentally reforming our broken campaign finance system.

Nearly forty years have passed since FECA, and there is now a good degree of inertia in the idea of using taxpayer dollars to finance presidential campaigns. Sure, Americans are eager to curb the influence of money in politics. Arguably, public funding obviates the need for candidates to raise private contributions from potentially dubious sources and wealthy bundlers who supposedly want something in return. And, with public financing, candidates can spend less time dialing for dollars and schmoozing at fund-raisers, and more time focusing on issues and shaking hands on the trail.

While there are significant advantages to public financing, our current system provides little of the benefit we want, with nearly all of the problems we hope to avoid. One reason is that elections have become exponentially more expensive, but public financing has not kept pace. In 2008, the public grant in the general election was $84.1 million—a small fraction of the hundreds of millions that were raised and spent by the presidential campaigns. Given this comparatively paltry sum, presidential candidates end up relying on party committees and independent expenditure groups to supplement their publicly funded campaigns. In 2008, public funds accounted for only a fraction of the money spent on behalf of John McCain in the general election. Presidential contenders continue to devote considerable time to fund-raising on behalf of political parties and the interest groups that support their efforts in the general election. And because the spending cap and public grant for the general election kick in only when a candidate accepts his or her party's nomination, this creates a loophole for candidates who refuse public funding during the primary—they can raise and spend as much as they like between the time they've secured the nomination, in late winter or early spring, and when they receive the nomination at the party convention, in late (and later and later) summer.

The media's knee-jerk reaction notwithstanding, Obama's decision was welcome news not only for First Amendment advocates in right-wing and libertarian circles, but also for left-leaning academics and respected campaign finance scholars. As Thomas Mann of the Brookings Institution noted near the conclusion of the 2008 primaries, "The presidential public financing system is largely irrelevant in this election cycle," citing the record sums raised through bundling and small contributions over the Internet as a positive alternative to the public finance system.[24]

I couldn't agree more. The amount of cash raised in 2008 and the way in which it was raised outside the public financing system are extremely positive developments, despite the blather of pundits. The rise of the small Internet donor is perhaps the single most empowering development for the average voter in generations.

Again, let's look at the numbers. In the past two election cycles, Internet donors who contributed $200 or less to presidential candidates have increased dramatically. Obama raised a total of $751 million in the 2008 cycle, $334 million of which came from small-dollar donations of $200 or less. Even John McCain, who hardly appealed to the young and Internet savvy, received $64 million from donors who gave at that level.[25] Perhaps the most exciting number in the data is the single-day record for Internet fund-raising. It's held not by a major party nominee, and not even by Internet fund-raising pioneer Howard Dean, but by Ron Paul, the Republican congressman from Texas whose conservative populism sparked his surprisingly successful haul. In 2008, Paul's campaign took in just short of $6 million in a single twenty-four-hour period, besting John Kerry's $5.7 million one-day take in 2004.[26]

The advent of Internet fund-raising has led to a positive feedback loop. Large numbers of small donations allow candidates to forgo public funding, and once outside of the public financing system candidates make extra efforts to speak to and engage the average voter, the source of those small contributions. As we can see from the numbers above, voters respond in kind, participating in the process and rewarding candidates who speak directly to them—with their credit cards and checkbooks. This mutually reinforcing process is now a staple of politics on the right and the left. And that's a good thing.

However, there is a ways to go before small-dollar donations reach the tipping point at which they are more critical to a campaign's success than large donations. In 2008, both Obama and McCain established joint efforts between their campaign committees and party committees, which are able to accept larger donations, spend limitlessly, and play a key role in advertising for their party's respective presidential efforts.

Both candidates in 2008 spent much time and effort targeting the donors who were able to write megachecks in the tens of thousands of dollars to these committees.

But the rise of small-dollar donors via the Internet has fundamentally
altered the financing of presidential campaigns, in many ways providing
the reform that Congress has never been able to bring about. As Cornell
University economist Robert H. Frank concluded following Obama's
record fund-raising from small-dollar donors, "Voters have the power to
eliminate the fundamental conflicts of interest that have corrupted
American politics in recent decades. Because of the First Amendment
constraint, that's something McCain-Feingold and other campaign finance
laws simply cannot deliver by themselves."[27]

The evolution of online fund-raising is overwhelmingly positive on a
number of levels. But there are, of course, problems we must consider at
the outset—namely, that Internet fund-raising renders our campaign
finance reporting rules and procedures increasingly anachronistic.
Internet fund-raising dramatically expands the sheer number of people
who participate in the political process. But campaigns are required to
report these contributions only quarterly. This means that campaign
finance watchdogs must pore through an increasing mountain of data
every three months to look for violations, inconsistencies, and red flags.
This mountain will grow exponentially with each election cycle, and as
such our reporting regulations make it exponentially harder to mine. As
the nature of campaign finance changes, so must the procedures by
which we report and regulate campaign cash.

FIXING THE MONEY GAME

Innumerable books have been written on campaign finance reform, and
it does not make sense to rehash the arguments here with respect to the
First Amendment, restrictions on political speech, the *Buckley v. Valeo*
case, the constitutionality of the Bipartisan Campaign Reform Act of
2002, and so on. Does it make a pragmatic difference to voters—or even
to donors—if current campaign finance laws are constitutional if, in the
end, they aren't serving the public good? My solution is simple: Expand
on what works; get rid of what is broken.

More, better, and faster campaign finance disclosure

To my mind, campaign finance disclosure works, and the more disclosure the better. In fact, between the Internet and the computer software that nearly every campaign currently uses to track their finances and generate quarterly FEC reports, there is no reason why we shouldn't have near-instant disclosure of contributions and expenditures.

Contributions should be reported within twenty-four hours. Donations increasingly take place over the Internet, and thus a twenty-four-hour requirement is not at all onerous for a presidential campaign. Expenditures should be reported weekly, instead of quarterly. In a modern presidential campaign, there is no reason why the public needs to wait three months to find out where the money is going. Increasing the frequency of reporting increases transparency, and it also reduces the inane political journalism that occurs around the quarterly reporting deadlines and the silly press scrambles by campaign communications operations. As an added bonus, if we are able to curb the horse-race stories about money in politics, it might contribute, over the long haul, to reducing the perceived and actual importance of money in politics.

Get rid of public financing as it exists today

The current public finance system for presidential campaigns is a waste of time and a waste of money. Today's system is structured around old ways of thinking and realities that no longer exist. For three decades, FECA has attempted to limit campaign spending, open up the playing field, and lessen the importance of fund-raising in presidential politics. It's failed on each and every count. The result is that a major party candidate has finally opted out of the system and won the election, putting the last nail in the coffin of the public finance system. Thankfully, voters have already devised a replacement, which reduces the amount of time that candidates have to spend hobnobbing with the superrich: small contributions from millions of people, from all walks of life. When the most effective use of the public financing system is as presumed collateral for a private loan, it's time to get rid of public financing.

Create a refundable tax credit for contributions of $50 or less

Small-dollar contributions and Internet fund-raising are already revolu-tionizing the way presidential campaigns are financed. Instead of issu-ing megagrants to candidates who no longer want or need them, the federal government should give a new tax credit to every American who contributes up to $50 to one or more presidential campaigns.

Sound far-fetched? Several states already do this, and studies prove that it is a successful means of increasing political participation. Minneso-ta's Public Contribution Refund Program gives an immediate $50 refund to political donors. For those on the right who think this is a ploy to en-courage donations to liberal candidates, consider that so far the refunded contributions have skewed heavily to conservative campaigns in the state. Ohio also gives a 100 percent tax credit for contributions up to $50, and $100 for joint filers. A survey of the Ohio program indicates that tax credits are more likely to bring in new donors than increase the size of donations from current contributors. And a 2006 study shows an increase in political participation when voters are notified of the tax credit by direct mail.

Historically, the campaigns with the most support from the estab-lishment and the wealthy have had the most resources to compete and thus the best chances to win. In a political environment where every American has either the means or an incentive to vote with his or her wallet, the campaigns with the message that best engages regular voters will also be the most well funded. To borrow the famous line from *Field of Dreams*, as the campaigns of Howard Dean, Ron Paul, and Barack Obama have already shown us, if you build it, they will come.

A tax credit for small-dollar contributions could lead to a presidential field of dreams. Candidates wouldn't have to hail from the ranks of mil-lionaires or party hacks to battle to the highest office in the land. It is not out of the question—in fact, it's an exciting possibility—that with a $50 federal campaign tax credit, the next election's presidential nomi-nees could credibly pledge not to engage in traditional fund-raising whatsoever. Instead of countless hours and dollars spent on throwing fund-raising cocktail parties and other events for the wealthy elite, can-didates will have more time to shake hands, kiss babies, and engage in the retail politics that are so vital to American democracy.

Ban coordination between the major national party committees that allow presidential candidates to skirt campaign finance limits

The explosion of small-dollar Internet contributions was the big story of the 2008 presidential campaign, but an interesting headline emerged late in the game: "In Fine Print, a Proliferation of Large Donors." While the Obama campaign was collecting record-smashing donations from millions of donors, it was also raking in five-figure checks from extremely wealthy contributors and bundlers. How could this be, if the individual contribution limit is $2,300? The answer is tricky accounting and unprecedented coordination between the various fund-raising committees of the party infrastructure.

During the general election, the Obama and McCain campaigns both organized so-called joint fund-raising committees—collaborative efforts between the presidential campaigns and national and state political party committees. Fat-cat donors used to have to write separate checks to separate committees; now joint fund-raising committees allow these donors to make a single, massive contribution of tens of thousands of dollars. The funds then get disbursed among the different campaign efforts that make up the committee, based on contribution limits under existing law.

For example, according to the *New York Times*, the "McCain Victory 2008" joint fund-raising committee accepted checks as large as $70,100, which was then split among the McCain presidential campaign, the Republican National Committee (RNC), and other state party committees.[28] According to the Center for Responsive Politics, McCain's campaign coordinated with ten different joint committees that collectively raised $177 million. The Obama campaign effort organized three of these joint committees, which raised a total of $184 million in a similar manner.[29]

Joint fund-raising committees are a disturbing trend that we need to eliminate. They represent an end run around campaign finance laws, and they give campaigns a new avenue to cultivate wealthy financiers. More important, these committees are an effort to maintain the status quo in presidential fund-raising at a time when the system has shifted in a dramatically new and positive direction with the influx of small Internet contributions.

Let's keep this momentum going. Joint fund-raising committees are a throwback to the old paradigm of presidential fund-raising, where campaigns relied on the wealthy and well heeled. Just as we should encourage more small-dollar donations through a refundable tax credit, we should tighten our campaign finance laws to ban joint fund-raising committees from our system.

Free airtime for presidential candidates

Forget about campaign spending limits, reducing the maximum allowable contribution to candidates, and the umpteen other regulations that have been proposed to cut campaign spending. The best idea out there is to give free airtime to candidates, which would drastically reduce campaign spending and fund-raising and would even the playing field for candidates.

There have been numerous attempts to force broadcasters to give free airtime to presidential candidates, which have been predictably met by fierce resistance from the industry. The National Association of Broadcasters has reportedly spent millions lobbying against free airtime.[30] And they have found some strange bedfellows among incumbents in Congress, who somewhat counterintuitively oppose the idea, because it would give a leg up to challenger candidates.[31]

Democrats and Republicans are equally to blame that this popular idea has yet to be implemented. Bills were introduced in 2002, 2003, and 2007, sponsored by some of the brightest and most powerful senators—including both 2008 presidential candidates, Russ Feingold (D-Wis.), Dick Durbin (D-Ill.), Dianne Feinstein (D-Calif.), and Arlen Specter (then R-Penn.). Regardless of the majority party, each attempt has died in committee.

It's not the amount of money raised and spent by campaigns that is a concern. It's the act of fund-raising in and of itself that has become problematic and all consuming. By reducing or eliminating the cost of airtime—a foremost campaign expenditure—we could reduce the amount of time that candidates are forced to raise money and increase the amount of time they spend interacting with voters and discussing the issues.

2

BREAK UP THE PARTIES
Reforming the Primaries

> We might as easily reprove the east wind, or the frost, as a political party,
> whose members, for the most part, could give no account of their position,
> but stand for the defence of those interests in which they find themselves.
> —RALPH WALDO EMERSON, 1844

There is no shortage of colorful ways to describe America's inane presidential primary system. In the run-up to the 2008 nominating contests, Larry J. Sabato, director of the University of Virginia's Center for Politics, wrote, "If the job of scheduling the presidential nominating contests were assigned to an insane asylum, this is pretty much what the patients would come up with."[1] Others have compared the primaries to a full-term pregnancy—it takes roughly the same amount of time, and it's just as painful.

Unfortunately, our presidential primaries are less amusing than they are complex, unfair, arbitrary, and undemocratic. In fact, they are far worse than undemocratic. Today's presidential primary system is one of the most *antidemocratic* features of our national politics.

Our primary system as we know it today unfairly benefits the voters of some states, while virtually locking out other voters. It forces candidates to purposely ignore issues important to vast swaths of the nation. The rules that govern the intricacies of this system make it impossible for many Americans to participate at all.

In 2007, several states—notably Michigan and Florida—tried to revolt against this terribly conceived system. Some pundits predicted a collapse of the primary nominating process. At the end of the day, to the surprise of many, the system didn't crash and burn. In fact, some believe it passed its 2008 stress test with flying colors. The system whittled an unruly field of twenty-one candidates down to just a few final contenders and ultimately two major party nominees. Barack Obama's unprecedented victory and John McCain's come-from-behind success suggested that our presidential primaries worked as designed.

Nothing could be further from the truth.

In 2008, a flawed system delivered two refreshingly surprising results. But the positive outcome of that year's nominating contests shouldn't be a reason to maintain the status quo. Nothing that happened in 2008 changed the fact that our primaries and caucuses are antidemocratic. It's time to reform our nominating contests so that they conform to our core democratic ideals.

TROUBLED HISTORY

The first primaries were held a century ago in a handful of states, as progressives tried to throw some light into the proverbial smoke-filled back rooms, where political bosses historically chose the major party nominees in a process largely closed to the public and the press. Ironically, the first state to adopt the presidential primary is everyone's favorite electoral troublemaker. In 1901, Florida enacted legislation to hold primary elections, followed by Wisconsin in 1905, and Oregon in 1911. In 1912, the Republican Party nominated President William Howard Taft in a closed-door process, angering supporters of popular presidential contender Teddy Roosevelt. By 1916, a populist movement had gained mass, and primaries were on the books in twenty-six states.

Yet primaries did not truly catch on as a means of nominating presidential candidates through popular vote until more than a half century later. In 1968, Vice President Hubert H. Humphrey of South Dakota became the Democratic nominee without participating in a single primary contest. The result was the tumultuous and violent 1968 Democratic Convention, after which the party instituted cascading reforms over a period of years. Pledged delegates from each state were, from then on, elected by popular vote. A certain number of party leaders became "superdelegates" and were allowed to vote for a nominee as they saw fit. The new rules required states to hold their primaries within the calendar year of the presidential election. Some state parties adopted caucuses in an effort to build party loyalty. And many states entered into a delicate dance to hold early primaries, hoping to exert more influence on the national nominating process.

In 2008, this dance turned into a brawl. After years of intense lobbying by Michigan senator Carl Levin and Michigan DNC member Debbie Dingell, the Democratic primary calendar was altered in 2008 to dilute the historic prominence of Iowa and New Hampshire. Nevada and South Carolina were added to the front of the voting pack. However, in violation of this tacit agreement, the Republican-dominated Florida legislature moved its primary ahead of South Carolina's. South Carolina retaliated, moving its primary ahead of Florida's. Then Michigan's party leaders, worried that their state would become completely inconsequential in the primary calendar, joined the fray, moving its primary before New Hampshire's. The DNC threatened both the Michigan and Florida state parties that their delegates to the national party convention would not be seated if they held their primaries before their originally allotted time.[2] In the meantime, some twenty-two states moved their primaries to February 5, or "Tsunami Tuesday," the new supersized Super Tuesday, the earliest date allowed by the DNC.

The uncertainty and acrimony surrounding the primary calendar signaled disaster. According to most political pundits, loading so many primaries on February 5 was the equivalent of setting a national primary. Both parties, it was believed, would have a nominee by the beginning of February, nearly a year before the general election. As veteran *Washington Post* political reporter Dan Balz summarized the convention wisdom, "Tradition, self-interest and pure envy have shaped the 2008 calendar and they ultimately could be the system's undoing. At some point there is likely to be rebellion against a process that forces voters to begin picking presidential nominees ten months or more before the general election. Can any state official truly justify asking voters to think seriously about presidential politics in the calendar year before the presidential election—and in the middle of the holiday season to boot?"[3]

The primary train wreck was averted thanks only to the historic candidacies of Barack Obama and Hillary Clinton, who excited Democratic voters and motivated them to turn out in record numbers. If one candidate had wrapped up the nomination based on low voter turnout in a handful of primaries before Tsunami Tuesday, it would likely have been the breaking point for the primary system. Voters would have been outraged that, yet again, a (most likely) well-funded front-runner walked away with the nomination before 98 percent of the nation had a chance to cast their ballots.

As it turned out, voting stretched on, to the near-comic point at which Montana and Puerto Rico became political battlegrounds in June. Instead of a primary disaster, what we witnessed in 2008 was a "soft break" of the system, where the political establishment was torn between its next in line and the new kid on the block. The viability of Obama's candidacy itself was created in large part by the customarily arbitrary primary process, which has typically favored establishment candidacies, silenced credible alternatives, and made the votes cast by the majority of Americans irrelevant.

A "soft break" notwithstanding, it would be a mistake not to learn from our experience in 2008 and make needed reforms to the primary system going forward. Both Democratic and Republican primaries exposed manifold problems in 2008—all of which have existed for decades. Unless we implement reforms, the vast majority of the country will continue to be disenfranchised, voters will become even more disillusioned, and our democracy will suffer for it.

ACCIDENTAL EXTREMES

There are three fundamental problems with the primary system as it exists today. First, it is the product not of design but of tradition, self-interest, and accident. Second, it is wholly undemocratic and thus lends itself to voter disillusionment and low turnout. And third, it has contributed to today's hyperpartisan environment by minimizing centrist voices.

It would be funny, in fact, if there weren't so much at stake.

In 1915, New Hampshire's primary was moved from the third Tues-

day of May to the second Tuesday of March, the date of the state's re-
nowned town hall meetings. As former New Hampshire governor
Hugh Gregg recalled several years ago, the rationale was parsimonious,
not hegemonic, as "frugal New Hampshirites had realized it was
wasteful to light the Town Hall twice."[4] Although New Hampshire's
first-in-the-nation status began as thrifty convenience, its place was
cemented less by tradition than by a law enacted by the state legislature in 1975. After other states encroached on New Hampshire's special status, lawmakers acted to *require* that the state's primary be held
a week before any other.

New Hampshire's haphazard climb to first in the nation has implications well beyond the realm of politicking. According to Andy Smith of
the University of New Hampshire Survey Center, the state ranks eighth
in the nation in overall congressional earmarks. This, despite the fact
that New Hampshire is the forty-first most populous state. As Smith
says, "There are a lot of politicians in the House and Senate with presidential aspirations who want to make friends with New Hampshire."[5]

Through tradition and attrition, New Hampshire, Iowa, South Carolina, and Nevada now hog the front end of the process. No great group
of intellectuals sat down and hashed out this system based on comple-
mentary demographics, voter participation, civic awareness, or any other
reasonable standard.

Yet, surprisingly, some exceptionally smart people have bought into
the early states' bogus argument that their citizenry is the best prepared
to winnow the field of candidates. Among New Hampshire's biggest
cheerleaders, for instance, is David S. Broder, the so-called dean of
Washington political reporters: "What is most needed is time—and a
place—for [candidates] to be carefully examined. Historically, New
Hampshire has fulfilled that responsibility. Voters there—in both parties and especially among the numerous independents that also vote in
the primary—take their role seriously. They turn up at town meetings
and they ask probing questions. So do the interviewers at local papers
and broadcast stations. So do high school students."[6]

With all due respect to Broder, it is tautological to argue that New
Hampshire's citizenry is more civically engaged than other states', when
the system all but ignores the rest of the nation. Why *should* voters in

Idaho or Washington pay attention to the primaries when they know they are effectively shut out of the process? I am quite sure the rest of America would prove their civic mettle if given an opportunity to have a real say in the outcome of the primaries.

Further, by shutting so many voters out, the primaries and caucuses are unfair to candidates as well. Each passing primary contest has shown that front-running candidates who do well in just a few early states are simply impossible to beat, no matter their popularity in more diverse and representative states elsewhere in the country. When front-runners win Iowa and New Hampshire, they build momentum and are able to raise the funds to compete in subsequent primaries. Their opponents, needless to say, are not. They lose momentum early, and their fund-raising dries up. Lo and behold, a presumptive nominee is anointed before tens of millions of voters in massively populous, important, and heterogeneous states, such as New York, California, and Illinois, ever enter a voting booth.

Historically, one of the parties' victors in Iowa or New Hampshire (or both!) has gone on to win the White House in all but one race since Iowa moved its caucus to January, in 1972—which is how Bill Clinton gained his nickname "the comeback kid," when he lost in 1992 to favorite son senators Tom Harkin (D-Iowa) and Paul Tsongas (D-Mass.). John McCain used this phenomenon to his distinct advantage in 2008, sky-rocketing from underdog to front-runner after Mike Huckabee's win in the Iowa caucus burst Massachusetts governor Mitt Romney's momentum, and McCain managed to hold on to his deep support, dating back to his 2000 bid for the GOP nomination, in New Hampshire. With a further victory in South Carolina, McCain became the candidate to beat. Illinois senator Barack Obama surprised the political world—and established the viability of his run for the office—with his upset win in his neighbor state of Iowa.

In the current primary system, not only are the majority of Americans disenfranchised, but minority voices and lesser-known candidacies are effectively silenced. The primary calendar is simply stacked against them. Unless you have the name recognition and the resources to make a strong showing in Iowa or New Hampshire, you are instantly relegated to also-ran status in the history books.

THE RULE OF PARTY CHIEFS

The caucus system is by far the most glaringly undemocratic component of both the Republican and Democratic presidential nominating races. In states such as Iowa, Nevada, and Texas, caucuses favor the views and the voices of party operatives over regular voters. Even the etymology of the word itself suggests an antidemocratic process: "Caucus" allegedly comes from an Algonquin word meaning "gathering of the ruling tribal chiefs."[7]

Caucuses are governed by intricate rules and require both a learning curve and a time commitment. Unlike a traditional primary, where voters can cast an absentee ballot, the caucus process excludes voters who work during the hours that caucusing takes place or who cannot afford child care. Some older voters are unable to make it to caucus sites in the dead of Iowa's harsh winters. Voting should be simple, quick, and accessible; caucuses are just the opposite.

For this very reason, turnout in primary states far exceeds turnout in caucus states. According to a report by the Pew Center on the States, some 57.9 million votes were cast in both the Democratic and Republican primaries in 2009.[8] At the same time, according to the Center for Politics at the University of Virginia, only 2.6 million people participated in Democratic and Republican caucuses.[9] To be sure, this is partly attributable to the fact that larger population states such as New York, California, and Illinois hold primaries, while smaller states such as Colorado, Kansas, and Maine hold caucuses—not to mention that most states hold primaries instead of caucuses. However, even with seventeen states holding caucuses for one or both party primaries, primary voters outnumbered caucus voters in 2008 by more than twenty to one.

It's telling to examine the results in the four states in the Democratic nominating contest that held both primaries and caucuses—Idaho, Nebraska, Washington, and Texas. Turnout was uniformly higher for the primary components of these contests than the caucus components. In Idaho, twice as many Democrats participated in the primary than the caucus. In Nebraska, Washington, and Texas, nearly three times the number of voters participated in the primaries than the caucuses. The results are also telling. The primary contests were much closer than the caucus contests. For instance, Obama won Nebraska's

Democratic caucus with 68 percent of the votes, but he won that state's Democratic primary with only 49 percent. This suggests that the caucus results reflect not necessarily the will of the voters but a candidate's supporters' ability to organize—and persuade—fellow voters.

	Dates		Democratic Turnout			Democratic Winners	
State	Caucus	Primary	Caucus	Primary	Caucus Turnout as Percentage of Primary	Caucus	Primary
Idaho	Feb. 5	May 27	21,224	42,882	49%	Obama (80%)	Obama (56%)
Nebraska	Feb. 9	May 13	38,670	93,757	41%	Obama (68%)	Obama (49%)
Washington	Feb. 9	Feb. 19	244,458	691,381	35%	Obama (68%)	Obama (51%)
Texas	Mar. 4	Mar. 4	1,000,000	2,874,986	35%	Obama (56%)	Clinton (51%)
Total			1,304,352	3,703,006	35%		

In the race for the 2008 Democratic nomination, most states held primaries, and some states held caucuses. Obama did uniformly better than Hillary Clinton in the caucus states, which had roughly a third as many voters as the primary states. Clinton fared much better in large-voting primary states. Ultimately, Obama bested Clinton in thirteen of fifteen Democratic caucuses, which gave him the edge in the overall delegate count on his way to securing the Democratic nomination.

Obama also benefited from another inegalitarian component of the Democratic primary—superdelegates. Superdelegates are voting members of the Democratic Party. They were created after the mess of the 1972 convention as a means of giving party leaders the deciding role in determining the nomination. As originally conceived, the superdelegates could steer the party away from a left-leaning candidate and toward a more centrist nominee who would fare better in the general election. Today, however, superdelegates represent another degree of separation between candidates and the public, adding to voter frustration at the stacked deck in primary elections. When Clinton began to collect superdelegates' promissory votes in 2007, it helped to fuel a backlash against her candidacy, and in the end the majority of superdelegates chose to support the candidate who had won the popular vote in their state—whether it was won via primary or caucus. That helped widen Obama's slight delegate lead and give him the Democratic nomination.

The Republican process that handed John McCain the nomination is frankly not much better. While Democrats have long since adopted proportional delegate allocation, Republicans continue to pick their nominees mostly through winner-take-all primaries and caucuses. Initially, it was thought that the winner-take-all system would offer some momentum to lesser-known candidates who are able to succeed in a small state, early in the process. Today, it basically shuts those candidates out of the process. Consider Mike Huckabee's run. In state after state, Huckabee was nipping at McCain's heels, coming in a close second among voters, but he could never catch up on the delegate board. Despite his better-than-expected placement in several early primaries, the system allowed McCain to amass all of the delegates in the contests he won.

Some argue for the winner-take-all system because it provides for an unambiguous winner. Others suggest that winner-take-all voting pushes candidates toward the center of the political spectrum, encouraging centrist campaigns and governments. While I agree with these arguments intellectually, on a practical level they simply don't work in a national presidential election. Our goal should be a system in which every voter in every state has an equal say in the outcome of the nominating contest. Today, winner-take-all voting in the Republican primaries and caucuses ensures that lesser-known and underfunded candidates will always be at a disadvantage, and voters who support them simply won't have their voices heard.

From winner-take-all to superdelegates to caucuses, this inherently undemocratic process has contributed to the rampant partisanship we bemoan today. Since the party apparatuses control the primaries, not surprisingly the system gives activists a disproportionate say in the outcome of the nominating contest, and those who get involved at the grassroots level are by nature the most partisan. There's nothing wrong in my book with partisanship. Real differences exist, and they need to be pointed out. I've spent my career poring through the numbers, identifying different constituencies and researching the push-button issues that drive them to the polls. The problem is that activists tend to represent the extremes of the political spectrum. And when the fringe is calling the shots, polarizing candidacies emerge, and the centrist views of the majority are infrequently represented.

THE GOLDILOCKS NOMINATION

Nearly everyone rejects the glaring flaws of the nominating system, yet no one who has the power to improve the system has an incentive to do so. Thus, in forty years of declining voter participation and increasing rancor, nothing has changed. The problem with our primaries is decidedly of the Goldilocks variety. We need primary elections that are long enough to give everyone a say and to road test our candidates, short enough to maintain engagement and excitement throughout the process, and inclusive enough that everyone feels the process is just right and chooses to take part as a result.

For both parties, the desire to avoid a messy fight has taken primary reform off the table. On the Democratic side, Senator Carl Levin, DNC member Debbie Dingell, and other party leaders in Michigan have long advocated reforms, to no avail. Since the reforms of 1968 and 1972, little has been done to shake up the primaries in either party. In fact, the last serious reform effort was put forth by several prominent Republican leaders in the run-up to their party convention in 2000. A commission led by former Tennessee senator and RNC chairman Bill Brock recommended the party adopt the Delaware Plan, which would create a four-tiered primary process, with small states voting first and large states voting last. This popular proposal was torpedoed by George W. Bush—then the presumptive Republican nominee—who wanted to avoid a potentially contentious debate on the Delaware Plan at his nominating convention.

Although the parties have not been able to forge a consensus so far, voters are nearly unanimous on this issue: the solution Americans support by a wide seven-out-of-ten margin is a single national primary day, with all states holding their primaries at the same time. Interestingly, President Woodrow Wilson first proposed a national primary nearly one hundred years ago, during his 1913 State of the Union Address, at the height of popular anger over the antidemocratic nomination process that had pushed aside Teddy Roosevelt. Wilson, an advocate of progressive politics, told a joint session of Congress: "I feel confident that I do not misinterpret the wishes or the expectations of the country when I urge the prompt enactment of legislation which will provide for primary elections throughout the country at which the voters of the several parties may choose their nominees for the Presidency without the intervention of nominating conventions."

A century later, Wilson's supposition is still spot-on. Americans by and large favor a national primary. The simplest solution is often the best, and it would be far simpler indeed to designate a single day on which the entire country votes for each party's nominee. No more scrapping for delegates and superdelegates, negotiating complicated state caucuses, or concentrating the decision-making power in the hands of an unrepresentative few. A national primary would certainly eliminate the current system's undemocratic components, as well as its sheer arbitrariness.

There is, however, a major complication with a national primary: it will never happen.

First of all, we are far from the day when parties and their leaders will relinquish all of their control over the process to the general public by way of a nationwide popular vote. More to the point, activists and elected officials from less populous states have a vested interest in maintaining a system that lofts their regional issues to the national stage. Look no further than Iowa's corn farmers and the ethanol-gasoline blend in your car's tank.

There are also reasonable arguments against a national primary election. First, a national primary would make it very difficult for dark horse candidacies to emerge. With the exception of politicians with tremendous personal wealth, it seems unlikely that an unknown candidate could capture the public's imagination in a national primary. Second, a primary structure in which candidates compete in different regions over an extended period has positive attributes. It gives the best opportunity for different voices to be heard along the way. And campaigning by region allows candidates to be thoroughly battle-tested on the path to the nomination.

REFORMING THE PRIMARIES

Over the course of the sixteen-month-long primary campaign of 2008, national opinion began to coalesce around certain reforms that would create a new, organized framework for picking our nominees. Editorial pages across the nation have been virtually unanimous in their position that a new rotating primary system would reinstate order and fairness to an otherwise chaotic and unwieldy process, while maintaining the few positive attributes of our current muddled system.

The four proposals that currently have the wind behind them are generally variations on a theme: break the country into regions, stagger the vote based on certain criteria, and then shuffle the deck four years later to give every state and every voter a fair shake. Each proposal has garnered the support of different political players. And each of them is flawed. They are alternately complicated, problem-prone, or inegalitarian. In order to preserve what is good in our current system—that it forces candidates to pay attention to smaller states and that it prepares them for a general election campaign—each proposal maintains a vestige of today's process, in some instances for better, but in most cases for worse.

Then again, all four proposals establish predictability and restore fairness, the essential criteria for any new system. It is difficult to effectively play a game if you do not know the rules—or if the rules keep changing.

The Regional Presidential Primary and Caucus Act, sponsored by Senators Lamar Alexander (R-Tenn.), Amy Klobuchar (D-Minn.), and

Joe Lieberman (I-Conn.), would divide the country into four quadrants roughly equal in population, each of which would vote during a different month on a rotating schedule. All states in one region would vote during the same week in their designated month, and Iowa and New Hampshire would continue to maintain their status as first in the nation to the polls. A lottery would determine the order in which the regions vote in the next presidential election, with the region going first moving to the back of the line in the next contest. The plan is based on the Rotating Regional Presidential Primaries Plan first adopted by the National Association of Secretaries of State in 2000, and it would allow more candidates to run while giving power to states other than Iowa and New Hampshire.

The Regional Lottery Plan is the brainchild of Larry J. Sabato of the University of Virginia. To rectify the insanity of our current situation, Sabato also proposes dividing the country into four geographical regions, each of which would vote over the course of one month, from April to July. On New Year's Day of each presidential election year, a lottery would determine the order of the schedule to help avoid early campaigning. Instead of Iowa and New Hampshire playing their traditional roles, two states with four or fewer electoral votes would be chosen at random to kick off the primary season.

These two regional plans would certainly bring order to our current chaos. They would confine the primaries to a reasonable time frame, allow a diversity of voices, and give every voter a chance to participate in selecting the nominees. But they simply do not lend themselves to a national consensus. Imagine if either regional plan had been in place in 2008. Conceivably, Obama would have won the upper Midwest and Great Plains, Hillary Clinton would have won the Northeast and the heartland, former North Carolina senator John Edwards would have fared well in the South, and the West would have been a toss-up, perhaps with the advantage going to New Mexico governor Bill Richardson, who would have polled well among Hispanics and voters in the Southwest, where he is popular and enjoys high name recognition. The 2008 primary might have been unusually contentious, but at least it weeded out the candidates who had only regional and not national appeal. In 2008, a regional system would likely have produced regional winners and risked leaving the party without a nominee before balloting began at the convention.

To address this problem, the two other popular reform measures take an interregional approach. They call for different states, of different sizes, from different regions, to vote at once over a period of a few months.

The American Plan, backed by the Center for Voting and Democracy and academics at Harvard's John F. Kennedy School of Government, ensures that candidates without megabucks can compete and make a name for themselves early in the process by pressing the flesh at state fairs, bus stops, and beauty shops in small states. The plan would break voting into ten rounds, with small states voting first and big states voting last, giving a leg up to candidates who don't have a national profile. The order of voting would be determined by the number of congressional districts in each state. In the first round, a group of states with a total of exactly eight congressional districts would vote—for instance, Alaska (one), Delaware (one), Hawaii (two), North Dakota (one), South Dakota (one), Montana (one), and Wyoming (one). In each subsequent round, the total congressional districts of the states would increase by eight, so that the second round would feature a group of states with sixteen districts, then twenty-four, thirty-two, and so on (with some variation to allow megastates like California an opportunity to vote earlier in the process, despite its fifty-six congressional districts).

The Interregional Primary Plan, first proposed in 1986 by Representative Sandy Levin (D-Mich.) and introduced in every congressional session since, would divide the primary voting into six stages, with the country similarly carved into six regions.[10] During each stage, one state (or block of small states) would vote from each region. Voting would start in March, end in June, and rotate every four years. The initial order of voting would be determined by lottery, and the system guarantees that every twenty-four years, every state will have had a chance to kick off the first wave of voting.

Adopt a new, interregional primary system by 2012

An interregional primary—which would eliminate the antidemocratic elements of the arbitrary primary calendar while creating an open, structured, and predictable process—is perhaps the only viable solution to the Goldilocks dilemma. Both the American Plan and the Interregional Primary Plan would fix many of the ailments the system suffers. Each state would have a chance to influence the process, each voter would be empowered to participate, and lesser-known candidates without massive war chests could ostensibly compete and win through retail politicking in smaller states.

Yet there is one major distinguishing feature between these interregional proposals. The American Plan, through its somewhat complicated formula, allows smaller states to vote first. Over the years, academics and politicians alike across the political spectrum have argued this is a good thing. *They're wrong.*

It's hard to swallow the argument that these small states should have such a large role in our national politics. For one thing, they have largely homogeneous populations that do not necessarily look like the rest of America. For another, smaller states are more likely to revolve around singular industries, such as agriculture in Iowa or natural resources in West Virginia. To my mind, the best primary system would allow voters in each state to have their specific concerns addressed, without entirely subverting the debate on issues of national and regional importance.

Besides, there's no indication that candidates and campaigns can't address more than one set of local concerns at any given time. Consider the wonderful accident we witnessed in 2008, as the voting dragged on. Obama and Clinton were forced to compete in states of different sizes, in different regions, on the same day. Hawaii and Wisconsin voted on February 19. Ohio, Texas, Vermont, and Rhode Island voted on March 4. Kentucky and Oregon voted on May 20. The result was that the primary continued on without a winner until every voter in every state had a chance to cast a ballot. If we should preserve any aspect of the current dysfunctional system at all, this is it.

In this way, the Levin proposal, while not perfect, is superior to the other possible reform ideas floated to date. It equally weights the impact of large and small states. It gives every voter a chance to be heard and every candidate a chance to compete. Critics might argue that the Inter-regional Primary Plan would force candidates to travel great distances in order to campaign in several states in different regions that would vote on the same day. Then again, this is nothing new to today's road warrior presidential candidates.

Iowa and New Hampshire will kick and scream the whole way, but at the end of the day, most Americans think their outsize influence in the process is unfair—and they're right. The only question is whether Congress or the national political parties will force Iowa and New Hampshire to give up their privileged positions. Frankly, it makes less difference which body brings these changes about than that they are put into action, but given the many years of earmarking on behalf of the two states by members of Congress, the swiftest course may involve pressure on the DNC and RNC from the state political parties. Indeed, special committees for both national parties began meeting in 2009 with the mission of putting in place new primary fixes in advance of 2012.

Make voting easier and uniform, and ensure egalitarian primaries across the nation

Presidential primaries are a confusing and unfair hodgepodge of rules and procedures. The cumulative effect is that "one person, one vote" is more myth than reality. Too many Americans are shut out of the process thanks to the structure of the primaries. But there are simple steps we can take to make our primaries more uniform and more democratic.

- *Eliminate caucuses:* Caucuses are a needlessly silly exercise that disenfranchises working-class voters and the elderly. Getting rid of them might be going against the grain of tradition in states such as Iowa, but doing so would dramatically open up the process to voters who for years have been forced to watch the nominating process from the sidelines.
- *Eliminate superdelegates:* As I noted earlier, superdelegates give party leaders more say than the average voter. Especially after the 2008 campaign, where it seemed for a time that superdelegates would be decisive

in the outcome, it's time to do away with this antidemocratic mechanism that concentrates power in the hands of party elites.

- *Eliminate winner-take-all voting:* Meant to protect minority voices, winner-take-all voting has effectively shut them out. Each party's nominee should be the clear winner of the nationwide popular vote.
- *Simplify ballot access:* Ballot access for candidates now consists of a confusing welter of rules that vary widely across the states. It would help reform the primary process if the barriers to entry were lower, or at any rate more rational.
- *Same-day registration:* Primary turnout is significantly higher in states with same-day registration, including Idaho, Maine, Minnesota, and North Carolina. Higher turnout would certainly be welcome in states in which labor unions and highly partisan special interest groups dominate get-out-the-vote efforts during the primaries, and it could help produce more centrist and grassroots-driven candidacies and campaigns.

These are commonsense measures that would increase turnout and improve voter confidence in our political process, and all of them could be put in place quickly.

Open partisan primaries to independent and unaffiliated voters

The two major parties have distinct rules in each state that determine who can vote in the relevant primary election. In some states, Democrats and independents are able to vote in Republican primaries, and vice versa. These so-called open primaries clearly were critical to facilitating John McCain's victories in Michigan and New Hampshire in 2000 and 2008. Open primaries encourage consensus, centrism, and, of course, bipartisanship, because moderate-minded independents are allowed to cast ballots for the candidates of their choice. Closed primaries, on the other hand, make it tougher for outsiders to run, participate, and win.

Both parties should welcome voters of any stripe to cross over and participate in their primaries. Independent and unaffiliated voters are the fastest-growing political group in America. Bringing these voters into the nominating process would increase turnout and dampen the overwrought partisanship in our presidential politics. The switch from closed to open primaries would be implemented state by state and would require wresting power away from entrenched state party leaders. But as more voters choose against declaring a party, it bolsters the case for opening party primaries to everyone—and truly putting the presidential nominating process in the hands of the people.

3

MAKE EVERYONE A SWING VOTER
Reforming the General Election

> I consider it completely unimportant who in the party will vote, or
> how; but what is extraordinarily important is this—who will count
> the votes, and how.
>
> —JOSEPH STALIN, 1923

In 2008, America witnessed a shocking aberration. After two bitterly contested, highly controversial presidential elections, the legitimacy of the
results on November 4 was not called into question by hanging chads,
ballot discrepancies, voting irregularities, the Supreme Court, or a diver-
gent electoral college outcome. That alone would have made the election
something to celebrate.

Yet in many respects, the fundamentals of our presidential elections
did not change. Despite the new enthusiasm and millions of new voters,
the system itself is largely unchanged.

- In the midst of two wars and economic collapse, nonissues and sideshows
  repeatedly sidetracked the public and the press, as they have in years
  past.
- Registration requirements continue to vary drastically across the nation,
  meaning that access to the ballot box was as uneven and unfair in 2008 as
  ever before.
- Our Constitution once again effectively disenfranchised millions of Americans thanks to the electoral college—an eighteenth-century idea that
  doesn't fit in our twenty-first-century democracy.

- The FEC, the institution meant to enforce our election laws, was missing in action for the majority of the 2008 campaign.
- Despite reforms after the 2000 debacle, an arbitrary patchwork of state rules and regulations that governs how votes are cast and counted continue to distort the outcome of our presidential elections.
- Turnout was slightly above average by U.S. standards and significantly below average by international standards.

Make no mistake, the inherent defects that bedeviled the general elections of 2000 and 2004 still mar the system. The illogical, disorganized way in which Americans elect the president of the United States has serious, long-term consequences for our democracy and calls into question the very authenticity of our presidential elections.

The 2008 presidential election is perhaps the very best case in point. Conventional wisdom would have us believe that record numbers of voters propelled Barack Obama to his historic victory. But the data don't support that conclusion. While millions of new voters were registered, the number of eligible voters who cast ballots didn't change much between 2004 and 2008. It's still a sad fact that, even in 2008, more than one in three eligible voters stayed home on Election Day.

In the most riveting election in decades, why was turnout so average?

In 1992, during a debate over voter registration laws, Senator Mitch McConnell (R-Ky.) memorably quipped, "Low voter turnout is a sign of a content democracy."[1] Given what we know about the sad state of our presidential elections, it's hard to take the senator's supposition seriously. In fact, we know the opposite is true. Turnout for our presidential elections is low in part because Americans are smart enough to see the truth: the outcome of the general election as currently devised is unfair and not always legitimate. From the institutions that run and manage the process of our general elections, to a tuned-out media, to rules and regulations that are applied unevenly across the nation, it's as if our entire system has conspired to suppress the democratic inclinations of the American people.

THE DEMOCRACY DEFICIT

It's not surprising that our reckless management of the centerpiece of America's democratic tradition—electing the leader of the free world—has resulted in dismal voter turnout and participation. We have a democracy deficit that's a direct result of our system of voting itself.

Much has been made of the "Obamamania" that swept America in 2008, and rightly so. More than 131 million Americans cast a ballot for president in 2008, representing some 63 percent of eligible voters—the highest voter turnout since 1960. Impressively, first-time voters counted for 11 percent of the electorate.[2] At first glance, these exciting numbers affirm what was by other measures deemed a very successful election.

But a deeper analysis of the numbers proves that the system of campaigns and elections has hardly changed. In 2004, African Americans made up 11 percent of voters;[3] in 2008, that figure climbed ever so slightly, to 13 percent.[4] Latinos made up 8 percent of voters in 2004 compared to 9 percent in 2008. Meanwhile, according to the Pew Research Center, while voters aged eighteen to twenty-nine voted overwhelmingly for Obama, turnout among young voters did not significantly increase in 2008.[5] Voter excitement in 2008 has been largely interpreted as the winds of electoral change. But the results of the 2008 election simply prove that even with exciting candidates, well-run campaigns, and a tumultuous political climate, something is terribly wrong with how our presidential elections engage American voters.

The year 2008 was one of the most momentous of the past three decades. For starters, it was the first time in eighty years that neither the sitting president nor the sitting vice president was seeking election. The nation was still at war in Iraq, and the situation in Afghanistan was becoming increasingly unstable. As the campaign entered the homestretch, the stakes increased dramatically. Our financial system imploded, entire industries failed, and Washington cobbled together the biggest bailout since the Great Depression. Given this calamitous environment, it stands to reason that the presidential campaign should have been the most substantive in recent memory, given the many issues of tremendous consequence on the table. Far from it, as it turned out.

Joe the Plumber. Wardrobe-gate. "That one." In November 2008, any

American with a cable box or an Internet connection knew the meaning of these phrases, which were coined during the general election. Today, this shorthand and the controversies associated with it have been all but forgotten. That's because when it comes to presidential elections, America has a short-term memory problem. Every four years, we fixate on issues and story lines that we immediately forget after the campaigns close shop.

Each presidential cycle produces its share of tropes and sensational stories that become national obsessions in the weeks and months before Election Day. They distract from the real issues at stake and then quickly fade once the election is over. The 2008 election was no exception to this rule. First there was the frenzy surrounding the Republican vice presidential nominee, Sarah Palin. Her six-figure wardrobe made headlines, and her Alaskan colloquialisms provided much fodder for late-night comedians. And Palin was, pardon the pun, just the tip of the iceberg. Consider:

- Samuel Joseph Wurzelbacher, the Ohio plumber who challenged Barack Obama's tax plan on the campaign trail, was transformed overnight into a celebrity everyman, "Joe the Plumber." He accompanied McCain at campaign rallies, was the subject of a front-page story in the *New York Times*, and was even discussed by the candidates *during the second nationally broadcast presidential debate.*
- As the campaign neared its conclusion, an Internet rumor that questioned Obama's citizenship generated dozens of news stories and nonstop cable coverage, ultimately prompting the Obama campaign to post a copy of the Democratic nominee's birth certificate online.
- In the closing weeks of the campaign, conservatives screamed bloody murder about the legitimacy of hundreds of thousands of fake voter registrations filed by the Association of Community Organizations for Reform Now (ACORN), a liberal voter outreach organization—evidence, they suggested, of a vast left-wing conspiracy to steal the election.

These media firestorms consumed the most important weeks of the general election, yet they're justly of little note today. Indeed, this cycle of obsessing and forgetting is a staple of modern presidential campaigns.

In part, this is a failure of the media, but it is also a failure of our system itself—debates that have been hemorrhaging viewers, voter turnout that has only modestly increased, and a variety of structural problems that Obama's victory did nothing to change.

THE SWEET SIXTEEN

Chances are, Barack Obama and John McCain didn't visit your hometown during the 2008 campaign. And if they did, it was likely to attend a fund-raiser instead of a town hall meeting.

It is a sad truth that if you live in one of thirty-four states, home to roughly two-thirds of the nation, your vote for president is, for all practical purposes, meaningless. Forget what your social studies teacher taught you in high school. Swing states decide the presidential election, and there are only sixteen of them by today's count.

This isn't the brilliantly devious scheme of a modern-era political consultant or a recent divergence from past practice. *It's the way our Constitution was designed.*

The fact is that voters like you and me don't vote for president. We vote for electors, who cast the only votes for president that matter. Today, electors are ceremonial positions that merely carry out the will of the popular vote in each state. And every state is assigned a certain number of electoral votes—one for each representative in Congress. To win the presidency, a candidate must capture not the popular vote, but the majority of the electoral college's 538 votes. As Hendrik Hertzberg noted in the *New Yorker*: "[The Constitution] says nothing about political campaigns, political parties, or nominating conventions. . . . Nor, for that matter, does Article II say anything about regular people voting. What it does say is 'Each State shall appoint, in such Manner as the Legislature thereof may direct, a Number of Electors.' As the Supreme Court pointedly reminded us on December 12, 2000, 'The individual citizen has no federal constitutional right to vote for electors for the President of the United States.'"[6]

In today's world of red states and blue states, the electoral college means the only votes that matter are the ones up for grabs in swing states such as Florida, Ohio, and Indiana. The Republican and Democratic nominees can each rely on about the same number of states to shift their way in any given presidential election. New York, Illinois, California, and other states in the Northeast, Upper Midwest, and West Coast are reliably in the Democratic column. Texas, Oklahoma, Kentucky, and other states in the Bible Belt and the Great Plains nearly always vote Republican. Kerry and Bush spent 99 percent their money on the sweet sixteen, and Obama and McCain devoted 99 percent of their campaign stops in the final eight weeks to these states.

If you think this system is stupid, you're in good company. Almost two hundred years ago, in a letter to fellow Virginia Republican George Hay, Thomas Jefferson essentially expressed the same sentiment: "I have ever considered the constitutional mode of election ultimately by the Legislature voting by States as the most dangerous blot in our Constitution, and one which some unlucky chance will some day hit and give us a pope and antipope."[7]

The most dangerous blot in our Constitution. Coming from the man who wrote the Declaration of Independence, it's hard to take this criticism lightly. Jefferson worried, rightly so, that the winner of the electoral college would not necessarily be the winner of the popular vote—as happened in the 2000 election between George W. Bush and Al Gore. But the college is an equal opportunity mess maker. In 2004, had John Kerry received just sixty thousand additional votes in Ohio, he would have been the forty-fourth president, despite Bush's substantial three-million-vote margin in the popular vote.

At this point, almost no one except a handful of purist political scientists seriously thinks we should maintain the electoral college. Over the years, politicians and pundits alike have complained that the electoral college gives undue weight to small states, which can and do usurp the will of the majority. Lawmakers have proposed eliminating or altering the electoral college *more than seven hundred times.* According to the National Archives and Records Administration, "There have been more proposals for constitutional amendments on changing the electoral college than on any other subject."[8]

America ranks an abysmal 139th among the world's democracies for voter turnout in national elections. Some see this as a sign of Americans' general political apathy. I see it as a mark of great intelligence. Americans have always been frugal, and when it comes to voting for president, the majority of voters are right to ask, "Why waste the time, when it's really the electoral college that makes the decision?"

THE DEBATE DEBACLE

Nowhere in the Constitution or in the Code of Federal Regulations is there any reference to presidential debates. But there's no question that they play an enormously vital role in our presidential politics. Televised debates have been a mainstay of our presidential campaigns since the Kennedy-Nixon race in 1960. Political junkies might tune in to the campaign coverage more than a year before the first votes are cast, but most Americans begin to focus on the presidential race when the debates begin after Labor Day. They have become a nationally unifying event, an important ritual of our civic religion, and a critical means to engage the public in our presidential elections.

And therein lies the problem with presidential debates as we know them today. They are mind-numbingly boring. They are tedious and uninformative. Instead of drawing everyday Americans further into the process—exciting them, engaging them, encouraging them to participate—today's presidential debates are a national political sedative. As Tom Brokaw once put it, "In 1992 someone asked me how I would change the presidential debate format. I proposed handing each of the candidates a double martini in the firm belief that would get them beyond their canned answers. I think in 2007 we can pair up the martini past and the electronic future. How long would Joe Biden talk on a cell phone after knocking back a big Gibson, straight up?"[9]

Over the past three decades, the viewing audience of presidential debates has dropped dramatically. Despite the historic nature of the 2008 campaign, the second televised debate between Barack Obama and John McCain ranks at the very bottom of the ten most watched presidential debates, according to Nielsen ratings—with neither of the other two debates making the list.[10] Approximately 63.2 million Americans tuned in to Obama and McCain's second debate, compared with 80.6 million who watched the debate between then president Jimmy Carter and Governor Ronald Reagan in 1980.

Rank	Year	Date	Candidates	Viewers
1	1980	October 28	Carter/Reagan	80.6 million
2	1992	October 15	Bush/Clinton/Perot	69.9 million
3	1976	September 23	Ford/Carter	69.7 million
4	1988	October 13	Bush/Dukakis	67.3 million
5	1984	October 21	Reagan/Mondale	67.3 million
6	1992	October 19	Bush/Clinton/Perot	66.9 million
7	1988	September 25	Bush/Dukakis	65.1 million
8	1984	October 7	Reagan/Mondale	65.1 million
9	1976	October 6	Ford/Carter	63.9 million
10	2008	October 8	Obama/McCain	63.2 million

America's population has increased by more than 30 percent since 1980, but viewership of our presidential debates has declined by more than 20 percent since then. Something is very wrong with this picture.

If there is a culprit to blame for this steady erosion in audience, the finger has to be pointed at the organization that runs our debates and the corporate sponsors that underwrite them. Since 1988, the general election debates have been organized—you could say monopolized—by the Commission on Presidential Debates (CPD), a private organization with a nonprofit charter that is accountable to no one. Its leaders—two former chairs of the Democratic and Republican parties—have succeeded in all but running the debates into the ground through the combination of a stifling format, open hostility toward third parties, and routine acquiescence to the major parties' nominees on virtually every aspect of the debates themselves. The result is a rather useless exercise in which fewer and fewer Americans bother to participate.

A coalition of prominent civic groups—including New York University's Brennan Center for Justice and the Center for Voting and Democracy (FairVote)—concluded in a 2004 report that the CPD hosts generally uninformative debates with rigid and stale formats that result in softball questions that avoid important issues. Their report concluded, "The CPD's formats prevent in-depth examination of critical issues, and allow the candidates to deliver pre-packaged sound bites during the debates that are repeated over and over again on the campaign trail." Liberal good-government types aren't the only ones who think poorly of the CPD. Right-wing politicians and activists, including Newt Gingrich and Alan Keyes, favor abolishing the CPD altogether.

It's impossible to know whether the CPD's useless debates actually depress voter turnout, but there's no question that the debates are an extraordinary missed opportunity to bring more people into the political process.

NO REFEREE ON THE FIELD

The 2008 election saw fund-raising record after fund-raising record fall. It started in June 2007, when Hillary Clinton set a one-day primary election fund-raising record. Then Ron Paul bested Kerry's all-time one-day money haul. Then Obama set a one-month primary election record: $55 million in February 2008. Then Obama set a one-month general election fund-raising record: more than $150 million in September 2008, mostly from small-money donors. It was the priciest presidential election in history. With this influx of cash came umpteen questions about how it could be spent and how it must be reported. Yet despite the feverish pace of presidential campaigning, the Federal Election Commission, which enforces the nation's election laws, was out of commission.

The FEC is a bipartisan body comprising six commissioners picked by the president and confirmed by the Senate. By law, no more than three members can belong to the same political party, and a four-commissioner majority is required to pass new rules, undertake investigations, or issue judgments against those who violate campaign finance laws. But in 2008, the terms of four of the FEC's six members had expired, leaving just two remaining commissioners. A partisan stalemate between Senate majority leader Harry Reid (D-Nev.) and minority leader Mitch McConnell (R-Ky.) resulted in a seven-month stretch during which the nation's election referees were on the sidelines, watching the game unfold, hamstrung. McConnell and Reid ultimately sorted out the issue in late June 2008, forcing the FEC to cram half a year's work into a few short months. Remarkably, when the Senate finally filled the four vacancies, it confirmed Donald

McGahn, a Republican campaign finance lawyer who had previously headed disgraced congressman Tom DeLay's legal team. McGahn was shockingly elected FEC chairman later that year.

There is quite possibly no issue less sexy than election law. But the FEC serves a vital function, and elections can easily be decided by the fine print of the FEC's rules and regulations, which determine what candidates can and cannot do. When McCain received the dubious bank loan to underwrite his flagging primary campaign and reportedly secured it by leveraging "incoming but unprocessed contributions," presumably including public financing, it would have been the FEC's job to decide whether the move was permissible under the law. But the political impasse over FEC appointments in 2008 left this issue unsettled, opening McCain up to attack from Republican and Democratic rivals. (The FEC eventually issued a letter stating that McCain did nothing improper—in February 2009, four months after he lost the election.[11]) Over the same months, FEC oversight was lacking on PAC and lobbyist contributions, let alone on contentious areas such as the activities of 527 political organizations, which are technically not regulated by the FEC as long as they do not coordinate their activities with a campaign, and bundling, around which new regulations could have been proposed during a campaign with two candidates willing to voluntarily disclose information about their donors.

Furthermore, given the FEC's role as the nation's elections referee, it's mind-boggling that it is a *bipartisan* commission instead of a *nonpartisan* one. It's a simple fact that the men and women who serve as FEC commissioners are unabashed partisans with a vested interest in the issues that come before them. Imagine the home-plate umpire at a ball game wearing the jersey of the home team, and the first-base umpire wearing the visiting team's jersey. Neither fans nor players would want to watch or play a game with this kind of biased officiating. Yet this is a fundamental reality of our presidential politics—and a recipe for stalemate and chaos.

THE BALLOT BOX BLUES

In a legitimate election, every vote should count equally, and every eligible voter should have an equal opportunity to cast a ballot. But when it comes to voting for president of the United States, each state has different standards for registration, different means for casting ballots, and different ways of counting votes. In 2008, Obama won by such a large margin that these irregularities seemed unimportant. But as with the elections in 2000 and 2004, these differences in voting procedure and election law literally decided the outcome of the presidential contest. Today, your ZIP code determines when, where, and how you vote for president—and if your vote will count at all.

My purpose here is not to dissect each specific state's dysfunctions, but to paint a broad picture of the inequitable system by which we as a nation elect our president. The main areas for concern in the nation's patchwork system are:

Registration. Registering to vote in the United States can be truly burdensome, depending on where you live. Federal law requires voters in every state to provide proof of identification—such as a driver's license, utility bill, or bank statement—at the time of registration or the first time they go to the polls. However, states are allowed to impose additional requirements, and many do.

For instance, Indiana requires a government-issued photo ID to register to vote. In the most extreme example, registration in Arizona requires *proof of citizenship.* Government-issued ID requirements are particularly onerous when you consider that more than one out of every ten Americans don't have driver's licenses or state ID cards. About three-quarters of those without photo IDs are women, and a third are senior citizens.

While policies in some states inadvertently disenfranchise women and seniors, others are extremely inclusive. Minnesota, Montana, and several other states allow voters to register at the polls on Election Day, and North Dakota doesn't require any registration whatsoever for voters to cast a ballot.[12]

Is it fair that residents of Arizona have more obstacles to registering to vote than folks in North Dakota?

Purging. Once registered, voters are included on voter registration lists (voter rolls) in each state, which are used in polling places on Election Day to determine those who are eligible to cast a ballot. Of course, these lists include millions of names and must be maintained to reflect current and accurate registration information. To that end, these rolls are "purged" periodically of voters who are no longer residents of a particular state, who have died, or who have been convicted of crimes that render them ineligible to vote.

However, such purges often result in registered voters being accidentally removed—through "near" matches of names or addresses as massive databases are compared. If mistakes are not caught before Election Day, purges can disenfranchise eligible voters. If you think this is a rare occurrence, think again.

According to the Brennan Center for Justice, between 2004 and 2006 thirteen million voters were purged from the rolls in thirty-nine states and the District of Columbia, which resulted in thousands of eligible voters being stripped of their right to vote. In Georgia, for instance, an election official removed seven hundred suspected felons from the list in 2008, although many on this list had no criminal record whatsoever.[13] And the *New York Times* reported that Colorado, Louisiana, and Michigan purged more people in 2008 than were estimated to have moved or died during the period in question.[14]

Provisional ballots. In an attempt to solve some of the issues created by our hodgepodge system of state-specific registration, federal law allows voters who feel they have wrongly been left off voter rolls to cast provisional ballots. These ballots aren't counted at the polling site. Instead, election officials can review provisional ballots at a later time, when they have all the information needed to determine the voters' eligibility. In the 2004 election, however, only 64.5 percent of provisional ballots were eventually counted.[15]

This is an important safeguard for voters who might be accidentally purged from registration rolls, but there's a catch: each state sets its own rules for whether a provisional ballot is ultimately considered valid. As the *New York Times* editorialized in 2004, "It's ridiculous . . . that a person who accidentally walks into the wrong polling place can cast a provisional ballot that will be counted in one state but thrown out in another."[16] Until presidential elections are no longer determined by the outcome in individual states rather than the national popular vote, these differences in arcane election law have the potential to decide the fate of the nation.

Voting. When it comes to the ballot box itself, innumerable problems associated with casting and counting votes plague us, despite a patchwork of reforms passed in 2002 as part of the Help America Vote Act (HAVA) after more than two million votes were thrown out of the 2000 election because the ballots could not be read.

Just as states set the ground rules for voter registration, they also determine requirements for voting once a person shows up at the polls. Eighteen states require voters to present identification to cast a ballot, and six of those states require a photo ID. Again, women and seniors are disproportionately shut out of the voting process.

States are also empowered to determine whether voters pull levers, fill in circles, or check the box on a touch-screen monitor to cast their votes—though HAVA requires that states upgrade punch-card ballots. States also determine how and when voters cast their ballots. Since 1998, all voting in Oregon is conducted by mail, with ballots sent to registered voters between fourteen and eighteen days before the election closes. Thirty-four states allow voters to cast ballots in person before Election Day, whereas four states lack early voting and absentee provisions altogether.[17]

From ballot access to the type of ballot—and all the various problems associated with counting them—whether you're allowed to vote for president and how is determined entirely by where you live.

FIXING THE BALLOT BOX

Reforming our presidential politics has always been an elusive endeavor. There is widespread confusion about what is truly problematic about our current system. In this way, significant energy for reform is diverted, and nonissues dominate much of the debate.

On the one hand, reform isn't lacking for want of ideas. Indeed, most proposals to fix our general election system have been around for years. It is interesting that few of these fixes are new, and fewer still have been implemented. It's time to consider a different approach. No more theorizing, analyzing, and agonizing over ideas that are never going to see the light of day. We already know what works, what is feasible, and, honestly, what is popular. Let's do what we can, as fast as we can, before the system deteriorates any further.

Then again, many analysts and observers are skittish about changing the historic institutions by which our nation selects its commander in chief. We've always done it this way, they argue. It's what our founders intended. Why change course after some 230 years of successful self-rule and peaceful transitions of executive power?

Except that's not true. For one, it was not until the Voting Rights Act of 1965 that the United States prohibited qualifying tests—including literacy tests, poll taxes, and grandfather clauses—to be used in voter registration. As Jill Lepore recounted in the *New Yorker*, there wasn't a secret ballot in the tumultuous years immediately preceding the Civil War. Men would get ballots from their parties' headquarters and carry them to the polls—sometimes risking physical assault from supporters of other parties. A Baltimore merchant, George Kyle, was "clobbered [and] drew a knife, but didn't have a chance to use it," she writes. "Someone else fired a shot, hitting Kyle in the arm. A man carrying a musket rushed at him. Another threw a brick, knocking him off his feet. George Kyle picked himself up and ran. He never did cast his vote. Nor did his brother, who died of his wounds." Later, "when the House of Representatives convened hearings into the election . . . [it] was upheld on the ground that any 'man of ordinary courage' could have made his way to the polls."[18]

I'm mindful of the gravitational pull of history and precedent that has previously prevented forward-thinking solutions to the problems ingrained in our voting process. But American democracy has been reinvented many times over the generations, and restoring fairness and legitimacy to our presidential elections, by ensuring that every American has the same opportunities to vote and have his or her vote counted equally, fits this grand tradition.

It's not an overstatement to say that the election of the president of the United States is the most important democratic exercise in the world. We simply can't afford to have a pall cast over a presidency because of the way an election is administered and how the voting process is structured. The following solutions address structural problems that remain unsolved, in order to ensure that America's presidential elections are fair, secure, open, accurate, and legitimate—not just once in a blue moon, but each and every time.

Bypass the electoral college to restore integrity and equality to our presidential elections

Nearly everyone agrees that the electoral college has outlived its usefulness. The problem is, the framers made it awfully difficult to get rid of the electoral college—not because they were especially enamored of that means of selecting the president (though some of them were), but because they were dedicated to the right of a strong minority of states in the republic to maintain the agreed-upon Constitution. Making a change to the Constitution was a significant decision, a potentially Union-ending decision, and could not be left to the simple majority of states or the federal government. The electoral college, in this sense, protected the voting interests and welfare of the less populated states.

Particularly today, an attempt to ditch the electoral college will face vociferous opposition from the "small" states. In 1790, at the time of the nation's first census, the differential between "small" states and "large" states was not nearly as great as it is now. Then, the least populous state, Delaware, had 7 percent of the population of Virginia, in which 747,610 people resided (excluding slaves). In 2008, Wyoming's 532,668 residents equal 1.5 percent of California's population. It is therefore hard to imagine three-quarters of state legislatures adopting a constitutional amendment to abolish the electoral college, let alone two-thirds of U.S. senators.

Fortunately, there is another way. States that have been forced to sit out the general election for years are starting to take action. Legislatures in several states have adopted an innovative interstate compact to bypass the electoral college.

In 2007, Maryland became the first state in the nation to adopt a national popular vote law. Instead of giving all of its electoral votes to the winner of the statewide vote, the Maryland law will give its ten electoral votes to the winner of the national popular vote. The law will take effect when enough states to represent 270 electoral votes—the number needed to win the presidency—adopt national popular vote legislation.

This is a viable solution that could easily be put into work within a few years, completely avoiding the mess of amending the Constitution. In fact, several other states have already followed Maryland's lead. In 2008, New Jersey, Illinois, and Hawaii signed on to the compact, accounting for 50 of the 270 electoral votes needed for it to take effect. Four additional states have passed legislation, which was subsequently vetoed by the states' governors.[19] In fact, California's state assembly has twice passed national popular vote legislation, in 2006 and 2008. The legislation would have added California's 55 electoral votes—20 percent of the entire goal—to the compact. On both occasions, Governor Arnold Schwarzenegger vetoed the legislation, despite endorsement from the *Los Angeles Times*.[20]

Legislatures in forty-three states have some form of the national popular vote act pending.[21] If a few additional large states pass this legislation in the coming years, it could signal a watershed moment for direct democracy.

Dismantle the FEC and replace it with a nonpartisan agency that we can trust to fairly monitor and regulate our presidential campaigns

We can't afford to have biased and ineffective arbiters overseeing our presidential elections. And we also can't afford to have the referees on the sideline during the biggest game of the year. In a system plagued by questions of legitimacy and fairness, getting rid of the Federal Election Commission is the right move toward restoring credibility to our presidential elections.

Of course, I'm not arguing that we go without any regulatory body whatsoever. We certainly need someone to call the shots. But we need an institution that will call them fairly and promptly. A nonpartisan commission, instead of today's bipartisan FEC, would give this important enforcement agency the credibility it needs to effectively patrol national campaigns.

Two Yale Law School professors, Bruce Ackerman and Ian Ayres, have proposed an interesting alternative to the current FEC. Instead of a six-member panel composed of equal numbers of Democrats and Republicans, Ackerman and Ayres have suggested a five-member commission of retired federal judges who are at least sixty-five years old. They argue, rightly, that these men and women are best able to do a credible job enforcing our election laws: "Such experienced judges would have compiled track records that permitted a full assessment of their fairness. By this stage in their careers, they would have their eyes on the history books and would be reluctant to tarnish their reputations by blatant acts of partisanship."[22]

Ackerman and Ayres also suggest that each commissioner serve a ten-year term, with one commissioner retiring every two years. This would not only prevent the "out to lunch" problem of the 2008 elections—it would also mean perpetual impartiality.

This is a smart solution to a chronic oversight problem inherent in our presidential elections, and it's a relatively simple step that would help restore citizen trust and confidence in a tarnished system.

Enact universal voter registration, to ensure that every American has an equal opportunity to cast a ballot

It is absurd that Americans are discouraged or prevented from voting because of different state laws that make registration burdensome. In presidential elections, everyone should have the same access to the polls. That's why we need to create a new system of universal voter registration for our national elections.

According to the Brennan Center for Justice, "the United States is one of the few industrialized democracies that places the onus for registration on the voter." In fact, voter registration itself has a tangled history in America, where it was most energetically instituted by segregationists, who wanted to suppress the black vote. In other Western nations, the government is responsible for compiling rolls of eligible voters, for instance, as in the United Kingdom, which sends annual registration cards to confirm the electoral districts of every possible voter.[23]

A system of universal registration would require that election officials in each state compile lists of eligible voters—so that voters need only show up at the polls, present identification, and vote. Such lists would be exceedingly easy to compile from U.S. tax records, utility companies, change-of-address forms submitted to the U.S. Postal Service, and state databases from agencies such as the Department of Motor Vehicles. Instead of different states creating different rules that govern voter registration, the government and citizens would work in tandem to make sure that every eligible voter is included on registration rolls.

Universal registration makes all the sense in the world. Plus, it's an especially attractive solution to those who are concerned about such fraudulent voters as the deceased woman who cast a ballot or the man who voted early and often, or voter registrations listed under Mr. Santa Claus or Ms. Minnie Mouse. We're right to be concerned about the legitimacy of our elections, but it turns out that voter fraud—the purposeful casting of an illegitimate ballot by impersonation or fraud—doesn't exist to any meaningful extent. According to Project Vote, from 2002 to 2007 only 52 people were convicted of voter fraud—*out of 196,139,871 ballots cast.*[24] The ACORN workers in 2008 who registered fake names weren't scheming to cast fake ballots; they were minimum-wage employees who decided it was easier work to find lists of names from, say, the phone book than it was to canvass the streets and knock on doors.

Fraud isn't a problem in our presidential campaigns. What is a problem are the widely disparate election laws that create second-class voters and that forcibly and covertly discourage civic participation. Universal registration would rectify the inequitable rules that have discouraged some fifty million Americans from even registering to vote. It would also prevent instances of false registration, by putting the burden of voter registration on the government, instead of on citizens and third-party organizations, such as ACORN.

Create a national standard for national elections

Our national elections suffer from extreme regionalism, and the presidency is today determined by voting standards that are contradictory from state to state. The good news is that Congress can adopt simple national standards that will fix the shortfalls of HAVA and give every citizen the equal opportunity to vote and have their vote counted.

- *Standard rules for provisional ballots:* As I noted earlier, an eligible provisional ballot cast in one state might not be acceptable across the border in a neighboring state. That creates a fundamental inequity that Congress must address. Creating a uniform standard for provisional ballots is the only way to ensure that every vote counts equally.

- *Establish early voting nationwide:* In 2008, voters across the country were met with long lines at the ballot box. To relieve congestion at the polls and to ensure that everyone has an opportunity to vote, Congress should require every state to offer early in-person or absentee mail-in voting.

- *Advance voter registration:* One measure that would encourage civic participation and learned voting behavior is a youth initiative championed by FairVote: advance voter registration, which allows teenagers to preregister at sixteen, with further provisions allowing them to vote in primaries at seventeen if they'll be eighteen by the time of the general election. Republican governor Charlie Crist signed a version of this proposal into law in Florida, so it certainly has cross-party appeal. Several others states, including California, Michigan, and Maryland, have considered this commonsense measure.

Make Election Day a national holiday

In 2008, 63 percent of registered voters cast a ballot for president, the highest percentage since the landmark elections of 1968. While it's good news that voter turnout has increased over the past three election cycles, it's also worth considering why, on average, more than one in every three registered voters—today, some fifty million Americans— fail to show up at the polls. One of the reasons, without question, is that for the vast majority of Americans, Election Day is just another workday.

If you think there's something sacred or special about the first Tuesday in November, think again. According to Why Tuesday?, a voting reform group, this day was picked back in 1845, in order to make it convenient for voters to get to the polls. To accommodate the time it took voters to travel by horse to the county seat, and so as not to interfere with other days of the week reserved for going to market or church, Congress chose Tuesday as Election Day. Today, instead of making it convenient for voters to cast ballots, voting during the workweek is simply an impossibility for millions of Americans—especially workers with children and families to care for who can't afford or are not given permission by their employers to spend hours in line at the polls.

The simple solution to this rather large impediment is to make Election Day a national holiday. Some say this is too expensive and would cost the economy billions in productivity. But, as Why Tuesday? smartly notes, "If we can move Columbus Day, Presidents' Day, and Martin Luther King, Jr.'s Holiday for the convenience of shoppers, why not make Election Day more convenient for the sake of voters?"[25]

Sack the Commission on Presidential Debates

Today, our presidential debates are structured by political elites and driven by a top-down model that has led to a stifling, uninteresting format. I've argued for years that our presidential debates should interact with voters rather than lull them to sleep. Involving more voters will result in debates that are far more memorable—and informative.

It all comes down to a misunderstanding of what presidential debates should be about. The Commission on Presidential Debates believes that the debates should be a dialogue between candidates and journalists that the public is able to view and evaluate. This is flat-out wrong. Instead, debates should be a two-way dialogue between voters and candidates, in which journalists simply serve as impartial moderators and hosts.

The latter was the model adopted during many of the 2008 Democratic and Republican primary debates. These debates—more than fifty of them, when all was said and done—drew amazingly high ratings. Some eleven million Americans tuned in to ABC's Democratic debate in Philadelphia, the largest audience of any debate during the primary season. What makes this figure astounding is that this debate was *the twenty-sixth of the primary campaign*. And consider that by April, most Democrats had already cast their ballots.

Clearly, one factor for the sustained interest among voters was the suspenseful, never-ending primary campaign. Yet something also must be said for the structure of the debates, which were managed and produced by the networks in partnership with Internet-based media.

In one debate, sponsored by CNN and YouTube, debate questions were solicited online, and viewers submitted videos of their queries for the candidates, which were shown at the debate. There was considerable candidate interaction, and in many of the debates candidates were given significant amounts of time to answer their questions. In addition, the debates themselves featured *all* of the candidates who participated in the primaries—even unlikely contenders. The result was not an embarrassing sideshow in which long shots and showmen ruined the debate for the serious candidates, as some predicted. The primary debates were serious and engaging, in a way that the CPD has failed to re-create during any of the general election debates it has sponsored.

That's why it's time to abolish the CPD.

Instead, the major broadcast and cable networks, with the oversight of respected, nonpartisan citizens groups such as American University's Center for Democracy and Election Management, should sponsor the presidential debates—and lots of them. Together, the media and democracy-promoting organizations can set the terms of engagement, design new formats, incorporate new technologies, and reach more voters as a result. Here are a few good ideas as a starting point.

- *Interactivity:* In the next presidential election, let's incorporate the information technology we all use every day into every presidential debate, in order to engage everyday citizens—technology that enables ongoing dialogue between candidates and voters. From webcams to instant messages, Facebook to Twitter, technology now gives us the means to dramatically open up the debates. The CNN/YouTube primary debates in 2008 were a great start—but much more needs to be done. A vast improvement would be to adopt the model pioneered in the fall of 2007 by 10 Questions (http://www.10questions.com), a collaboration between techPresident, the *New York Times* editorial board, and MSNBC. The Web site allowed individuals to submit video questions, which were then ranked by the site's thousands of users. For the 2007 launch, the top ten questions had a tech focus. (The number one question was about the candidates' stances on an open Internet, which makes sense for an online start-up—just as in the early days of Amazon, the site's best-selling books catered to a tech-savvy audience.) As more people become aware of 10 Questions and similar Web sites, regular citizens—instead of journalists and TV moderators—will be able to collectively determine the most important questions to ask our presidential aspirants.

- *Town hall format:* At the onset of the general election in 2008, John McCain challenged Barack Obama to a series of town hall debates across the country. It was an exciting proposition that would have truly engaged voters, but Obama regrettably declined the invitation. I can't think of a better way to engage voters and to create the time and the space necessary to allow the candidates to spar at length on a number of important issues.

- *Third-party candidates:* Presidential debates should feature only candidates who might win enough ballots to capture the White House—but it can't be overlooked that participating in a debate vastly improves a candidate's chances. The current 15 percent polling threshold, set by the CPD, is far too high if you believe the point of the debates should be to boost the public's interest in the election. In 1992, independent candidate Ross Perot went from having support from 7 percent of the public before the first debate to 19 percent on Election Day, and two of the three debates in which he participated, alongside George H. W. Bush and Bill Clinton, rank in the top ten in Nielsen's ratings. Instead of the 15 percent threshold, candidates should have to poll at 5 percent and to have gotten on the ballots in enough states to conceivably win the White House if their polling numbers improved. Allowing independent and third-party contenders to participate engages voters and increases viewership. Even in 2008, 56 percent of people hoped that a major third political party would emerge in the United States—and among younger Americans and independent voters, the percentage was higher (65 percent and 72 percent, respectively).[26]

Develop integrity standards for voter-registration drives

The flap over ACORN's phony voter registrations in 2008 proved not to be the electoral cataclysm that many on the right believed. Nonetheless, until universal registration is enacted, it's worth taking a hard look at new integrity standards that would prevent groups like ACORN from mucking up the system with voters that don't exist and creating more needless distractions during presidential elections.

ACORN's sloppiness and malfeasance put a serious strain on the election boards that were required to go through its blizzards of bad paper. That costs taxpayer money. It also promotes cynicism about the integrity of the franchise when a voter-education organization is discovered to have "registered" the entire Dallas Cowboys lineup, as agents of ACORN did in 2008.[27] Worse, every fake registration provides an easy cudgel to those right-wing activists who are bent on discouraging minorities from registering because they will likely vote Democratic.

Groups such as ACORN can't be barred from registering voters. However, both political parties and voter-participation groups can develop voluntary policing standards in order to keep voter registration issues from becoming a distraction for law enforcement officials, secretaries of state, and the public at large. Ultimately, our goal should be universal registration. Until then, we should set our sights on ensuring integrity in registration procedures, and indeed in every aspect of our presidential elections.

4

KILL THE SAFE SEATS
Reforming Congressional Elections

> The purpose of our lobbying laws is to tell the public who is
> being paid how much to lobby whom on what. That purpose is
> not being served under the status quo as we now see it.
> —SENATOR CARL LEVIN, 1992

In 1994, Republicans, under the leadership of Newt Gingrich, took control of Congress for the first time in decades, promising to put the interests of Americans first and reform the ways of Washington. Twelve years
later, Democrats led by Nancy Pelosi promised a return to sensible,
consensus-driven government, and the American people again handed
the reins of congressional power to one political party. Yet, as I write
this, we're back to square one. According to the Gallup organization,
Americans continue to have a lower opinion of Congress today than
during virtually any other time in modern American history.[1]

Democrats and Republicans alike have earned the mistrust of the
American people after decades of historic unresponsiveness and abuse.
But as tempting as it might be, we can't just blame the politicians.
Americans' low opinion of Congress is a direct result of the way elections are fought and structured, campaigns are financed, party committees are operated, and lawmakers collude with lobbyists, among a
number of challenges. It's not about ideology or which party happens to
be in charge. It's about the structure of our legislative system.

The disillusion, distrust, and disgust that Americans feel toward

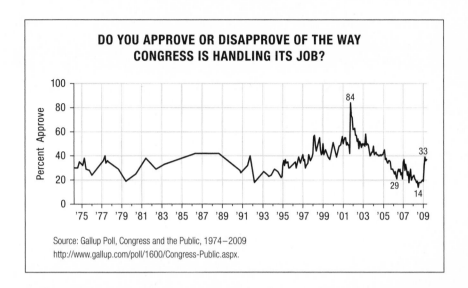

**DO YOU APPROVE OR DISAPPROVE OF THE WAY
CONGRESS IS HANDLING ITS JOB?**

Source: Gallup Poll, Congress and the Public, 1974–2009
http://www.gallup.com/poll/1600/Congress-Public.aspx.

the nation's legislative branch has less to do with the party in power than the gridlock and partisanship that has crippled Washington. If New York is the city that never sleeps, Washington is the city that never works. Members of Congress and the major parties have more incentive to pick political fights than find common ground on pressing issues. In our dysfunctional system, the rewards for winning partisan battles far outweigh those for responding to the needs of the American people.

There's an important difference here between identifying with a particular ideology and blindly following the will of a political party. Rampant partisanship is the latter. I have no problem with Republicans and Democrats whose conscience dictates that they take up a particular position. But rampant partisanship—the kind that has overwhelmed Washington for the past decade and a half—goes beyond ideology to simply walking the party line because to deviate would seem weak. This brand of thoughtlessness and pettiness has infiltrated our politics.

And it has serious consequences. On the one hand, out-of-control partisanship has led to unethical behavior by our representatives, compounding the distrust of Congress that Americans already feel. Despite small reforms in recent years, special interest influence is pervasive not only in determining our congressional elections but in determining the outcome of legislation on Capitol Hill. The cost of running for the

House or Senate has quadrupled, elections are nastier than ever, and our leaders continue to waste billions of taxpayer dollars on pet initiatives and projects.

On the other hand, Congress has utterly failed to confront the issues facing the nation. More Americans today are uninsured, underemployed, underpaid, and unemployed than at any previous time in recent memory. Just three days after Barack Obama was elected president, unemployment hit 6.5 percent, a fourteen-year high, and it rose to a twenty-six-year high of 9.7 percent by the fall of 2009. If there ever were a bipartisan issue, one would think it would be saving the country from a crippling repeat of the Great Depression. Yet in the early months of 2009, the newly minted administration was forced to muscle through an economic stimulus bill without any Republican support in the House and with only three Republican votes in the Senate. Partisanship prevented Congress from reforming our health care system before its summer break and from enacting more effective economic policies to reverse the trend of declining wages and stagnant job creation. Furthermore, as the rest of the world takes action to confront the climate crisis, America is still debating its first legislative effort to confront the problem, the "cap-and-trade" bill passed in the House in June 2009 and still in contention in the Senate as of this writing.

We need realistic solutions that take into account some straight truths about Congress that reformers have generally failed to acknowledge. Yes, special interests, lobbyists, out-of-control politicking, and unethical officials plague our government. But influence peddling is not our main problem. In fact, special interests are an important part of our democracy and the legislative process. Our representatives and senators are by and large right-thinking people who are operating in an environment that encourages and even requires misbehavior as a means of survival. We have to change the game, not the players, to bring about real reform.

What does real reform look like? To change the Washington culture, we need to:

- *Shake up our congressional elections,* by banning special interest contributions and changing the way our districts are drawn. We need to give congressional candidates free airtime and shift to them the public funds that have previously gone to presidential races.

- *Change the way Congress does business,* from a budget-drafting process that is a major target of partisan bickering to a law-drafting process that is far too secretive.
- *Tackle ethical lapses by members of Congress*, by forcing them to disclose all of their contacts with lobbyists and banning lobbyists from all political fund-raisers.

Instead of spasmodic reactions to our reoccurring problems, this chapter and the next present an agenda of comprehensive reform, with a singular goal: a fair and open legislative system that ameliorates the problems endemic to our unjust and closed system. The steps I outline here are decisive measures, but they're not divisive. They combine the best thinking from the left, right, and center—which together will bring about the comprehensive change needed.

THE ELECTION THAT DOESN'T COUNT

The first thing you need to know about congressional elections is that they generally don't matter. By the time you get into the voting booth to mark that circle, the outcome has largely been predetermined by some very powerful people in Washington, D.C., whose names you have likely never heard. This isn't a conspiracy theory; it's the truth. Our system is set up to lock you out and perpetuate itself, and it does an excellent job on both counts.

In theory, on the first Tuesday of November every two years, voters in each of the nation's 435 congressional districts pick between a Democratic nominee and a Republican nominee to represent them in Congress. Unfortunately, theory differs decidedly from reality in House races, thanks to a long tradition of congressional gerrymandering—the process by which state legislatures purposefully draw districts to favor one party or the other.

This is something that I know a good deal about. During my career as a political consultant, I've worked at charting public opinion, plotting strategy, and guiding candidates through the shoals of electoral politics. Together with my former partner Mark Penn, I developed the practice of "microtargeting" voters by their demographics and "psychographics." By identifying a person's economic, cultural, and social status, often summarized by their ZIP code, we developed techniques to target voters in a way never before possible. Where people send their children to school, where they shop and what they buy, and any number of additional data sets offer insight into how certain people in certain areas vote—and why. Using that information enables a politician to send a particular message to particular voters. Our pioneering use of microtargeting in the political sphere revolutionized modern campaigning. The technique has become widespread, and with the help of sophisticated computer tools, political consultants were able by the early 1990s to identify the political preferences of voters on a *block-by-block* basis.

Since that time, state lawmakers have applied that same technology to redraw the lines of congressional districts to make it easy for incumbents to win reelection. They use census data and voter files maintained by state election officials to craft districts that contain a majority of voters from one political party—all but guaranteeing that an incumbent of a particular party in a particular district will always prevail. Take the extreme case of congressional redistricting in Texas in 2003, when then House majority leader Tom DeLay helped his fellow Texas Republicans redraw district maps that eliminated safe Democratic districts and created impenetrable Republican ones. Several Democratic state legislators literally fled the state of Texas in a last-ditch effort to stop DeLay's map from being passed. DeLay's effort targeted several incumbent Democrats, forcing them to compete in newly minted Republican districts, and many lost their seats as a result, including the venerable and long-serving Martin Frost.

The result of modern gerrymandering is that today, especially in "off-years," also known as nonpresidential election years, only a relative handful of seats in the House of Representatives are true toss-ups. The rest—typically between 370 and 400—are highly predictable contests, thanks to districts in which either Democrats or Republicans have been handed a significant advantage by their states' legislatures. In 2004, for instance, leading candidates were in a "close" race—within ten percentage points of each other—in only 31 of the 435 seats in the U.S. House.[2] Even in 2006, a very active election year in which Democrats took back the House and the Senate, only fifty-eight House races were decided by a margin of ten percentage points or less.[3] And in 2008, the year when history was made and change swept through the nation, only sixty-six House and eight Senate races were truly competitive. The data clearly show that most congressional races are highly predicable blowouts. In House races, incumbents won 95 percent of the elections, and in openly contested House seats, the candidate that raised the most money won 84 percent of the time.

The effect of gerrymandering is especially apparent when you compare the outcome of races in the House and the Senate in any given election year. Because senators compete for votes statewide, there are no districts to gerrymander, which means their races are impervious to the partisan manipulations that have plagued House contests. In 2000, only 10 percent of House races were decided by ten points or less while 29 percent of Senate races were decided by the same margin. In 2008, one-quarter of House candidates did not face any opposition *at all*.[4]

Granted, other factors affect the competitiveness of Senate contests. But because of gerrymandering, it doesn't matter how unpopular Congress is; the system is rigged to perpetually reelect incumbents to the House and maintain one-party control in the vast majority of congressional districts.

THE SECRET PRIMARY

Even if our gerrymandered congressional districts render most general elections moot, at least voters have their voices heard in the primary election, right? Wrong. To be sure, each party holds an important primary election—but not one in which you or I get to participate.

The truth is, there is a secret primary that you've never heard about. Citizens don't run for office; party leaders adopt them. The first primary in a congressional campaign is an informal and unwritten one held by party heavyweights alone. It doesn't quite amount to the smoke-filled back rooms of yore, but the outcome is largely indistinguishable.

One-party, gerrymandered control of congressional districts is an essential precondition for the secret primary. When district lines are drawn to favor a particular party, suddenly the national parties have outsized influence and control over the primary process.

With party control firmly cemented through redistricting, four committees in Washington take over—one for each party and each house of Congress:

1. Democratic Congressional Campaign Committee (DCCC, or "D triple C" as it's often referred to)
2. National Republican Congressional Committee (NRCC)
3. Democratic Senatorial Campaign Committee (DSCC, or "DS")
4. National Republican Senatorial Committee (NRSC)

Each of these committees has a singular task: win as many races as possible to gain a majority in its respective chamber. To achieve this goal, each committee raises and disburses massive amounts of money. For instance, in 2008 the DCCC raised and spent more than $176 million in support of Democratic candidates for the House. The NRCC, struggling in one of the worst years for Republican candidates in recent memory, spent *only* $118 million.[5]

The secret primary kicks off as early as eighteen months before a general election, when these committees begin what amounts to a party-wide talent search. The committees hunt likely winners to whom they give essential support—namely, those millions and millions of dollars. Having spoken at great length to committee insiders over the years about what they look for in a candidate, I know that there are a variety of traits they seek. The first is a candidate's ability to raise money. The second is their ability to raise money. And probably the third is their ability to raise money.

But there are some very important criteria beyond money. One is something I call "clubability"—that is, will they work for the party, will they fit in, and will they get along? That is especially important in circumstances where a number of candidates are vying for party support and all are deemed just as likely to raise about the same amount of money. Who will be most controllable or amenable to the party plank and party program? Who will be most supportive of the party leadership? In some congressional districts, finding a candidate with clubability is a luxury;

the committees simply don't have a choice of candidates. In that instance, they look for people who will at the very least stay on message.

Staying on message is critically important, because the committees are controlling the funding for multiple districts, and they want to know that a particular candidate won't undermine their efforts in other competitive races—or, in the worst-case scenario, put a safe seat into play. With the party committees investing tens of thousands, if not hundreds of thousands, of dollars in a candidate, they want to know that the candidate will stick to the committee's script.

A certain degree of freelancing and local color is necessary and indeed even desirable. But I've had many experiences where a committee staffer would call me early in the morning, having read an obscure press clipping, to say that the candidate is off message and threatening to jeopardize critical funding in the waning days of a campaign.

Rest assured—or not—the candidates themselves understand that sticking with the script is nonnegotiable. If, as with most challengers, they are reliant, at least in part, on the committee's funding, it's very unlikely that the candidate will even consider deviating from the party line. Simply put, gerrymandering and the secret primary encourages party discipline, which fosters the division and partisanship that makes it so difficult to pass substantive legislation on Capitol Hill. Whereas citizens tend to grumble that candidates cynically take positions just to get their votes at the ballot box, candidates often fearfully take positions just to win party leaders (and their cash) in the secret primary.

Almost invariably, the winners of the secret primary are previously elected officials, well established in the party, with high name recognition and the ability to raise quick cash; or they are wealthy, powerful individuals with partisan leanings and political ambitions such that they'll never stray far from party orthodoxy. But who are these nameless actors who are secretly calling the shots? Some of them are representatives or senators, trusted by the party and therefore put in charge of party committees. In 2006, for instance, long before he was named White House chief of staff, then congressman Rahm Emanuel (D-Ill.) was tapped by Nancy Pelosi to run the DCCC. Emanuel's success in the 2006 elections, during which Democrats recaptured the House, laid the groundwork for his continued rise through the ranks of the Democratic establishment. In addition to the actual members of Congress themselves, the political directors, finance directors, and communications directors of the parties and the committees play important supporting roles in determining who gets financial and logistic support and who doesn't.

Without the stamp of approval from one of the four gatekeeping committees, it's nearly impossible to win the actual primary campaign, for several reasons:

- The committees play an extremely important role in raising and spending money on behalf of candidates. Joint fund-raisers headlined by party leaders help bankroll campaigns, and the committees tell the party leaders who they need to stump for.
- Party committees run television ads and send direct mail appeals on a candidate's behalf, often costing hundreds of thousands of dollars.
- The support these committees provide to campaigns is as much tactical as it is financial. The committees help candidates recruit staff and consultants, who essentially remain part of the party apparatus and thus help the committees control the campaigns from afar.

Election law prevents campaigns and committees from coordinating these expenditures, but in reality it's not a difficult thing to accomplish within the bounds of the law. In fact, *de jure coordination doesn't happen, because de facto coordination naturally occurs.* Committee staff and campaign staff know one another, share talking points, and openly discuss which races are being targeted as competitive. They work with preferred vendors, who end up being hired by party committees and the campaigns themselves. I can't count the number of times that Mark Penn and I would have a promising meeting with a candidate in his or her home state. Weeks would go by, and we'd finally hear from the campaign manager. Invariably, the candidate would have been steered to a different polling firm, which happened to also have a contract with one of the party committees. The firms weren't allowed to plug a question on behalf of the candidate into the committee's poll—that would be inappropriate coordination—but the firms were intimately aware of the questions and scripts that the committee was pushing. If it happened that the party committee's and the candidate's messaging reinforced each other, it wasn't against the law, because only *direct* coordination of expenditures is prohibited. But this brand of *informal* coordination stands as the real law of the land. Candidates endorsed by the major party committees benefit from it significantly.

Almost without fail, these preanointed individuals become their parties' nominees. The support of the DNC or the RNC gives a candidate a significant advantage over any other primary challengers. Often, independent-minded candidates, knowing full well they can't win without the support of the national committees, simply step aside. And when they don't, the resources of the party committees overwhelm them, and they lose. Consequently, voters are seldom given a real choice between toe-the-line partisans picked by the party leaders and true advocates of reform.

No one knows how the system is stacked better than Paul Hackett. Hackett, an Iraq war veteran, narrowly lost a whirlwind grassroots campaign for Congress in 2006 against a formidable Republican incumbent in a heavily conservative district in southwestern Ohio. After Hackett's impressive showing, then Senate minority leader Harry Reid and DSCC chairman Chuck Schumer (D-N.Y.) recruited Hackett to run for Senate against the vulnerable Rebublican incumbent, Mike DeWine. Hackett— the first Iraq veteran to seek national office and a virulent critic of the Republicans' war efforts—was considered a strong challenger to the unpopular DeWine. In a shocking turn of events, however, Senators Reid and Schumer reversed their decision and decided to back longtime Ohio congressman Sherrod Brown. According to Ohio's Democratic Party chairman, the decision came down to the highly subjective question of "electability" and Brown's demonstrated ability to raise significant funds. Democratic officials urged Hackett to drop out and asked his donors to stop financing his race. As Hackett told the *New York Times*, "This is an extremely disappointing decision that I feel has been forced on me. . . . For me, this is a second betrayal. First, my government misused and mismanaged the military in Iraq, and now my own party is afraid to support candidates like me."[6]

The Hackett experience is common. In 2006, Schumer publicly backed Jim Webb for U.S. Senate in the Virginia primary, a deathblow to businessman Harris Miller, the first candidate to challenge Republican senator George Allen. Schumer's DSCC also gave early backing in the Rhode Island primary to Sheldon Whitehouse over two other qualified challengers, including Carl Sheeler, a former marine. Senators Webb and Whitehouse are, without question, fine public servants. They are also loyal Democrats (a particularly interesting twist for Webb, a late convert to the party).

As chairman of the DCCC during the 2006 cycle, Rahm Emanuel threw the party establishment's weight behind another Iraq war veteran, Tammy Duckworth, in the primary race for Illinois's Sixth Congressional District. Duckworth narrowly beat her popular opponent, Christine Cegelis, after prominent Democrats such as Hillary Clinton and Barack Obama were brought in to campaign on Duckworth's behalf. (Despite this celebrity heft, Duckworth lost the general election.)[7]

The fact remains that the national party committees loathe the notion of truly independent and independent-minded candidates. In this furtive game, partisanship rules. After getting the nod, candidates are beholden to the committees. Party leaders in the capital can choose at any time to increase or decrease the amount of funding they allot to certain campaigns. When reporters handicap a race, the first thing they look at is whether a race is "targeted" by the party committees as one of its "top-tier" races. If a race is targeted, it has instant credibility in the eyes of journalist-pundits, despite whatever the polls might show. This credibility increases the candidate's press coverage, which increases the candidate's name recognition. Name recognition jump-starts a campaign's fund-raising and get-out-the-vote efforts.[8] And the national committee then showers more money, staff, and media support on the candidate as the polls tighten.

Are there exceptions? Absolutely—if you're a multimillionaire. Ned Lamont was able to win his primary challenge against Connecticut senator Joe Lieberman in 2006, but only because he spent a chunk of his personal fortune to do so. Fundamentally, the secret primary is a closed process, designed to work surreptitiously as it perverts our politics.

DOLLARS MAKE THE DIFFERENCE

Once a congressional candidate has survived the secret primary, his or her true beliefs, values, and passions, and the problems the candidate wanted to solve given a chance to serve the people of his or her district, become quaint afterthoughts. In the run-up to Election Day, the campaign's message, themes, and policy positions are almost always determined *for* the candidate. The first order of business is raising money—for the candidate's own campaign and for the party committee—and that means courting the special interests that write checks. In fact, the influence of special interests on a congressional candidate's platform is more insidious than you probably ever thought.

Nobody likes to back a losing racehorse. It takes a lot of money to run for Congress, and the numbers never lie. Winners spend more than losers—about twice as much, in fact. According to the Center for Responsive Politics, the average winning House race spent $1,253,031 in 2006; in 2008, the number rose to $1,361,687. The average losing campaign in 2006 spent $622,348. The same is true in the Senate, where the average winner spent $9,635,370 in the 2006 election cycle, and the average loser spent $7,406,678.[9] (The 2008 figures are not yet available as of this writing, due to the lengthy recount in 2008's most expensive Senate race, the $35.4 million contest between Republican incumbent Norm Coleman and Democratic challenger Al Franken.) The more money raised and spent, the greater the likelihood of victory.[10]

For a challenger or first-time candidate, the figures above are daunting. Raising $1.3 million is a tremendous feat. If a candidate were going to raise that money from small donors who gave $200 or less, it would take 6,500 donors. That might not seem like a lot of people after contemplating the millions of donors to Obama's presidential campaign, but that would be an unheard-of level of support in a congressional race. Moreover, challengers often have to raise and spend even more than the averages noted above if they have any hope of winning. Note that in 2006, the average amount spent by a House challenger who successfully beat an incumbent was more than $1.8 million. In the Senate, the average was more than $10 million.[11]

It's easy to see how even populist and reform-minded candidates are forced to turn to the "usual suspects" to raise this kind of cash—interest groups that are reliable sources of PAC funds or extremely wealthy individuals who have a vested interest in a particular industry or issue. PACs are essentially the means by which industry groups such as the oil and gas industry, labor groups such as the Teamsters, and ideology-driven groups such as Second Amendment advocates and pro-choice organizations exert influence over the shape of the nation's legislation. These groups can offer contributions of up to $5,000 in each of the primary and general elections, as well as important endorsements and political connections that drive additional large-dollar donations. They fuel nearly every congressional campaign and represent an astounding percentage of overall fund-raising for House and Senate races.

In 2006, PAC contributions accounted for roughly 42 percent of contributions to both Republican and Democratic House races. Contributions from wealthy individuals—including lobbyists and many others who donate to candidates at the direction of PACs—made up another 44 percent of fund-raising for Democratic House candidates and nearly 43 percent for Republicans. On the Senate side, PAC contributions represent a smaller but not insignificant share of contributions—about 14 percent for Democrats and 24 percent for Republicans in 2006. However, Senate campaigns still rely heavily on well-off individual donors—54.6 percent of contributions for Democrats, and just under 56 percent for Republicans, come from donors who write four-figure checks.[12]

For candidates committed to grassroots campaigning, small donations won't cut it. This is an instance in which presidential campaigns and congressional campaigns are different. In 2006, small donations accounted for just 8.5 percent of fund-raising for Democratic House candidates and 10 percent for Republicans. As a candidate, if you're serious about winning and you don't have a vast personal fortune or political base, you need to court PACs and win their endorsements.

Incumbents have other advantages that can only be surmounted by challengers with deep pockets. Those advantages amount to experience and relationships. Fund-raising consultants will tell you directly that they much prefer to work with incumbents for precisely this reason. First, incumbents know the rules. They know how to solicit, they know how to court, and they know how to close the deal. But there is more to it than that. Most politicians understand that quid pro quos are not only unseemly but also inappropriate and illegal. For every lobbyist like the incarcerated Jack Abramoff and for every politician like the indicted Tom DeLay and the scandal-plagued John Murtha, there are scores who understand that explicitly linking gifts to support is off limits. On the other hand, I've also heard Representative Barney Frank (D-Mass.) say that "politics is the only business where contributors are expected to give large sums of money to virtual strangers and *not* seek anything in return." This is an absurd proposition. Fund-raisers know that introducing their candidates to PAC directors who are of a like mind is the easiest way to win support—and reelection.

Fund-raisers also understand that by having their candidates meet with friendly PAC directors, they build a network of information that reaches across the larger PAC community. This process creates a multiplier effect in donation receipts. As one fund-raising consultant put it to me, "It's just easier with incumbents. They know the rules, they know the game, they know the process, and they are in a position to help right away."

Indeed, there is a symbiotic relationship between PAC directors and Congress members' offices. I have seen PAC directors summoned to members' offices to take orders and instructions quite unrelated to the solicitation of the gift. It's more of a business relationship that is ongoing, with periodic infusions of cash, than a straightforward solicitation. For challengers, it is necessary to quickly establish that relationship to get into the game.

The predominance of special interests in the financing of congressional elections has nasty side effects. One is that most candidates for Congress raise a significant percentage of their campaign funds from donors *outside* their local districts. And it's not just names like Pelosi, Clinton, or Kennedy that draw national support. In 2006, Representative Frank Pallone (D-N.J.)—someone you've likely never heard of, but who is currently serving his tenth term in the House—received more than 40 percent of his $1.04 million haul from *out-of-state* donors. Why does a twenty-year veteran of Congress need donors from other states to fuel his reelection campaign? The answer is simple: If you want to be reelected, you need an astronomical amount of money, and the easiest way to get it is from interest groups, their PACs, and affiliated wealthy donors and lobbyists, irrespective of where they happen to live. In this way, a candidate in suburban Phoenix or rural Nebraska can easily raise large sums from ideology-driven donors around the nation and from thousands of lobbyists at their doorsteps in Washington. Candidates get a huge portion of their campaign cash from donors who can't even cast a vote for them.[13]

Because dollars make the difference and interest groups are the major source of those dollars, much time and effort is spent courting PACs. The early stage of any campaign involves the highly time-consuming process of candidates, staff, and consultants filling out dozens of PAC questionnaires, in which candidates are asked to attest to their positions on issues critical to the groups' missions. The right answers on the forms are a precondition to getting the $10,000 in combined primary-general contributions from any individual PAC. To find those right answers, and that five-figure payday and a stirring endorsement, candidates will often bend their views to match those of the interest group in question. As you may have already figured out, it takes maximum contributions from only 130 PACs to raise the $1.3 million congressional race average. With 4,611 registered PACs to choose from in the United States, the odds are pretty good for a candidate to raise a good portion of the necessary money that way.[14]

On the one hand, it's an obvious political reality that's existed since time immemorial. On the other, it's a pernicious outcome of a failing system that has grown worse. Candidates will do much worse than change their positions to win PAC money and endorsements. One widespread practice is the use of polling to convince interest groups that a campaign is viable enough to receive their support and that the issues pertinent to that group will drive voters to the polls. I used to think that when you polled for congressional candidates, whether incumbents or challengers, the purpose was to better understand their districts. In large part, that remains the case. But the real questions candidates, particularly challengers, ask potential pollsters in the interview are, "Do the PACs know you? Will they listen and respond to you?" If the answers are no, you can usually hear a chilling of the voice, a withdrawal of interest, and a dismissive, "We'll get back to you real soon."

Today, sitting members in the House and Senate, as well as challengers, want reliable pollsters who have earned a measure of respect from key PACs. Frequently, pollsters are asked to include questions that will appeal not just to the electorate but to one or two targeted PAC directors—those who are party stalwarts, known for making or breaking a bid for office, or who haven't yet committed to an opponent—as well. If a PAC director who has not yet ponied up some money is interested in building support for a weapons system, a pollster might frame a question to show that the candidate is seen among likely voters to support strong national defense. The PAC contribution and endorsement won't raise alarms—and it will make working on legislation down the road go much more smoothly. If a PAC director represents a union, a pollster might ask constituents about whether workers should be free to join a union if they like, without intimidation from their employer—a way for the candidate to indicate support for using the union-supported "card check" system for a membership drive. Ultimately, the pollster will frequently put questions in polls that are designed principally to serve the interests of a PAC. In the end, these questions are less about shaping a candidate's stances in response to the voters' responses than they are about demonstrating that the candidate and his or her likely voters *believe* that the candidate's positions match those of the PAC.

Which leads us to the art of the PAC memo. Every candidate who hires a pollster gets an analysis of the data and a hardheaded assessment of the chances for victory on Election Day, but as part of the package the candidate also gets a PAC memo. The memo is crafted to build support among relevant PACs for the candidate. The pollster presents all the data collected in a way that makes the candidate appear most favorable to the widest variety of PACs possible, in the current circumstances. Both sides know what is going on. The PAC directors know how to read these memos and to read between the lines for the soft promises and even softer positions of the candidates, and the candidates understand how to present the data in ways that are honest and credible, yet also attractive to a particular cause.

I've been in situations where the actual analysis of the poll data, however insightful and useful they could be to building the campaign's field operation or name recognition, takes a backseat to the PAC memo's

job of raising fat checks from interest groups. The candidate or campaign manager will spend hours revising the memo to make sure it is
exactly on message, while the actual analysis of the data and strategy
goes stale. The seeming malleability of the PAC memo is how many
politicians are able to persuade themselves that pollsters simply "cook
the numbers."

Still, the memo isn't about creating phony data; it's about using real
data—which the campaign has paid for—to woo interest groups, PAC
support, and major donors. Sadly, favoring "good numbers" over real
numbers has become standard operating procedure in political polling.
In modern campaigns, polling is used less to determine campaign strategy and more as a propaganda and fund-raising tool.

PUTTING POLICY BEFORE POLITICKING

It's not that we don't know how to fix our politics. It's that we haven't yet
summoned the will to do what needs to be done. We know where the
special interest money comes from. We know how it gets from a lobbyist's pocket into a lawmaker's campaign account. We know how the
money is used and why members of Congress are so desperate for it.
And we know how this process amplifies political discord and puts politics before policy, creating devastating gridlock that impedes Congress
from solving the challenges facing our nation.

The problems we face are not only a matter of common knowledge in
Washington—they're a matter of common acceptance. After all, real
change would require real sacrifice. It would mean politicians giving up
power and perks, interest groups giving up their ability to curry favor
with campaign contributions, and political parties giving up the control
they exert throughout the process.

I've described from experience the lack of appetite for reform, and
the failure of reformers. I also know from experience that a few smart
and simple solutions can dramatically change how Washington operates,
how candidates are elected, and how our system functions by ratcheting
down political bickering, beating back the influence of interest groups,
and increasing transparency and accountability.

End gerrymandering—permanently

Allowing Tom DeLay to have input in drawing congressional districts is like letting Kobe Bryant officiate an NBA play-off game in which he's playing. Unbelievably, that's the system we have today when it comes to drawing congressional districts. Letting lawmakers handpick their voters is inverted democracy, and it must be stopped. We have to kick the legislators out of the redistricting process before we can usher in a new age of competitive elections.

Every state needs to take the urgent and necessary step of creating an independent commission to oversee political mapmaking. To my mind, the size, composition, and scope of the redistricting commissions don't matter as long as they share an essential attribute—they take the power to draw maps away from politicians. In fact, it's important that each state have the ability to tailor its own redistricting effort to its unique geography and demographics. For instance, a state with a relatively equally disbursed population—New Jersey—would rightly place emphasis on districts that are contiguous. On the other hand, a state with a population unequally disbursed over a wide geography—California—would perhaps be more concerned with ensuring districts that are competitive than contiguous.

There's no question that this can be done or that it leads to fairer elections. Several states have already taken away mapmaking powers from partisan legislators, with positive results. In fact, there's no lack of redistricting proposals that would both insulate the process from partisan politics and create more competitive elections. According to the National Conference of State Legislators, eight states have implemented serious redistricting efforts, each with different systems.

If I had to choose the system I most preferred, I would pick Iowa's model. Iowa is unique among the states that have ended gerrymandering in that it leaves the mapmaking to bureaucrats and computer simulations. Politicians are completely out of the picture. The state's nonpartisan Legislative Services Bureau is prohibited from using partisan data of any kind in drawing districts, and it submits its proposal to the legislature for an up-or-down vote. That way, lawmakers aren't able to twist the maps to their (or their parties') advantage.

As other analysts have also noted, I believe Iowa may have taken the antipartisan mission a step too far, since completely blind mapmaking might yield just as many noncompetitive districts as a gerrymandering process. So I would tweak Iowa's model slightly, to ensure that districts are drawn purposely to be competitive. This is especially critical in states that are more heterogeneous than Iowa, where not having access to "partisan" information could inadvertently disenfranchise certain racial, ethnic, and socioeconomic constituencies.

While bureaucrats control Iowa's mapmaking, six other states appoint commissions of different sizes and compositions to draw district maps, which are subject to judicial oversight. Arizona's constitution re-quires the state's redistricting commission to consider the competitive-ness of the districts it draws. That differs from the redistricting process in Iowa. While it had a number of flaws, I generally support California governor Arnold Schwarzenegger's proposal to give the task of district drawing to a panel of retired federal judges.[15]

In the run-up to the 2008 congressional elections, *USA Today* re-ported that increasing voter anger was creating newly competitive elec-toral districts across the country.[16] Indeed, the election saw a number of competitive races in typically safe districts. Yet there were still many uncompetitive elections that year, despite the rampant voter disgust and desire for centrist politicians who might heal the nation's partisan divide. The power of the national party committees makes it hard for centrists and outsiders to organize and compete. The first step in bust-ing the secret primary system is to dismantle gerrymandered districts and pry control out of the claws of the party committees.

Ban all PAC contributions to congressional candidates

Banning special interest contributions will have a huge impact on our political marketplace. In one bold move, eliminating PAC donations to congressional candidates would do away with the primary source of influence peddling in Washington and bring a sea change to the way cam-paigns are conducted and the way government functions.

Just think about the impact. On the campaign trail, candidates for office could take on issues that are important to them, instead of to their special interest backers. In Washington, members of Congress would no longer have to consider the effect of their vote on the source of nearly half the average member's reelection campaign contributions. And if members no longer have to chase after interest groups for dollars, their calculus in considering legislation becomes much more practical and much less political, reducing needless partisan bickering and enabling Washington to get to work.

Banning PAC checks isn't a pie-in-the-sky idea. It's a reform that's well within reach. In 2008, the presidential nominees and standard-bearers of both major parties took a hard line on special interest contributions. John McCain has long favored restrictions on PAC contributions, and President Obama, while a senator, instructed the DNC to stop cashing and start returning interest group checks. Neither side wants to unilaterally disarm, but a universal ban is something both parties can agree on.

Create a sensible and *optional* system of public financing for congressional candidates

I'm a political pragmatist, and I've been around Washington long enough to know that if we don't tackle the campaign finance issue, nothing will ever change. It's essential that we give congressional candidates the ability to sell themselves to the public without selling out. If we don't take this fundamental step, all of our other reform efforts combined will be meaningless.

It's not enough to limit the supply of special interest campaign contributions. We also have to limit the demand for it. That's why we need to give candidates for Congress the option of receiving public financing.

Here's my solution: If you want to run for office and can meet a standard threshold of credibility, the federal government should give you the cash you need to make your bid to voters. It's that simple. And if you want to raise money the old-fashioned way—dialing for dollars late into the night and collecting checks from donors at lavish fund-raisers— that's okay, too. I see no reason to force candidates to run publicly financed campaigns. Knowing the way politicians think, however, I can tell you that most will take the path of least resistance and opt for public financing.

The devil is always in the details, but in this case the details are relatively benign. Candidates for the House or Senate apply for public financing to the FEC, which certifies that they have met the standard threshold that is a prerequisite for financing. In my view, this threshold should be threefold:

- Candidates should be required to collect a minimum number of signatures. It strikes me that the required number should be two signatures for every one hundred residents. Congressional districts vary somewhat in size, but they are generally in the ballpark of 650,000 residents. That means candidates would need to collect, on average, about twelve thousand signatures—a reasonably high but very attainable number.
- Candidates should be required to raise a minimum of $50,000 in small-dollar donations, of perhaps $200 or less—starter funds to be used for basic and immediate campaign expenses.
- Candidates should agree to a minimum of five public debates per election cycle.

In primary elections, this standard will be high enough to prevent marginal candidates from wasting taxpayer dollars and reasonable enough that grassroots candidates can prove themselves eligible for financing through community activism and organizing—either online or on the ground. It would also require officeholders who take public financing to publicly debate their primary and general election opponents, which happens only occasionally if not rarely in modern congressional campaigns. Upon meeting this universal test of electoral credibility, qualifying campaigns would be given a lump-sum grant, the size of which would be determined by the size of the congressional district or state in question.

I'm painfully aware that there is a significant portion of the voting public that is against using public money for any political candidate. But the benefits of public financing would be tremendous. First, it would help candidates do what they're supposed to do: campaign. Instead of spending hours on the phone and running between fund-raisers, candidates could attend more community meetings, participate in more debates, and shake hands with—and serve—more constituents.

Second, it would mean the beginning of the end of the need to chase down interest group money as a precondition of running for election or reelection. No more hustling for PAC checks, no more stalking lobbyists and bombarding them with invitations to fund-raisers, no more special treatment for special interests.

Finally, imagine how public financing would open up the primary process. Party committees could no longer block moderates and independents from competing against dyed-in-the-wool candidates who have the backing of the national parties. Anyone could run, and anyone could win. This would open the doors to candidates who don't have a vested interest in joining the partisan wars driven by the major party leaders and ideology-based interest groups. Public financing would do more than decouple the sinister link between money and politics; it would be water on the partisan fire that has all but consumed Washington.

Others will note that the idea of public financing for congressional elections has been around for years. What's to make us think that it has a better chance of being enacted today than ten or twenty years ago? In fact, there is significant bipartisan support for one aspect of campaign finance reform among members of Congress: politicians openly hate fund-raising. For that reason, many more candidates are speaking out about the money race, which escalates with each passing election cycle. As Senator Bob Casey (D-Penn.) put it: "I am sick and tired of fund-raising. When you sit in a room for four hours making calls, it kind of has a deadening effect on you. Anything that reduces the amount of time that you are spending fund-raising is good for the country, and it is definitely good for me."[17] Senator George Voinovich (R-Ohio) agrees with Casey about the money chase: "It's out of control. We all hate it. And it's about time we collectively think about how we can get off the treadmill."[18]

As you can imagine, political fund-raising is now a multi*billion*-dollar industry. And I know a lot of people—political fund-raisers, lawyers, and special interest lobbyists—who would rather see that industry carry on unchanged by reformers. It pays their bills and certainly affords them and their families a comfortable life, to say the least. But why turn those running for office into full-time panhandlers? There must be a middle ground.

Indeed, liberals and conservatives alike have rallied around the concept of "fair elections," which are similar in structure to the public financing scheme I proposed above. In fact, Senators Dick Durbin (D-Ill.) and Arlen Specter (then R-Penn.) have introduced the Fair Elections Now Act. In short, the legislation, if passed, would require candidates to raise a minimum amount of seed money in small-dollar donations to prove their viability as a candidate—at which point they would be given funds based on an equitable formula. House candidates would receive $900,000, 40 percent of which could be used for a primary election. Senate candidates would receive a base grant of $1.25 million and an additional $250,000 for each congressional district in their state. An attractive feature of this legislation is that candidates would be able to continue to solicit small-dollar donations, which would be matched four to one with additional public funds.

Those opposed to public financing of congressional elections often say it would be too expensive but, if anything, these figures indicate that it would *save* taxpayer dollars. Even if the federal government took on the expense *in full*, a tax increase would not be required—assuming, of course, that the existing presidential election fund is converted into a congressional election fund.

Free airtime for congressional candidates—to dramatically *lower* the cost of campaigning and *raise* the level of discourse

The reason candidates for Congress are cash crazed is that the cost of campaigning has skyrocketed. And it's no secret that the culprit is television ads, which account for the bulk of every campaign's balance sheet. It's just plain common sense that if elections were less expensive, there would be less of a need for financial backing from interest groups. Fortunately, there's an easy way to dramatically cut the cost of running a competitive campaign. It's time to end the free ride for broadcasters and give free airtime to candidates. The public owns the airwaves, and we should put them to public use in order to curb the mad dash for money, the influence of special interests, and the partisan rancor that is a direct result of both.

Politics is a recession-proof industry, and campaign ad revenue has been a consistent cash cow for broadcasters struggling to turn a profit in the Internet age. As Dick Durbin put it to his Senate colleagues:

> In 2002 the total amount spent on Senate races was a bit less than $300 million. Four years later, total spending approached $550 million. We are not far away from the election in which we spend $1 billion on Senate campaigns. . . . Why has the cost of running for the Senate risen so quickly? The primary reason: to pay for television ads. The total amount spent on all political ads in 2002 was just shy of $1 billion, for all campaigns. In 2006? $1.7 billion. If the money spent on ads nearly doubles in four years, I think that is a pretty good indicator that the overall cost of campaigns is going to rise as well.

There's no shortage of blame to go around for our system of elections driven by special interest money, but broadcasters own a fair-sized piece of it. It's time to end their payday at the expense of good government, and there are a few ways to do it. One popular proposal previously sponsored by Senator McCain would create a tax and voucher system. Unlike the cell phone industry, which purchases licenses from the federal government for billions of dollars, broadcasters receive their licenses for free with limited guidelines for the privilege of their use by the federal government. The McCain proposal would give candidates vouchers to purchase free airtime. And the vouchers themselves would be financed by a federal tax that amounts to a tiny fraction of a broadcaster's overall profits.

Of course, another means of achieving free airtime for candidates would simply mandate that broadcasters set aside a certain amount of time for political ads, and each station would be responsible for dividing the time equally between qualifying candidates. The Durbin-Specter proposal for fair elections also includes a provision to provide vouchers for free airtime to candidates that would qualify for public financing.

Needless to say, none of the above is going to be popular among broadcasters. Tough luck. Appealing to their civic duty clearly hasn't worked and won't do so in the future. We have enough data and enough ideas to act quickly, and any of the proposed solutions for free airtime would slash campaign expenses by a significant margin. As a result, the special interest power brokers that finance campaigns would have less influence over our politics.

Bring real-time transparency to the system

Today, it can take months to wait for FEC reports and then dig through them to find out who made a contribution, to what candidate, and when. Senate candidates file campaign finance reports by paper. Congressional candidates report their campaign donations and expenditures quarterly. All of this amounts to a seemingly concerted effort—since Congress writes the campaign finance regulations—to obscure important information from the public. It's a systematic means of preventing campaign watchdogs from following the money trail to sniff for fraud and abuse, but by using the Web to increase campaign finance transparency we can finally change it.

It's insanity that in our digital society, where information is instantly available, the FEC requires candidates to report their contributions and expenditures *quarterly*. That means contributions made in the last months of a campaign aren't reported until the campaign is well over. To make matters worse, after Senate candidates file the paper copies of their campaign finance reports, the FEC has to spend timing scanning them and saving them as PDFs.

There's just no excuse for this. We get real-time stock quotes on our cell phones. Satellites navigate our rental cars to the nearest Chinese restaurant in an unfamiliar city. A quick Google search can tell you how much your neighbor's house is worth. Practically the only thing we *can't* access online instantly and with ease is from whom our elected representatives are taking money and how it's being spent. Since an increasing number of campaign contributions are made online with a credit card, the electronic data are available.

It's time to bring campaign finance disclosure into the twenty-first century by requiring near-instant online disclosure of donations and expenditures. All candidates should be required to report all contributions and expenditures within twenty-four hours, and this information should be available immediately to the public in a searchable online database. For the first time, voters and journalists would be able to connect the dots in real time and hold officials immediately accountable.

Raise the cap on individual contributions to congressional candidates

As a lawyer by training, I don't buy the argument that campaign contribution limits are unconstitutional. And neither does the Supreme Court. But I do believe that they are arbitrary. As a pollster by trade, it's hard for me to ignore the data, both empirical and anecdotal. There is simply none to suggest that limiting individual contributions to $2,300 has done anything to limit the influence of money in congressional politics. Meanwhile, our elections are increasingly uncompetitive, partisanship is as bad as it's ever been, and interest groups continue to fuel our campaigns. All this, despite recent reform efforts that have put a limit on "soft-dollar" contributions to political committees, as well.

As a longtime Democrat, part of me hates to say it, but the right wing is right—it's time to raise the cap on individual contributions to federal candidates. Congress created the donation cap years ago as a seemingly smart way to reduce the influence of wealthy contributors and level the playing field. At this point, the jury is in—it didn't work. More to the point, small-dollar Internet contributions will continue to make mega-contributions from multimillionaires an irrelevant concern. If a wealthy person writes a big check, it will make news and then the public can evaluate it, pro or con.

Campaign finance law, as noted earlier, currently limits individual contributions to federal candidates at $2,300 for both the primary and general elections. That means you can give up to $4,600 to any one candidate per election cycle. These figures merely represent an evolving consensus on where to randomly cap contributions, not a well-reasoned limit based on research or analysis. It seems to me that, as with the presidential election, we could reasonably raise the contribution limit significantly, to $7,500 for the 2010 cycle, $10,000 in 2012, and then tied to inflation thereafter. Why these specific figures? Admittedly, they are "Goldilocks" in nature—not too big, not too small. Hopefully, they'll be just right, in that by 2012 the maximum contribution will have more than doubled, giving candidates access to larger donations but not significantly increasing the influence of well-heeled donors.

The right wing has argued for years that higher contributions that are disclosed fully and timely to the public are the only way to truly rid our system of special interest money. I clearly don't believe this is the panacea they think it is. But I do agree with those on the right who argue that Americans are smart enough to sort it all out if given the information in a timely fashion. So for the good of democracy, this fix must be made alongside the creation of real-time, online disclosure of congressional contributions and expenditures.

5

SERVE THE PEOPLE
Changing How the Legislative System Works

I have a Congress on my hands.
—GROVER CLEVELAND, 1893

The broken system that has brought us congressional elections that don't really count gets, if anything, even worse when members arrive in the swampland of Washington. Just as the chase for dollars is more important than the chase for votes in elections, the same is true of day-to-day business on Capitol Hill. Wheeling and dealing in reelection cash trumps the business of the people. The handful of newcomers who make it into office every two years quickly discover that to win reelection—as well as important appropriations and projects for their constituents—they have to play by a very archaic set of rules. Otherwise they don't come back.

Those rules do not include bipartisanship or thoughtful consideration of the issues or finding legislative partners (of either party) with whom to develop an agenda. No, the rules they learn to play are once again all about raising money—to pay for their own reelection campaigns, the campaigns of their fellow partisans, their leadership PACs (the perfect vehicle for contributing to party colleagues), their national party committees, and their general party coffers. Suddenly, instead of hunting checks to fund one election budget, they're endlessly dunning. In order to raise that money, they must court interest groups some more and assiduously heed their preferred policies. This is the first (and some-times only) concern of the men and women whom the American people send to Washington to represent their interests.

Most people think special interests are throwing money at members of Congress and that members passively accept campaign contributions from Washington insiders who will do anything to buy influence. In reality, it's the other way around. Members themselves actively solicit the help of interest groups with deep pockets. They round up lobbyists at political fund-raisers and unabashedly hit them up for campaign contributions. There is such a thirst for interest group donations to fund reelection campaigns that members of Congress themselves are anything but shy about pressing lobbyists for donations to their cam-paign coffers. As *BusinessWeek* reported in 2006: "One prominent business lobbyist was so aggravated by attacks on his brethren by money-raising members of Congress that he collected every fund-raising invi-tation letter he received for a month. The total for January: more than sixty. He dutifully sent checks for most even though he says that he has never asked half of those lawmakers for anything. 'I'm doing it because it's expected,' he laments. 'If you want to be in the game, you've got to pay.'" Another anonymous lobbyist described meeting with a Demo-cratic senator and later that day receiving a voice mail from that same senator's office with instructions on where to mail the contribution.[1]

Consider, for a moment, those sixty invitations for political fund-raisers sent to a single lobbyist over the course of a month. Each invi-tation represents thousands of dollars spent in assembling a political fund-raiser for just one member's leadership committee—hiring graphic design firms to create invitations and fund-raising consultants to orchestrate the event, renting a venue, picking up the catering tab. An entire industry has been spawned. Hundreds of businesses and thousands of people support, and are supported by, the Washington money chase. So it's no surprise that efforts to reform campaign fi-nance have been a nonstarter. Even if politicians want it, those who earn their bread and butter from residual campaign expenditures don't. After all, Congress is nothing if not an excellent customer to print shops, caterers, and event planners.

POLITICAL PARALYSIS

There are five major consequences of this cash-driven system: abuse, waste, corruption, gridlock, and total meltdown. Our legislative branch is no longer what it was designed to be: a deliberative body that is responsive to the will of the American people. Today, it is a self-interested institution, fueled by politics and responsive only to partisan interests, and one that fails to take on the serious issues facing the nation. As our elections have been overrun by special interest cash, so, too, has the legislative process, and the American people have suffered as a result.

Abuse. The Republican Congress led by Dennis Hastert (Ill.), Tom DeLay, and Bill Frist (Tenn.) was well known for lending a sympathetic ear to interest groups and their lobbyists. But the extent to which these groups not only influence legislation but also *write it* has become a deplorable bipartisan tradition. For instance, in 2008, ninety-four House Democrats reversed their opinions and their votes on immunity for the telecommunications industry in domestic surveillance lawsuits after receiving a deluge of campaign contributions from telecom industry PACs. According to MAPLight.org, a nonprofit watchdog group, the dots weren't hard to connect. An analysis of campaign contributions shows that telecom PACs gave an average of $8,359 to the ninety-four Democrats who had a change of heart. Meanwhile, PAC contributions to the 116 Democrats who opposed immunity on both occasions averaged significantly less—$4,987. In short, PACs double the bounty if you play along.

Three of the most powerful Democratic leaders were among the top recipients of PAC dollars from the telecom industry between 2005 and 2008, and all of them flip-flopped on the issue. James Clyburn of South Carolina, the House majority whip, received $29,500 from the telecom industry; Maryland's Steny Hoyer, the House majority leader, received $29,000; and Rahm Emanuel, then DCCC chairman and the fourth-highest-ranking Democrat in Congress, received $28,000.[2] Never mind that opposition to telecom immunity was a key Democratic talking point from the moment the issue first arose. When push came to shove,

Democrats gave in, and the system worked as designed—to fail the average voter and reelect the average member.

Waste. Partisan politics has directly led to the explosion in recent years of "earmarks"—tens of billions of dollars in pet projects that lawmakers quietly insert into bills to gain favor with constituents and interest groups. The earmarking process is a bit technical, but the earmarks themselves are not: they increase government waste.

Traditionally, earmarks have been inserted into appropriations bills, often thousands of pages long, during closed-door conference committee meetings, where a small legislative group meets to reconcile the two chambers' versions of the same bill. Because the process has been secretive—and because party leaders control it—earmarks have become a favorite source of partisan influence peddling. According to the watchdog group Citizens Against Government Waste (CAGW), in 1995 these projects totaled $10 billion. In 2006, they reached an all-time high of $29 billion.[3]

Pork barrel legislation has been with us for years, but it only recently grew into a touchy subject with the voting public. Why? There's nothing easier to attack than your opponent's vote in favor of a "Bridge to Nowhere" or research studies on grizzly bear DNA that may appear to have no immediate benefit. In the 2008 general election, McCain/Palin and Obama/Biden went after each other on their support for silly earmarks, including McCain's quip in the first presidential debate that he didn't "know if [the DNA study] was a paternity issue or criminal, but it was a waste of money."[4] Politicians know that people hate waste in government, and nowhere is this more important than in the pork written into bills. But to put it into perspective, this kind of federal spending amounts to just a bit more than 1 percent of the federal budget. A half-percent increase in the Social Security withholding figure—which none of us has much say in—accounts for more than all the pork barrel spending in a given year.

Democrats were handed majorities in both the House and Senate in 2006 after campaigning on government reform, from ethics to earmarks. And to some extent, Democrats delivered on their campaign pledges. They made good on their promise to make the earmark process transparent, by identifying earmark sponsors and posting conference reports that include earmarks on the Internet forty-eight hours before a scheduled vote. And senators are now able, for the first time, to oppose individual earmarks.[5] These are positive reforms.

Unfortunately, these reforms have done little to curb the *number* of earmarks themselves—they still drive partisanship, and they can still be traded in illegal and unseemly quid pro quos. According to CAGW, earmarks hit nearly an all-time high in fiscal year 2008, at 11,610, second only to 2005, when Congress passed 13,997 earmarks. While total spending on earmarks is down significantly—$17.2 billion in 2008, from the high-water mark of $29 billion in 2006—this is hardly the wholesale reform that many voters expected. Despite all this, legislators are still judged in their home districts by how much bacon they bring home every session.

It's notable here that there's nothing wrong with earmarks per se. Indeed, many of the projects they pay for are worthwhile and even necessary. For instance, after speaking out against earmarks early and often on the campaign trail, President Obama signed a number of welcome earmarks into law in 2009, including a $350,000 upgrade to the Los Angeles County 9-1-1 system and an $800,000 new air traffic control tower in Palm Springs.[6] These are good and worthy projects that are necessary to keep Americans safe. But the process that begot them is illegitimate and in need of serious reform—reform that both parties continue to promise but fail to deliver. So long as earmarks are inserted through a secretive process, hidden from public inspection and open debate, they will continue to breed partisan intrigue and mistrust.

Corruption. The first decade of the twenty-first century—a time of exponential growth of campaign costs, lobbying on the Hill, and political fund-raising in general—was a banner era for political corruption. From California Republican Randy "Duke" Cunningham, who is currently serving eight years for collecting $2.4 million in bribes, to Louisiana Democrat William Jefferson, who was caught hiding obscene amounts of cash *in his freezer*—the payoff from shady business deals he was attempting to orchestrate in Africa—both parties have done their part to shatter Americans' faith in what is arguably our most important civic institution. Criminal activity is no doubt the exception rather than the rule. But, like excessive pork barrel spending, its symbolism sends a powerful message to the voters.

This explosion in scandals and troublesome ethics violations are a direct result of the way we run our congressional elections. Indeed, if you've ever wondered why it seems like politicians of both parties seem to make the same mistakes over and over again, there's a simple answer: our system encourages these abuses. The pressing need to raise campaign cash drives candidates to cut corners wherever possible. Significant loopholes in our lobbying laws encourage politicians and lobbyists to collude at political fund-raisers. The prevalence of pork barrel spending makes it tantalizingly easy for members of Congress to engage in quid pro quos. *Everyone else seems to be doing it, so why not?*

With that mentality, Congress has proven inept at policing its own members. The fox has been guarding the hen house for far too long. In 2008, House Ways and Means chairman Charlie Rangel (D-N.Y.) came under fire for renting campaign office space at significantly below the market rate from what the *New York Times* dubbed a "major real estate developer." Rangel allegedly received the equivalent of an illegal campaign contribution from a well-heeled supporter. He angrily denied any violations and took the unprecedented step of requesting the House ethics committee to investigate the arrangement. On the face of it, Rangel appeared sincere. But it seems considerably less noble when you learn that the House ethics committee has a track record of ignoring violations and almost never initiates investigations.

In fact, according to the *Hill*, the last such complaint was filed in 2004, by one-term congressman Chris Bell (D-Tex.) against Tom DeLay.[7] The *New York Times* reported that a "half-dozen other members plus staffers [were] brought down while the House ethics committee looked the other way." The committee even failed to investigate former representative Rick Renzi (R-Ariz.), who in 2008 was "indicted on thirty-five counts of fraud, money laundering and extortion for allegedly netting $700,000 in a political land scheme."[8]

The problem isn't that all politicians are inherently corrupt—it's that the system breeds corruption. To make matters worse, reformers have consistently taken a "bad apple" approach to ethics violations: remove the rotting apple to prevent the barrel from spoiling. What we really need is a new barrel.

Gridlock. Contrary to conventional wisdom, politics has only *partially* paralyzed Washington. When Congress sniffs out a hot-button political issue, it roars into action. In 2005, Congress swiftly interceded in the legal battle between the husband and parents of Terry Schiavo, a young Floridian who had been in a vegetative coma for ten years. Schiavo's husband was hoping to take her off the feeding tube that was prolonging her life, and her parents were attempting to block his move in court. What on earth would make Congress get involved in such a deeply personal, tragic, and complicated situation? Pander politics at its worst. A memo by an aide to Florida Rebublican senator Mel Martinez that was leaked to ABC News revealed the Republican strategy to insert Congress into this difficult ethical and legal dilemma: "This is an important moral issue and the pro-life base will be excited that the Senate is debating this important issue. This is a great political issue, because Senator Nelson of Florida has already refused to become a cosponsor and this is a tough issue for Democrats."

The Schiavo vote was a despicable bit of politicking, meant solely to please pro-life conservatives who continue to be a major source of campaign contributions for Republicans.[9] It also illustrates the most troubling and frustrating consequence of such political games: Congress's increasing inability to address real issues. Look no further than the fight to increase the minimum wage. If there ever was an issue that had consensus among voters across party lines, this is it. Despite a continually devaluating dollar against other currencies, as well as modest annual inflation, it took a full ten years for Congress to nudge the wage for hourly workers from $5.15 to $7.25—basically, a belated cost-of-living raise. (Employers who don't offer health insurance must pay $7.55 per hour.) Our reelection- and money-fixated system encourages members of Congress to pander to their bases. Until we make structural changes to the entire election process, politics will always be paramount, and the hard work of compromise and negotiation will always be on the back burner.

Total meltdown. Clearly, I've saved the best (read: worst) for last. The doomsday scenario of our political paralysis unfortunately came to pass in 2008. Decades of political malfeasance of every variety culminated in the financial crisis that America and the world is still reeling from. No doubt, you have likely been personally affected by this crisis.

The financial crisis resulted from a perfect storm of intense special interest lobbying and extreme unchecked partisanship. And forget about federal bailouts—the real crisis at hand won't be solved until both parties own up to their roles in bringing it about and make a serious stab at attacking the root cause of the problem together: our broken political system.

To flesh out this story, let's start with a look at the unprecedented lobbying effort of Fannie Mae and Freddie Mac that fueled the subprime mortgage lending at the heart of the credit crisis and recession that sunk in during the fall of 2008. Fannie and Freddie together spent an astounding $200 million over the course of ten years lobbying Congress against instituting more oversight and regulations that could have prevented risky loans and the subsequent foreclosures. As Politico duly noted, "Fannie and Freddie's aggressive political maneuvering has helped stave off increased regulation and preserve special benefits such as exemption from state and local income taxes and the ability to borrow at low rates."[10]

Fannie and Freddie bought tremendous influence, mostly with Democrats. According to the Center for Responsive Politics, seven out of the top ten recipients of contributions from Fannie and Freddie from 1989 to 2008 were Democrats—including Senator Barack Obama.[11] Jim Johnson, who was tapped by candidate Obama to lead the committee charged with vetting potential vice presidential running mates, was forced to resign from that effort when it was disclosed that he had received millions—reportedly as much as $21 million—in compensation through a deal with Fannie and mortgage giant Countrywide Financial (now part of Bank of America).[12] Republicans, too, were part of the Fannie and Freddie extended family, if you will. Arne Christenson, a former top aide to Newt Gingrich, was handsomely compensated for his work on behalf of the mortgage giants.[13]

The contributions from executives at Fannie and Freddie certainly didn't curb the Democrats' push for expanding the opportunity for home ownership among low-income families. But, as the main recipients of financial-industry largesse, the GOP shoulders as much blame. It was Republicans who allowed the investment banks and other firms to shirk regulation, which enabled them to become dangerously overleveraged and develop the opaque financial securities and other instruments that packaged and disseminated the bad housing debt throughout the economy. As Martin Wolf noted in the *Financial Times*, "In the United States, influence comes as much from a system of beliefs as from lobbying (although the latter was not absent). What was good for Wall Street was deemed good for the world. The result was a bipartisan program of ill-designed deregulation for the United States and, given its influence, the world."[14]

Greed and abuse were likely factors in the lack of oversight with respect to the mortgage and financial industries, but rampant partisanship also played a key role. Over the years, deregulation became an entrenched stance among Republicans, an ideology with which to prove party loyalty regardless of whether it led to sensible policies. We know today it didn't. Likewise, home ownership became an unimpeachable goal among Democrats, regardless of whether the means used to achieve this laudable end were fiscally prudent. We know today they weren't.

Ultimately, partisans on both sides who blindly adhered to party orthodoxy and bowed down to the financial lobby created the economic meltdown of 2008. As former New York attorney general and governor Eliot Spitzer put it: "The new line from Washington and Wall Street is that hamstrung regulators lacked the power to stop malfeasance before the crisis. This is wrong. Washington had enormous power over the misbehaving investment banks, commercial banks, and ratings agencies. It just refused to use that power."[15]

How exactly did Congress acquiesce to the whims of the Wall Street lobby and the antiregulation crowd? There were two major missteps driven by special interests and enabled by blind partisanship. First, the financial crisis was in many ways the culmination of a decade of deregulated financial practice, facilitated by the Gramm-Leach-Bliley Act of 1999 (GLBA). Among other things, GLBA notably repealed the Depression-era Glass-Steagall Act, which for more than sixty years had required banks to be categorized and regulated according to the type of business they conducted, separating commercial banks from investment

banks. GLBA removed that distinction, and with it an important regulation that kept the securities industry from running amok, by letting
single holding companies conduct business in the fields of banking,
securities, and insurance. As Senator Carl Levin put it, GLBA "allowed
for a relatively small number of U.S. firms to become giant financial
conglomerates involved in collecting deposits, financing loans, trading
commodities, and buying, selling, issuing, underwriting, and insuring
billions of dollars in stock, debt instruments, insurance policies and
derivatives."[16]

Second, more deregulation was enabled on December 21, 2000,
when Congress passed the Commodity Futures Modernization Act of
2000 (CFMA), which created the loophole allowing "credit default
swaps," now a household word, by exempting certain investment instruments from regulation. As Securities and Exchange Commission (SEC)
chairman Christopher Cox told Congress during the height of the crisis
in 2008, "Knowing what I know now . . . I would have urged Congress to
repeal the swaps loophole in the 2000 Commodity Futures Modernization Act. As you know, in this loophole in this bipartisan law passed by a
Republican Congress and signed by President Clinton, Congress specifically prohibited the Commission from regulating swaps in very precise
language."[17] These legislative time bombs came about after fierce lobbying by Wall Street and thanks to fierce partisanship in Washington. Out-
of-control special interests and rampant partisanship not only create
real-world problems—they prevent solutions to them, as well.

In the wake of the financial crisis, both political parties should have
seized the opportunity to take responsibility for their mistakes and
work together toward a common solution. Yet the crisis and subsequent
bailouts have led to even more furious politicking. Republicans tried to
blame the whole crisis on the Democrats; Democrats angrily pointed
the finger right back at them. Even with their joint culpability, given the
way Congress currently works, Republicans have no incentives to join
with Democrats in fashioning solutions. And Democrats have no incentive to involve Republicans. Look no further than the bailout legislation
championed by President Obama during his first weeks in office, written by senior Democratic legislators, and unanimously voted against by
House Republicans.

The consequences of this political dysfunction, as 2008 taught us all too painfully, can be a monumentally serious meltdown. The financial crisis is the most recent and perhaps the best example of a meltdown scenario come to pass, but it won't be the last—unless we make systemic changes to the way Washington works. Indeed, it's clear what we need now is a total overhaul of our regulatory system—an overhaul that's unlikely to be as robust as it must be given the state of partisan division and special interest influence that still exists despite the aftershocks of the financial meltdown.

REFORM IN RUINS

The failure of reformers to fix what ails our politics boils down to the simple, fundamental fact that most people have very strong and wrong opinions about the political and legislative process. Indeed, there are three major misconceptions to my mind, each of which becomes painfully obvious when you look at previous (and proposed) reform efforts that were meant to fix our system but failed to do so.

FALSE ASSUMPTION #1:
"THE POLITICIANS ARE TO BLAME"

In the end, it doesn't matter who we send to Washington or which party controls Congress; it's the *system*, not the *individuals*, that needs to change. Reforms that target the actions of individuals instead of the system itself will always fail and don't deserve our serious attention. One such proposed reform would term-limit members of Congress in an attempt to break the cycle of incumbency and prevent individuals from accruing the power that can lead to abuse. Congressional term limits were part of the Republicans' "Contract with America" in 1994 and are today supported by some two-thirds of voters. It's easy to see why this idea is politically popular. If we could break up the incumbency racket by limiting the amount of time any one representative can serve in Washington, some reformers argue, it would reduce the influence of interest group campaign contributions and PAC checks.

In reality, though, term limits are a terrible idea rooted in misunder-standing. As I've demonstrated above, special interest influence is not merely the product of individual members' need for campaign cash to secure incumbency. Terms limits would do nothing to dismantle the nexus between partisan politics and interest group contributions. After all, you can't term-limit a political party, and the entanglement between national party committees and their interest group backers will perpet-uate itself whether individual members are allowed to serve two terms or twenty. It's easy to blame members and their drive for incumbency for the influence of special interests today, but in reality we know the problem is much more complex.

FALSE ASSUMPTION #2:
"IF ONLY [INSERT PARTY HERE] WERE IN CHARGE"

Forget about your partisan inclinations. If you think Democrats have all the answers or Republicans will always do a better job at running Con-gress than Democrats, you're naive. As I've demonstrated above, both parties are equally capable of—and equally responsible for—hijacking our system to their own ideological end. The partisan seesaw we experi-ence (usually during the election cycles between presidential contests) is this misconception manifest. When things are bad, it's natural to think the other team could do a better job. This is one reason, experts agree, that Obama was so successful in commonly "red" districts against McCain. But you don't need a Ph.D. in political science to know that it never works out this way. The balance of power isn't what's wrong with our politics. In fact, our problems have nothing to do with big govern-ment or small government, liberal politics or conservative politics. We are, somewhat paradoxically, confronted by a number of political prob-lems that require nonpartisan, nonideological solutions. And any pro-posed reform that has a partisan underpinning is a losing measure.

Look at the most recent effort to reform our campaign finance laws, the Bipartisan Campaign Reform Act of 2002, aka McCain-Feingold. While there were some positive features of the law—such as the ban on soft-money contributions to political parties—the law itself has failed to meaningfully transform our politics. And the reason is right there in its name: it was a *bipartisan* effort instead of a *nonpartisan* effort. While I disagree with many of his conclusions and much of his writing, John Samples, director of the Cato Institute's Center for Representative Government, gets it dead right in his recent book, *The Fallacy of Campaign Finance Reform.*

> Like earlier campaign finance restrictions, McCain-Feingold was a product of partisanship: congressional Democrats believed Republicans were likely to have an overwhelming advantage in soft money fundraising. Hence, more than 90 percent of Democrats in Congress voted to ban such fundraising. But McCain-Feingold showed that incumbency could trump partisanship. . . . In the end, the Democrats could expect something from the bill (a ban on soft money), and Republicans in general could expect something (a minor liberalization of contribution limits), but vulnerable Republicans in both chambers of Congress could expect the most. Because of McCain-Feingold, these Republicans could expect to be much less likely to face soft money spending by Democrats, hostile advertising funded by the Democratic National Committee or interest groups, or a wealthy opponent with money to spare and a willingness to spend.[18]

When evaluating a particular reform effort, it's only natural for partisans to first consider whether it would help or hurt their parties. But this is a dangerous urge we must collectively resist. Meaningful change will be driven only by a nonpolitical agenda that puts the greater good ahead of political consequences. In fact, in the end, doing so may help politicians that are serious about reform appeal to the independents and moderates that always decide the outcome of competitive elections.

FALSE ASSUMPTION #3:
"SPECIAL INTERESTS ARE DESTROYING OUR DEMOCRACY"

Actually, special interests are an important, essential, and positive component of our politics and government. And as the nonprofit, nonpartisan advocacy organization Public Citizen has correctly observed, lobbying is far older than American democracy. The right of individuals and groups to petition government was enshrined in the Magna Carta nearly eight hundred years ago.[19] Today, in a country of 300 million people and 535 federal lawmakers, we've handed over the daily duty of educating, pressuring, and, yes, influencing our representatives to some 30,000 registered lobbyists who are hired to represent various points of view in our nation's capital. And what we commonly call "special" interests are a lot less special than we give them credit for. Every industry and every profession—from chiropractors to teachers to welders—hire lobbyists to educate legislators and congressional staff about issues important to their ranks. If you're a parent with a child with Down syndrome and you're calling your local representative to support a disability bill, you're an individual lobbyist, and nobody would dare challenge your motives.

During the summer 2007 Yearly Kos candidate forum, organized by the political Web site Daily Kos, Hillary Clinton said, "[A] lot of those lobbyists, whether you like it or not, represent real Americans. They actually do. They represent nurses. They represent, you know, social workers. They represent . . . yes, they represent corporations. They employ a lot of people."[20] Clinton was heckled by the collected left-wing bloggers—and unfairly. While some lobbyists clearly are over-zealous, most play an important role in our legislative process.

Worse, the generally held, and terribly distorted, view of lobbyists as something between petty thieves and highway robbers has led to some particularly wrong-minded reforms. In the wake of the Jack Abramoff pay-to-play scandal, and with new scandals seemingly emerging each month, in 2007 Congress adopted a series of reforms, the Honest Leadership and Open Government Act. The new law doubled the reporting requirements for lobbyist activity, quadrupled civil penalties for violating the disclosure requirement, and set harsh criminal penalties as well. However, these useful reforms were fundamentally undermined by other measures in the law that look great on paper but actually open the door to making lobbying influence worse. Congress barred its members from accepting gifts from lobbyists, including meals or privately funded trips. But at the same time, it created a loophole large enough to drive all of K Street through. Lobbyists can't fete a member of Congress, but members can throw lavish parties to benefit their reelection campaigns and invite as many lobbyists as they like. As one lobbyist put it: "Members can't socialize with you, they can't go to dinner with you. . . . Nobody wants to be seen with a lobbyist right now because of the perception issue. You can't even get a staff member to have lunch with you in the cafeteria. But if I write a check, I can go to a fundraising event and have face time with them. At the end of the day, is that what was intended?"[21]

To answer this lobbyist's rhetorical question: Yes, that's exactly what Congress intended. In fact, that's the preferred way of conducting the business of politics in Washington today. As Penelope S. Farthing, a lobbyist at mega–law firm Patton Boggs, told the *National Journal*, "The ethics rules, which now ban most meals and gifts to members and staff, clearly will have the effect of driving social exchanges into fundraising. . . . If you need to really sit down and explain something to a member, that will now take place at fundraisers." Another lobbyist, Republican Lanny Griffith, put it even more succinctly: "What is more pernicious? A lunch at [Capitol Hill watering hole] Charlie Palmer, or a fundraiser? A fundraiser is likely to have more influence than a forty-dollar steak."[22]

The net result of the new law is that it has induced lawmakers to continue to openly solicit contributions from lobbyists. Just throw a fundraiser. The reality of the lobbying reform law is that it encourages—and, in essence, requires—members of Congress to corral special interests at political fund-raisers, the exact place where we should prevent the commingling of political and private interests. Congress addressed the perception issue that was most problematic in the minds of voters—gifts and junkets paid for by special interests—but it did nothing about the real problem: interest group financing of our elections, which perpetuates incumbency, fuels partisanship, and makes Congress responsive to special interests instead of average voters. Laws that prevent lobbyist abuse and political corruption are a good start, but we need more than lobby reform. It doesn't change the fundamentals. We need *congressional* reform.

RETHINKING THE POWER OF THE PURSE

Congress is charged with drafting legislation, the most important of which—the first two powers under section 8 of the Constitution—are the laws overseeing the funding of the U.S. federal government. But in our highly charged political environment, Congress is today utterly unable to deal with federal spending that has gone through the roof or implement reforms to Social Security, Medicare, and Medicaid, all of which are nearly insolvent. Congress must retreat from picking political fights over the fiscal problems we face and get back to solving them. Here are several solutions that amount to bypass surgery for legislative arteries that are clogged with partisanship.

Create a nonpartisan congressional solvency commission to cope with fiscal crises

We are in a fiscal crisis that may be long-term. The problems we're facing today will not be with us only for the foreseeable future—they're likely to get worse. From a near-depleted Social Security Trust Fund, to Medicare and Medicaid programs that are projected to be in the red within a decade, the federal government faces a number of significant fiscal challenges that have spiraled out of control.

Thanks to our political dysfunctions, we currently lack the means to deal with these challenges. Partisan bickering means nothing gets done while disaster looms. To circumvent political roadblocks, we should heed the advice of conservative voices such as the Peter G. Peterson Foundation and the Concord Coalition to create nonpartisan coalitions to brainstorm our way out of impending fiscal disaster. To that end, Congress should create an expert, nonpartisan congressional solvency commission to study the fiscal problems we face, recommend solutions, and put their recommendations to an up-or-down congressional vote.

Congress faced a similarly impassable dilemma in the late 1980s, when the Department of Defense began to reassess its domestic infrastructure and determine which military installations should stay and which should go. If you have ever lived near (or on) a military base, you know that they are massive operations that are essentially huge regional economic engines. In addition to the members of the armed forces who work on base, they indirectly support thousands of civilian jobs. Robins Air Force Base in Georgia, for instance, employs nearly twenty-six thousand people and is the largest industrial complex in the state.[23] It's no wonder that no member of Congress wanted to vote to close a base in his or her state.

The solution came in the form of the Base Realignment and Closure Commission (BRAC), a nonpartisan group of civilian and military experts who created a comprehensive plan to shutter certain bases across the country based on the needs of the military. BRAC's plan was presented to Congress for a simple up-or-down vote. To be sure, partisans reacted strenuously to the recommendations of this apolitical committee. But in the end, the system resulted in a fair, sensible, and nonpartisan way of reallocating federal resources.

Like BRAC, a congressional solvency commission would help Congress tackle a sensitive issue by removing it from the system that time and again has ensured that nothing gets done. The commission would be composed of experts from both parties, would conduct hearings and studies, and would assemble plans to solve the impending entitlement crises. Congress would appoint the members of the commission and, of course, would have the power to implement or reject its proposals. Dave Walker, president of the Peter G. Peterson Foundation and a former U.S. comptroller general, and others on the right and the left support similar commissions.

Managers to answer to a federal fiduciary standard when they invest on behalf of others

"How could so many highly skilled, highly paid securities analysts and researchers have failed to question the toxic-filled leveraged balance sheets of Citigroup and other leading banks and investment banks?" John Bogle, investor and founder of the Vanguard Group, has asked. And it's a good question. His point is elemental. Without trying to prejudge or determine the specific types of legislation that should be passed, a fiduciary standard for money managers would require that they act on behalf of the people they are supposed to serve—investors—rather than just allowing them to pursue profits at the expense of sound and practical business solutions.

Indeed, it seems to me that this is the thrust of the legislation proposed by President Obama to overhaul the institutions that govern the nation's financial system. Obama and Treasury Secretary Timothy

Geithner have proposed a new Consumer Financial Protection Agency, a Financial Services Oversight Council, and other measures intended to provide stronger and better regulation to prevent banks and other non-banking financial institutions from wreaking havoc on consumers and the economy. What form this well-intentioned legislation takes is another question entirely. After just a few months, it is clear that the major players in the debate—Geithner, Fed chairman Ben Bernanke, FDIC chair Sheila Bair, and ranking members of Congress—can't agree on how to accomplish a generally positive and shared goal of protecting the public and preventing future financial disaster.

According to Bogle, "We need Congress to pass a law to establish the basic principle that money managers are there to serve their shareholders. And the second part of the demand is that fiduciaries act with due diligence and high professional standards. That doesn't seem to be too much to ask."[24] By imposing these two standards, we can avoid the egregious abuses of the past few years that led to the creation of highly complicated securities, whose existence had as much to do with the needs of Wall Street financial houses as it did with the desire to serve the needs of both the economy and the investing public. As Bogle has said, this "is not a regulatory solution, it is a principles-based solution."

It's simple: consumers come first. Whether you're applying for a mortgage or investing in the stock markets, if consumers come first, we'll be on our way to stabilizing our financial markets with a regulatory system that puts the economy ahead of the interests of well-heeled Wall Street bankers.

Create a nonpartisan commission to overhaul the financial regulatory system

There are two problems with America's financial regulatory system, as we know it today. First, it doesn't work. As SEC chairman Christopher Cox noted in 2008, "Government intervention, taxpayer assumption of risk, and short-term forestalling of failure must not be a permanent fixture of our financial system."[25] Instead, a systematic reform of the entire federal, state, and private regulatory system is desperately needed.

This brings us to the second problem with today's regulatory system. It simply can't be fixed well, given our broken legislative process, which continues to be overrun by special interests and plagued by partisanship.

After the crash of 1929, the country faced a similar challenge to figure out what went wrong and implement needed solutions, in the midst of heightened partisanship and an unprecedented economic crisis. The Senate banking committee began investigations in 1932, which faltered repeatedly until Ferdinand Pecora was appointed to take over the investigation in 1933. Pecora relentlessly pursued the biggest financial moguls of the era and won bipartisan praise for his efforts, which ultimately resulted in Glass-Steagall, the formation of the SEC, and other long-standing and effective regulatory instruments.

Similar to the congressional solvency commission I proposed previously, Congress should create a Pecora-style commission to conduct a thorough nonpartisan investigation of the financial crisis and propose meaningful solutions that are not tainted by industry lobbying efforts or the political influence of partisan ideologues—solutions that would then be presented to Congress for a simple up-or-down vote.

What would these solutions looks like, if untainted by special interests and Wall Street lobbyists? In my view, they would preferably reinstate the regulations that were successful for six decades before their repeal at end of the 1990s. In the run-up to the financial crisis, agencies that were supposed to manage risk instead advocated and supported the deregulatory policies that allowed private financial institutions to engage in risk on a systemic level. A Pecora-style commission could change that, and it could also recommend that financial advisers be federally regulated fiduciaries, instead of independent actors with no legal responsibility for their actions, as they are today.

Bailouts and stimulus packages will be insufficient to restore the health of the financial markets if significant regulatory changes are not enacted into federal law. The initial reaction of federal policy makers was to address the crisis in the short-term through government bailouts, which don't address the root problem. A Pecora-style commission will make long-term reform possible in an environment that is too poisonously partisan and compromised to get the job done otherwise.

Ban congressional earmarks, which encourage ethics abuses and lead to unnecessary government waste

Earmarks should be illegal. Their only function is to allow members to sneak appropriations into law without proper review and to give ranking party members the ability to mete out favors or punishment. Nothing should be secret or hidden from voters by the members of Congress who we send to Washington—least of all the process by which hundreds of billions of tax dollars are spent on pet projects.

As I argued earlier, earmarks have a snowball affect. They rile up partisanship and represent an avenue for ethics abuses. Things are better today than they were before, but not by much. We need nothing less than a total ban.

Implement biennial budgeting to strengthen bipartisanship and enhance oversight

Congress has the power of the purse. But with a federal budget of $3 *trillion*, the process of creating and passing spending bills consumes a significant amount of time and results in equally significant acrimony. The budget process is one that always involves posturing and brinksmanship—see 1995, when President Bill Clinton and House Speaker Newt Gingrich twice shut down the federal government, for a total of twenty-two days, over partisan budget disputes.

Instead of annual appropriations, Congress should pass biennial budgets, which would result in a more thoughtful process that encourages cooperation and enhances congressional oversight. Budgeting every two years would almost eliminate the possibility of a government shutdown. Furthermore, biennial budgeting that takes place during an "off year" in which there are no federal elections would add another layer of insulation from the politics that all too often degrade the budgeting process.

As Brian M. Riedl of the Heritage Foundation has rightly noted, "Biennial budgeting would free lawmakers to spend more time overseeing federal programs and reforming failed or unnecessary programs."[26] Several liberal thinkers and policy makers agree. Leon Panetta, a chief of staff to President Clinton and Obama's CIA director, and Jack Lew, director of the Office of Management and Budget from 1998 to 2001, spoke out in support of biennial budgets during the previous Democratic administration. Riedl has another good idea that I'm sure most liberals would agree with—make Congress institutionalize its oversight responsibility by issuing public oversight reports: "Congress is supposed to oversee the executive branch, but few congressional committees produce reports determining whether the agencies that they oversee are effectively and efficiently accomplishing their goals. Semiannual oversight reports would strengthen oversight," he said.

During a time when we've seen a dramatic expansion of the federal budget and the size of executive branch agencies—from the Department of Homeland Security to the Office of the Director of National Intelligence—increased oversight is badly needed.

FIXING THE POLITICS OF MAKING LAW

Congress is a complex body. In many respects, the *way* it works sometimes *stops* it from working altogether. Both the House and the Senate operate on the sometimes archaic rules of parliamentary procedure, and members unnecessarily manipulate procedural rules. While some of these procedures—such as the filibuster—are necessary, others do more harm than good. We need to make it harder for members of Congress to manipulate rules for partisan gain.

Ban "holds" that allow senators to stall the chamber's legislative work

Holds are a tradition of the Senate that allows any one member of that chamber the ability to block a piece of legislative business from proceeding to the floor for full consideration. Sometimes they're used to kill a particular law, and sometimes they're used as political leverage to force a bill's sponsor to change its language substantially or to make a concession on an unrelated piece of legislation. Holds encourage logrolling. Typically, Senate holds have been secret, known only to the objecting senator's majority leader. All a senator has to do is tell the party leadership that he or she objects to a particular piece of legislation, and that legislation is automatically frozen until that senator drops the hold.

Case in point: In 2006, a bill sponsored by Tom Coburn (R-Okla.) and Barack Obama to create an online database to track federal spending was blocked by a secret hold. Internet activists supportive of the bill strenuously objected and ultimately discovered that Alaska Republican Ted Stevens and West Virginia Democrat Robert Byrd were blocking the measure. Outed by the blogosphere, Stevens and Byrd revoked their holds, Congress passed the bill, and the database is now online.[27]

Partially in response, in 2007 Congress changed the rules to force senators to reveal any holds they place on legislation after a few days. Even though holds are no longer secret, they still promote partisanship and foment gridlock. Let's just do away with them. Senators can change Senate rules and abolish holds with a simple majority vote. Stalwarts might object, but it's impossible to deny that this is a straightforward, pragmatic change that will end one of the most pernicious Senate procedures and make members of Congress much more responsive to their constituents.

Ban secret conference committees that allow members of Congress to conduct the people's business in private

According to the Senate, a conference committee is technically "a temporary, ad hoc panel composed of House and Senate conferees which is formed for the purpose of reconciling differences in legislation that has passed both chambers . . . convened to resolve bicameral differences on major and controversial legislation."[28] They're also the usual mechanism for inserting earmarks and other hidden measures into legislation. While these committees are required to hold at least one public meeting, most of the real work—that is, partisan handouts to special interests—happens in closed-door sessions. As the *New York Times* reported: "Often any public meetings are as much about show as substance, with the real dealing done in secret by top staff members and chairmen of the relevant committees. The conference rules, dating back to Thomas Jefferson's time, are often bent, with lawmakers making last-minute additions and reaching beyond the scope of the legislation passed by either the House or Senate."[29]

Here's an infinitely simple and smart solution to eliminate this avenue for partisan abuse: Force these committees to hold all their meetings in public, open to reporters and citizens alike.

ENDING THE PRIVATE INTEREST

In fairness, Congress has done much to improve the regulations that govern interactions between lobbyists and members of Congress. The system today is better than it was. But problems remain, and today there are still too many incentives for Congress and lobbyists to collude. A few easy fixes will tighten our laws, limit the influence of special interests, and reduce incentives to violate the public trust.

Ban lobbyists from attending political fund-raisers

It goes without saying that we should simply hold Congress to the same standard that we hold lobbyists. Yet in 2007, Congress pulled a fast one on the American people by creating a new standard of conduct for lobbyists but not for lawmakers. It was a brazen abdication of responsibility, which we can see today in the number of loopholes and double standards that allow legislators to use lobbyists as virtual ATM machines for their reelection campaigns.

The language of our lobby laws should be unequivocal. No interactions between members and lobbyists at fund-raisers of any kind. Period. While the Honest Leadership and Open Government Act of 2007 intended an outright ban on lobbyist-funded meals, travel, entertainment, and other gifts meant to influence members, it's not quite working. At the 2008 Democratic Convention in Denver, a law that prohibited members of Congress from attending convention events funded by lobbyists in honor of a *particular* member was railroaded when lobbyists threw lavish parties in honor of a *group* of members. It was a perfectly predictable and infuriating end run around the law.

These abuses can be stopped with clear and simple language that says lobbyists *cannot* attend political fund-raisers and by passage of a new law that prohibits members of Congress from treating lobbyists to meals, travel, entertainment, and other gifts. It might be unconstitutional to ban lobbyists from donating to the election efforts of candidates (including incumbents) for Congress. But it's legal to ban members of Congress from playing host to lobbyists at political fund-raisers.

Require members of Congress to disclose their contact with lobbyists on the Internet

Lobbyists are required to disclose their contact with members of Congress, but members are never required to report their contact with lobbyists. It's another loophole that Congress built into the law in order to make it easier for them to hit up lobbyists for campaign cash with total impunity. Again, we need to hold members to the same standard as lobbyists, this time by putting a burden of disclosure on members, too.

This important reform proposal has been championed by former Speaker of the House Newt Gingrich. Gingrich's proposal would:

1. Require that all lobbying contacts between government officials (elected and unelected) and lobbyists be posted on the Internet weekly so people can understand who is doing what.
2. Require that the lobbyist file one report and the member or staff file a parallel report so there is a continuous process of confirming accuracy and honesty in reporting, and
3. Make it a felony to deliberately misreport.

These excellent recommendations deserve serious consideration from conservatives and liberals alike.

Create an independent ethics commission and appoint a congressional ethics ombudsman to investigate wrongdoing by legislators

Despite recent reforms in Congress, the Senate and House ethics committees are still arms of Congress—not independent bodies granted the means and the will to investigate corruption and abuse. We need an independent ethics panel to investigate ethics violations in Congress and ensure that unscrupulous members can't abuse the public trust.

Democrats promised ethics reform when they reclaimed majorities in the House and Senate in 2006, and they delivered—in part. In 2008, the House narrowly created the Office of Congressional Ethics, an eight-member panel jointly appointed by the Speaker and the minority leader. In an important change from past practices, appointees must be former members or other nonelected officials. This represents the first quasi-independent panel on congressional ethics. But the panel is charged with referring complaints for further investigation to the House ethics committee, and you can immediately see that we're far from solving the real problem. The new office has no subpoena power, cannot take testimony under oath, and doesn't do any investigating itself. The House still runs its own investigations, though Joe Citizen can now file ethics complaints that are reviewed by an independent panel made up of the former colleagues of the politician in question.

Necessary, but insufficient. So long as members of Congress are allowed to police themselves, they can rely on a gentleman's agreement to look the other way on many indiscretions. Accountability ultimately rests with voters, but two years is too long to leave certain allegations and transgressions unresolved. Congress should take a cue from the thirty-three states that have created independent commissions with the power to investigate state lawmakers, government officials, and civil servants.[30]

An independent ethics commission should be federally funded, fully empowered, and wholly autonomous. Ideally, it would be composed of retired judges, drawn from the U.S. Court of Appeals for the Federal Circuit in Washington, D.C., who are appointed by the president, thereby ensuring that members of Congress and interest groups are not colluding to undermine the public trust. I'm also partial to Thomas Mann and Norman Ornstein's idea, discussed in their book *The Broken Branch*, that a new ethics commission should include a "chief ethics officer."[31] A congressional ethics ombudsman should head the new independent ethics commission, and commissioners should hold the ombudsman role for rotating two-year terms.

In 2004, an adviser to President George W. Bush told the *New York*

Times that while some in the "reality-based community" are content to study how things work to identify solutions to the challenges we face, the administration's official policy was to "create our own reality."[32] Unsurprisingly, critics clung to this revelation of policy making by selectively ignoring the facts, and it became a rallying cry for a return to common sense in government.

We need a similar return to the reality-based community in our politics. It's easy enough to ignore the facts and hope that a Band-Aid here and there will patch up the holes in our broken system. But it won't stanch the bleeding. What I've proposed is a reality-based approach that takes into account how and why our system malfunctions and exactly what we need to do to repair it.

The conventional wisdom is that the way things are today is the way they always were and always will be. And this sense is reinforced by our reformers—on the left and on the right, in Washington and in the states—who have continually failed to bring about meaningful change. But as I've tried to show, we know how the system fails us, and we know how to change it. By taking a hard look at the realities that confront us, we can and we will be able to transform congressional politics with solutions that limit the influence of special interests and put an end to the partisanship and gridlock that have paralyzed our government.

6

TAKE POLITICS OUT OF JUSTICE
Ending the Crisis in the Courts

> There is hardly a political question in the United States which does not sooner or later turn into a judicial one.
> —ALEXIS DE TOCQUEVILLE, 1835

Tocqueville's observation is quite the opposite today; there is hardly a judicial matter in the United States that doesn't eventually turn into a political one. This is not wholly surprising given the way judges are elevated to the bench. The Constitution specifies that the president nominates and the Senate confirms judges to the federal courts. It also provides that states are entitled to choose whatever system they see fit to install judges. Overwhelmingly, states have settled upon some form of election. Voters in thirty-nine states elect their judges directly, through contests in which political parties nominate candidates for judge or in nonpartisan elections. Even in states where judges are nominated by governors and confirmed by legislatures, judges must often go before the voters for "retention elections," in which the public has an opportunity to approve or remove an appointed jurist. In sum, 90 percent of states give voters a role in selecting their states' judges through partisan, nonpartisan, or retention elections.[1]

America is almost alone among the major industrial democracies in electing the preponderance of its judges in this way. And it has ramifications for the system as a whole—which has increasingly taken on a populist cast. Because so many judges or would-be judges face the voters, they tend to pander to the most vociferous, organized, and punitive elements of the public: victims' groups, police associations, and law-and-order advocates. Naturally, our judicial system reflects the influence of these forces. America is the only major Western democracy that retains the death penalty, which it applies with a gusto outstripped only by the world's dictatorships.

Our incarceration rates, similarly, mirror those of less-free countries. Legislatures, responding to popular pressures to "get tough" on crime, have enacted a variety of mandatory-minimum and "three strikes" sentencing laws that hamstring jurists and expand prisons, often to the detriment of justice and even common sense. Laws named after spectacular and often lurid murder and kidnapping cases proliferate, channeling public outrage but doing little to enhance public safety. Judges themselves have joined the popular culture—preening for the camera in televised cases and even transforming their courtrooms into reality shows. It's easy to see why this tabloidized judicial system might attract judges who often, alas, wind up in the tabloids themselves.

While our justice system has often been a model to emerging democracies in the developing world, other countries have decidedly rejected the elections used in the vast majority of states to staff the bench, precisely because they compromise the independence of the courts and invite political influence, even corruption. As former Oregon Supreme Court justice Hans A. Linde said, "To the rest of the world, American adherence to judicial elections is as incomprehensible as our rejection of the metric system."[2]

For years, judicial elections were of little note at home or abroad, and federal judicial nominations were a slow but not entirely disagreeable process. Today, "utter collapse" is not an unfair description of our system for selecting the men and women in whom we entrust the fair administration of justice, a linchpin of our democracy. From the stinted process of nominating and confirming judges for federal district and circuit courts, to out-of-control state judicial elections that break new records each year for cost and negativity, judicial appointments have been overwhelmed by politics in every conceivable way.

Why the dramatic departure from the relatively timid proceedings of the past? The same political crisis that has disfigured our presidential campaigns and put a choke hold on Congress is now causing massive damage to our courthouses. And if the rapid nature of our courts' decline is somewhat mystifying, the effect is not. In the mind of the public, the intensely political climate of judicial elections and appointments no doubt makes our system seem troubled, if not downright illegitimate. But it's *inside* our courtrooms where the worst repercussions of this broken system are manifest. For one, our judges are no longer the best and brightest. Many are political survivors who are willing and able to claw their way to the bench through questionable tactics, dirty campaigning, and power politics. The rest are ideologues whose fidelity to a particular political ethic makes them attractive candidates for political parties to elevate to the courts. In this highly partisan system, serving justice becomes an afterthought, the legitimacy of our justice system becomes suspect, and our democracy suffers for it.

STATE BY STATE

State judicial elections are now virtually indistinguishable from races for Congress or state legislatures. They are increasingly expensive, increasingly negative, and increasingly detrimental to the impartiality of the justice system. Just as in contests for the House and Senate, judicial candidates are forced to turn to special interests to finance their campaigns—a recent turn of events that has had a disastrous effect on the administration of justice.

A 2006 landmark report on state judicial campaigns by New York University's Brennan Center for Justice and the National Institute for Money in State Politics uncovered a number of troubling trends. First, judicial campaigns are becoming increasingly expensive with an explosion of television expenditures. In 2000, only four of the eighteen states that held supreme court elections that year featured TV ad campaigns; in 2006, on-air campaigns ran in ten of eleven states. Total spending on television by judicial candidates, their parties, and interest groups across the nation hit an all-time high of $16.1 million in 2006.[3] As a result, five of ten states that held competitive judicial elections in 2006 broke new records for fund-raising.[4]

After the 2008 elections, I spoke to Hank Sheinkopf, who made his career running supreme court elections in the states, particularly in Texas and Alabama, about these trends. "The system is now out of control—it has run amok," he said. "These elections now cost millions of dollars, not $500,000 or $1,000,000, but tens of millions of dollars. I've won some and lost some, but I'll never forget the day that I walked into a meeting in Alabama. I told them that I needed a half of a million dollars to get started, and the next day the money was in the account. Those sorts of things don't just happen. They happen for a reason, and those reasons are much more bad than good."

This record spending has hardly contributed to a positive or constructive debate about which judicial candidates are most qualified to be impartial arbiters of justice. Quite the opposite: recent ads for state court contests are some of the most distasteful and dishonest that I've ever heard of—and after thirty years on the campaign trail, I've seen some nasty ads in my day. A few examples:

- In a 2008 supreme court election in Wisconsin, one ad accused Justice Louis Butler of giving a new trial to a convicted rapist and murderer. While technically true, the ad ignored the fact that DNA evidence presented by the prosecution didn't match the convicted man—hence the new trial ordered by Butler.[5]
- In a 2004 West Virginia campaign, the incumbent chief justice was the target of an ad in which one of his speeches was digitally altered to have him emitting a scream reminiscent of Howard Dean's much ridiculed and campaign-ending utterance that same year.[6]
- A 2006 primary campaign in Alabama featured an ad that accused a judicial candidate of being soft on crime, while an image of a knife-wielding hand flashed on screen.[7]
- Another West Virginia ad accused circuit judge Bill Cunningham of putting six rapists up for parole and insinuated that one parolee raped a fourteen-year-old just hours after being released—even though the crime was committed years before.[8]

These advertising anecdotes are proof points of another unsettling development unearthed by the Brennan Center and the National Institute for Money in State Politics. In 2004, the campaigns of state judicial candidates were directly responsible for airing only 10 percent of the negative television advertising that cycle. The other 90 percent was paid for by the usual coterie of special interests and political party committees. Two years later, however, candidates themselves aired 60 percent of negative ads. On a similar note, the study found that only half of the ads aired in 2006 focused on the subject of the candidate's "qualifications, experience, or temperament." The rest were ad hominem diatribes on personal values, religion, and other characteristics that should have no bearing whatsoever on a judge's ability to hand down just and unbiased rulings.

In short, we now see that influence buying has crept into the courts in the same manner as it has saturated Congress.

With the sharp increase of television advertising in these races, it's clear why interest groups have come to dominate the process of financing judicial campaigns. During the 2006 cycle, PACs newly created by special interests in Washington State ran attack ads against the state's chief justice, Gerry Alexander. One such group, called ChangePac, accused Alexander of literally letting killers walk the streets; the Building Industry Association of Washington, which cut a $400,000 check to ChangePac, was conveniently located at the same address, which saved them the postage for mailing the donation. Another group, Americans Tired of Lawsuit Abuse, which spent $320,000 advertising against Alexander, was a cover for the D.C.-based American Tort Reform Association. And to counter all of this special interest influence from the business community and the right wing, Democrats rallied liberal interest groups—including the Service Employees International Union—to air counterattacks under the banner of Citizens to Uphold the Constitution.[9] In total, special interests on both side of the partisan divide spent $2.7 million in Washington State's judicial election that year.[10] And the special interest involvement in Washington was a trend seen around the nation. As the Brennan Center reported, "Trial lawyers and corporate interests in a southern Illinois race combined to give more than $3.3 million to two candidates for a seat on the state court of appeals, quadrupling the state record. Madison County witnessed a $500,000 trial court campaign, and a Missouri trial court judge was defeated after an out-of-state group poured $175,000 into a campaign to defeat him."[11]

Record amounts of money raised and spent, special interests climbing over one another to get a piece of the action, candidates going negative early and often—what does all of this add up to? In short, our courts are now for sale to the highest political campaign contributors. And while that might sound hyperbolic, the data prove that the loss of an independent judiciary is a direct and terrible consequence of our dysfunctional system of government, politics, and justice.

Vernon Valentine Palmer, a Tulane University law professor, and John Levendis, a Loyola University economics professor, studied the nexus between political contributions to Louisiana Supreme Court justices and their decisions. They found that two times out of three justices voted in favor of their campaign contributors, and that between 1992 and 2006 half of the cases before the court featured at least one party who had contributed to the campaign of at least one justice.[12] An investigative report by the *New York Times* discovered a similar trend in Ohio, where supreme court justices sided with their contributors 70 percent of the time. The *Times* also revealed that "in the 215 cases with the most direct potential conflicts of interest, justices recused themselves just nine times."[13]

There's little recent or comprehensive data from other states, but individual stories lead me to believe that Ohio and Louisiana are not anomalies. In West Virginia, for instance, a campaign contributor spent $3 million to support the election of supreme court of appeals justice Brent Benjamin. It seems that contribution paid off when Justice Benjamin cast the deciding vote that overturned a $50 million verdict against a company in which the contributor in question happened to be none other than the CEO.[14] In 2009, the U.S. Supreme Court ruled that Justice Benjamin should have recused himself. In a nearly identical scenario in Wisconsin, a supreme court justice refused to sit out a case involving a defendant who spent $2 million in support of her campaign—more than her own campaign itself spent on her election effort.[15] These aren't just a few examples cherry-picked to make a point. A poll conducted in 2001–02 found that 46 percent of state court judges believe their colleagues are influenced by political contributions.[16] Can we definitely prove a quid pro quo in these instances? Probably not. All the same, these contrasts do not instill any sense of judicial fairness in reasonably objective observers.

If judicial fraud and injustice weren't tragedy enough, the system is also forcing truly decent men and women out of our courts. Louis Butler, the supreme court justice in Wisconsin who, according to his opponent's bogus attack ads, let rapists run wild in the Midwest, was Wisconsin's first African American to sit on the state's supreme court. He was also the first justice to lose a reelection campaign in forty years, thanks to those and other attack ads, all overwhelmingly financed by special interest groups.[17] Judicial candidates today face the same dilemma as congressional candidates: If you want to win, you have to play the game. As a result, our nation's courts are being depleted of talented and independent-minded jurists.

Of course, some of these jurists will eventually rise through the courts, making it onto a long list—or a short list—for a U.S. Supreme Court nomination. Even if one doesn't live in Wisconsin, that state's bench (like any other's) could end up having a significant effect on how all Americans experience justice. Based on how "justice" is administered in the United States today, if you're a judge and you want to keep your job, you have to cozy up to a special interest. If you're a business and you want a favorable hearing, break out your checkbook. And if you're an everyday citizen and you want a fair hearing by an impartial arbitrator, well, try Judge Judy.

FIXING THE JUDICIAL SYSTEM

I'm the first to admit that we can't just ask our members of Congress to legislate a solution to the problem of judicial elections. Each state has its own constitutional parameters that determine the means by which judges are selected, and changing those means in many instances requires amending the state constitution. But there are a few universal reforms that are extremely compelling for their simplicity and their utility in cleaning up our state courthouses and purging politics from the judicial system.

Replace judicial elections with merit selection of judges subject to legislative oversight

There's only one foolproof way to ensure the independence of our judiciary and restore credibility to our courts: *eliminate judicial elections.* I don't buy the argument that the public needs to directly elect its judges. Most of our citizenry don't have enough time to adequately analyze such elections—they're too busy muting the ugly TV ads anyway.

There are credible ways to ensure citizen oversight and judicial accountability without opening up the process to partisan warfare and corporate special interests. I'm convinced that we have to do away with elections entirely in order to guarantee the fundamental independence and impartiality of our courts. Merit selection of judges is the only system that guarantees independence, ensures the appointment of qualified men and women, and still gives the public a say in the process.

Today, there are practically as many different ways of selecting state court judges as there are states. California's judges are selected by gubernatorial appointment, but judges are also reappointed by voters in retention elections every twelve years; elections are also held when judges retire. The legislature in South Carolina appoints its judges. A cluster of states in the Northwest hold nonpartisan elections. The national picture is a patchwork of partisan and nonpartisan contests, nominating commissions, legislative oversight, and citizen approval at the ballot box. The vast majority of these systems feature a popular election in some way, shape, or form.

Merit selection is simple and safe. It calls for expert nominating commissions of nonpartisan attorneys, legislators, judges, and others who together select a pool of the best candidates based on nonpartisan, nonideological criteria. The state's governor then chooses from among this pool. There could be a special oversight committee within the commission, as well, to ensure that the governor is not favoring a cadre of campaign contributors. Give this committee a couple of vetoes to discourage overzealous governors.

States that use the merit selection system have nominating commissions that vary. For instance, Iowa's commission comprises the senior justice of the state's supreme court, seven commissioners appointed by the governor and confirmed by the senate, and seven commissioners selected by the state's bar association. Arizona has three separate commissions that handle appellate, county, and trial court appointments. As long as the commissions are nonpartisan and diverse, I'm not especially concerned with how they're structured.

What I am concerned with are retention elections. In some states, these are held several years after a judge's initial appointment—enough time for a judge to amass a record of decisions on the bench—and periodically thereafter. They're meant to give the public an opportunity to weigh in, which on its face is a good thing. However, they also give special interests the same opportunity. It's not difficult to imagine a business group using a retention election as an occasion to retaliate against a judge for an unfavorable ruling.

A much better system is to give state legislatures the power to review and retain judges. This allows for indirect citizen oversight, without the problems that are introduced in a popular election. Legislatures could also adopt judicial performance review commissions—like those in Arizona—to help make a case for or against retaining a judge. Legislative review of this nature every six years is sensible.

What doesn't make sense is the argument that judicial contests should be or could be any cleaner or more harmonious than any other kind of election. That logic flies in the face of everything we know about politics. When candidates identify with a certain political party, they are stating their allegiance to a particular ideology. Our judges, however, should be apolitical agents committed to justice, not doctrine. Likewise, if given an opportunity, we know that special interest money will always find a way to pervade the process and distort the outcome. In legislative or executive elections, we can (and must) take steps to curb the influence of interest groups. But in judicial elections, we can't afford even the possibility of such influence.

Reform the process of electing judges

Merit selection is the closest thing to a panacea that you'll find in this book. It's the best way and the only way to ensure that state judiciaries are composed of the most qualified, the most diverse, and the most impartial jurists.

That said, we're a long way from the day when merit selection is the national standard. In the meantime, there are two important interim steps we can take to restore credibility and independence to our courts, by reforming the way our judicial elections are conducted.

Public financing. Instead of doing away with elections entirely, some states have tried to make them less prone to abuse by implementing public financing of judicial campaigns. For years, Wisconsin was the only state in which voters picked up the tab for these elections. North Carolina followed in 2002, and then Arizona, Maine, and Massachusetts. In North Carolina, the new system has been heralded a success. In 2004 and 2006, twenty of twenty-eight candidates for the state's supreme court and court of appeals participated in the public finance system. Of eleven races held during those years, nine of the winners were publicly financed. More important, the system has purged special interest money from the process. In 2002, contributions from attorneys accounted for 73 percent of campaign funds. In 2004, that figure plummeted to 14 percent.[18] I'm opposed to public financing of judicial campaigns as an ultimate solution because interest groups can still make independent expenditures but, as an interim measure, I can't argue with the numbers.

Judicial campaign conduct committees. As judicial campaigns have become increasingly negative and our courts increasingly politicized, some states have tried to reverse this tide of destructive partisanship by creating campaign conduct committees that police the activities of candidates. According to a 2008 survey by the American Judicature Society, these committees are extremely effective: "Without exception, active committees believe that oversight committees positively influence judicial campaign behavior. For example, the Dade County, Florida, committee responded that it has deterred inappropriate campaigning and its members believe it is an extremely worthwhile activity. There is an incentive to sign the campaign agreement and reap the favorable publicity that signing brings. The agreement establishes normative conduct and imposes restraint; and the committee is the cop on the corner that deters candidates from doing what they might otherwise do to win."[19]

Again, let me be perfectly clear: I am a strong proponent of merit selection of judges. But until all states move to merit selection, any measure that will help curb the sharp increase in despicably negative campaigning is worth consideration and implementation. Campaign conduct committees and public financing are two interim measures that have already had a positive impact in several states and should be implemented widely wherever judicial campaigns are held.

Institute online disclosure and recusal standards to ensure impartial justice

The idea that a judge could rule on a case in which he or she has a financial stake, or in which one of the parties in question is a campaign contributor, seems so ludicrous as to be impossible. But in many states these scenarios are not only legal, *they're commonplace.* With a few simple yet comprehensive steps that improve judicial disclosure, we can make sure that the only thing our judges have a stake in is serving justice.

According to a 2007 study by the Center for Public Integrity, forty-seven states require judges to disclose their finances, but only thirteen states make that information available to the public online. In the remaining states, the information is difficult to find, at best. There's no reason to reinvent the wheel here. There should be a national standard for disclosure—say, the annual financial disclosure form that senators file with the Senate ethics committee—and those disclosures should be available via the Internet.

Second, judges should have to disclose all campaign contributors. Today, there are uneven reporting standards among the states. In some cases, judges are not required to report any campaign finance information at all. Until merit selection is implemented nationwide, states should require candidates for judge to report all contributors, contributions, and expenditures in a timely manner—reports that should be available to the public online through a national center for judicial independence.

Third, states should automatically disqualify judges from hearing cases that involve campaign contributors or in which they have a financial interest—as a stockholder or an investor. With enhanced disclosure of judges' campaign and personal finances and easy access to this information online, scenarios in which disqualifications are necessary become easy to identify. So easy, their clerks could do the vetting in minutes. Automatic recusal will give every litigant and defendant the confidence of a fair trial.

Create a national center for judicial independence, a federally funded research center and clearinghouse for information on the influence of elections on judicial impartiality

As a pollster, I know that compelling data and thorough research can shape debates and change minds. And when it comes to overhauling the system of selecting state judges, we need much more data to mount an effective campaign for change. Judicial elections weaken our democracy, but as I noted above, eliminating them altogether means changing state constitutions. That's going to require substantial public pressure to bring about reform.

Today, there is a dearth of research on whether judges routinely decide in favor of campaign contributors or fail to recuse themselves in cases involving donors. Apart from the conclusive evidence collected and analyzed from Ohio and Louisiana, there have been no comparable studies in other states. A federally funded national center for judicial independence could:

- Undertake studies of the independence of judiciaries in every state with judicial elections on a regular basis. That way, we can assess the problem and build a case for a comprehensive solution.
- Serve as a clearinghouse for hard data and case studies on the influence of campaign contributions on our judicial system. In fact, the center could keep files and post disclosures from judges for "one-stop shopping" online.
- Help citizens and journalists raise awareness about the need for judicial election reform by providing the empirical evidence that the current system is far from meritocratic.

I'm sure judges will bristle reading this—and I certainly don't mean to suggest that they're an easily corrupted bunch. But the trend lines are clear, and a national center for judicial independence would go a long way toward spreading awareness of the problem and giving citizens the leverage to demand reform.

According to the political scientist Michael J. Gerhardt, "The recent history of the federal appointments process suggests, contrary to Abraham Lincoln's famous declaration, that ours is a government of men and not laws. . . . Conflicts between presidents and senators have intensified over appointments generally and with particular ferocity over judicial nominations."[20] I'm not sure that I agree that we are no longer a nation of laws, but the point is well taken. Politicians in Washington today use federal judicial nominations as a tool of political gamesmanship. The result has been not only the further politicization of our justice system— bad enough in and of itself—but Washington grinding to a halt as it deals with confirmation crises that are invented to score political points.

It's unclear if our framers could have foreseen the level of discord and disruption brought on by the federal appointment process today. Gerhardt writes that, to some extent, this clash between the executive and the legislative branches is by design. The appointments clause of the Constitution "creates a realm of shared authority that plainly invites conflict."

Nationwide, there are 870 federal judgeships, from the circuit courts to the U.S. Supreme Court. The Constitution requires that the president nominate candidates for these positions and that the Senate give its "advice and consent" to confirm the president's nominees. Shared authority is necessary to ensure that one branch of government can't lord over the process of appointments. But our system of checks and balances has lately become a maze of barricades and cordons. Political conflicts over judicial appointments in the past ten years have repeatedly tied Congress in virtual knots and prevented action on issues of national importance.

It's all but certain that with President Obama's election the complexion of the federal courts will begin a pendulum swing to the left. "The change will be most striking on the Richmond-based U.S. Court of Appeals for the Fourth Circuit, long a conservative bastion and an influential voice on national security cases, where four vacancies will lead to a clear Democratic majority."[21] At the time of this writing, Democrats were expected to gain more judgeships on influential lower federal courts in New York, New Jersey, and Pennsylvania. The Republicans still control the appellate courts, and this will likely continue. But there is some chance that the 56 percent majority they now enjoy can swing the other way by the time Obama's term expires, and this is certainly more likely if he is reelected.

Politics on the federal courts generally emanate from two societies, the conservative Federalist Society and the liberal counterpart, founded in 2001, the American Constitution Society. Young lawyers who are looking to expand their résumés and eventually land a court seat look carefully at these two groups, knowing that whichever party is in power will study the appropriate membership credential. Maybe the two societies do make helpful suggestions and provide guidelines, but the message is still clear: where you hang your coat indicates where you lean politically. According to the *New York Times*, "Some law professors privately bemoan the rise of both societies, saying they are helping to polarize the law by making ambitious students think they have to pick sides early—before their thinking may have matured, and in a public way that affects which judges will hire them as clerks."[22]

We can see how the system itself creates gridlock. Under Senate rules, any senator can block any piece of business before the Senate through the little-known but often used parliamentary procedure known as a hold (which I discussed in chapter 5). In a wonderfully absurd example of judicial stalemate, in 1997, Illinois's Democratic senator Dick Durbin placed a hold on a Republican education bill because Senator Phil Gramm (R-Tex.) had placed a hold on two judicial nominees from Illinois. Gramm, it turns out, was blocking those judicial nominations only because the junior senator from Illinois—Democrat Carol Moseley Braun—had blocked the appointment of Gramm's friend and a fellow Republican to the Commodity Futures Trading Commission. That's right. One senator miffed by a colleague unilaterally retaliated by using judicial appointments as a political chit, and he brought the whole Senate to a screeching halt.[23]

Of course, this example from the Clinton years is tame compared to what happened during the confirmation battles of 2005. Democrats opposed to several of President Bush's nominees proposed to block them by filibuster. Republicans, to retaliate, threatened the so-called nuclear option—changing Senate rules that require a sixty-vote supermajority to end a filibuster for the first time in Senate history. Democrats, in response to this brinksmanship, made a threat of their own: a total shutdown of the Senate except for matters of essential national security.

The solution came via the "Gang of Fourteen"—seven Democrats who agreed to support a filibuster of judicial nominees only under "extraordinary circumstances," and seven Republicans who, in turn, agreed not to vote to circumvent Senate rules and tradition by eliminating the traditional filibuster. The members of this group included moderates on both sides of the aisle—including Democrats Mary Landrieu of Louisiana and Mark Pryor of Arkansas and Republicans Lincoln Chaffee of Rhode Island and Susan Collins of Maine. Together, these middle-of-the-road senators helped to confirm several of President George W. Bush's political nominees, including Chief Justice John Roberts and Associate Justice Samuel Alito. Not everyone was pleased with this compromise, but it succeeded in averting a political showdown that would have had disastrous and unpredictable consequences.

Much of the analysis of these breakdowns in the judicial confirmation process—and in the hampered productivity of Congress that is a direct result—has been off the mark. It's tempting to blame the simple and predictable forces of partisanship and to view this situation as the fault of the political parties themselves. When Democrats threatened to filibuster President Bush's nominees in 2005, Republicans tried to paint them as obstructionists. At the time, former Republican presidential candidate and conservative activist Gary Bauer said, "What we have is an uneven playing field where the liberals get away with these kinds of tactics, and the conservatives never use these tactics because they approach the controversy in a much more gentlemanly fashion."[24] Likewise, former senator and Democratic majority leader George Mitchell wrote, "In 2000, the last year of Bill Clinton's presidency, Republican senators filibustered two of his nominees to be circuit judges. They also prevented Senate votes on more than sixty of Mr. Clinton's judicial nominees by other means."[25]

With due respect to these gentleman, they're both wrongheaded. Partisan politics isn't to blame, and neither party is at fault. The fact that the business of government can be so easily overwhelmed and usurped by the politics of judicial nominations today is proof that *our system is the problem.*

There's nothing unusual about the sport of politics being played in Washington or members manipulating congressional procedure to accomplish their partisan goals. There's nothing atypical about filibustering judicial nominations, a relatively common occurrence since 1968, when senators used the filibuster for the first time to block President Johnson's nomination of Abe Fortas to the U.S. Supreme Court.[26] But it's amazing to think that something as relatively straightforward as a judicial nomination virtually shut down Congress *during a time of war.* We can't afford for Washington to be paralyzed by the process of judicial appointments any more than we can afford to allow rampant ideologues to determine the men and women who serve on the federal bench.

One of the most disturbing features of the judicial confirmation process in today's hyperpartisan environment is that judicial candidates are bluntly asked by senators to pick sides in ideological wars. During confirmation hearings and in committee questionnaires, nominees are asked to state their personal positions on abortion, the separation of church and state, teaching evolution in our schools, and a host of other hot-button issues. Most recently, Associate Justice Sonia Sotomayor was bombarded by senators about her personal opinion on whether *Roe v. Wade* had been wrongly decided, among other issues. She effectively parried these questions, which have much less to do with a nominee's ability to effectively execute the law than with political posturing for constituents. The result is that the White House is more likely to nominate and the Senate is more likely to confirm fellow ideologues than coolheaded legal minds—Sotomayor being a notable exception to this rule. The repercussions should be frightening to all Americans—Democrats and Republicans—who value an impartial system of justice.

RESTORING JUSTICE

The way forward involves structural changes to ensure 1) that neither the White House nor individual senators can torpedo the nomination process to score political points; and 2) that highly qualified federal judges are confirmed quickly and without the bitter political haranguing

and litmus tests that have stalled numerous nominations and contributed to congressional gridlock.

Get rid of procedural anachronisms that allow individual senators to hijack judicial nominations

Senators love nothing more than reminding us that they are members of
"the world's greatest deliberative body." And it's quite true that the Senate
has been shaped through the decades into an institution quite unlike any
other. It's governed as much by tradition as by the rules it adopts for itself
or the constitutional parameters that define its place in our democracy.
Unfortunately, some of these traditions give individual senators the power
to single-handedly stop judicial nominations, thereby turning the process
of confirming judges into a political circus. And increasingly, senators who
are more interested in politics than the people's business abuse this power.
As fond of tradition as the Senate may be, it's time to undo two longtime
parliamentary procedures that have significantly contributed to congressional gridlock and the political rancor surrounding judicial nominations.

Tear up Senate "blue slips." A blue slip is an old Senate tradition that
enables home-state senators to block judicial nominees. While they're
nowhere to be found in the Senate's bylaws, blue slips have been
around for more than ninety years, and today they allow senators to
block qualified nominees for blatantly political or personal reasons.
The Senate Judiciary Committee is the first stop for a president's judicial nominee, and before the committee considers whether to recommend a nominee to the full Senate, it issues a blue slip to the nominee's
two home-state senators. If either blue slip comes back with a "no,"
the chairman of the committee can decide not to send the nominee
for a vote in the full Senate. As George Washington University legal
scholar Jonathan Turley noted, "This means that judges who may rule
in your case often are selected to meet senatorial, not professional,
demands." And those senatorial standards can be, well, anything.
With a simple stroke of a pen on a blue slip, Turley wrote, "a senator
can block a nominee for the most nefarious or arbitrary reasons, including a personal grudge, a bargaining tool with the White House or

failure of the nominee to be sufficiently fawning in the senator's presence."[27]

Abolish Senate "holds." This reform, which I proposed in the previous chapter, is just as relevant—if not more so—to saving the justice system from politics. According to the Congressional Research Service, "Nowhere in the written Senate rules is the tradition of 'holds' to be found, and it is not clear when the practice began."[28] While its origins are in question, its effect is not. As I noted earlier, holds can lead to a Twister-like series of retaliatory moves that end up tying up the Senate. Senators simply tell their parties' leadership that they object to a nomination moving forward, and, until recently, these holds were entirely hidden from the public. Today, a senator has five days in which he or she must publicly acknowledge a hold. But even when made public, holds are still pernicious, and they give individual members of the Senate far more power than was ever intended by our framers.

Eliminating blue slips and holds are easily made changes that will have a dramatically positive effect on how the Senate operates. They require only a majority of senators to get rid of. Today, any one senator can railroad the nomination process for any reason and at any time. The only people who are hanging on to these old traditions are power-hungry sentimentalists. Eliminating holds would mean that individuals opposed to a particular judicial nominee would have to build bipartisan consensus. That's the kind of Senate tradition we should encourage.

Create bipartisan nominating commissions to fast-track well-qualified and uncontroversial judicial nominees

The best way to take the politics out of the judicial appointment process is, quite simply, to remove it from Washington. Bipartisan nominating commissions at the state level offer a political buffer that's badly needed. State commissions could identify highly qualified and uncontroversial nominees to senators and the White House—and a nominee that comes before the Senate and has the stamp of approval of a state's official bipartisan commission should be fast-tracked for confirmation.

On paper, there's nothing wrong with the way we appoint our federal judges. Home-state senators make recommendations to the president. The White House reviews the candidates and the FBI vets them as well. The Senate then has the opportunity to provide its advice and consent, approving well-qualified judges and rejecting problematic ones.

But in reality, as I've discussed, the process is far less democratic and consensus-driven than it seems. Political parties create litmus tests for judicial nominees and oppose them for strictly partisan and ideological reasons. Quite often, qualified candidates go unconfirmed, and the process leads to harmful gridlock in Congress.

The best way to deal with these issues is by creating bipartisan panels to help senators make strong judicial recommendations to the president. Currently, according to the American Judicature Society, eight states have ad hoc commissions with bipartisan representation that help senators recommend nominees to the White House. The commissions are composed of lawyers, retired judges, politicians, academics, and others who are concerned only with candidates' standing and performance, not their political ideologies or whether they pass partisan litmus tests. Their only job is to pick qualified candidates who are acceptable to the White House and can stand up to Senate scrutiny.

Today, federal judicial appointments amount to something in between a high school popularity contest and a secretive Masonic ritual. Bipartisan nominating commissions would all but eliminate the partisan considerations that lead to confirmation battles that can literally last years. By creating these commissions in each state, we could ensure a speedy nomination and confirmation process and sidestep the politics that have often led to judicial stalemate in the Senate.

Institutionalize the "Gang of Fourteen" compromise to prevent filibusters of judicial appointments

The seven Democrats and seven Republicans who came together in 2005 to prevent the Senate judicial showdown were on to something. The Gang of Fourteen solution is a smart way to avert the rancor that has plagued the Senate's review of judicial nominations and the politics that have infiltrated the process of selecting our federal judges.

At the outset of each new session of Congress, the chair of the judiciary committee and the ranking member should together identify members from their respective parties to keep the compromise intact in each Congress. With both filibusters and the nuclear option off the table for practical purposes, home-state senators and the president will have the incentive to appoint moderate judges who are palatable to all parties and can win quick confirmation.

7

TAKE JUSTICE OUT OF POLITICS
Changing How the Justice System Works

> The complete independence of the courts of justice is
> peculiarly essential in a limited Constitution.
> —ALEXANDER HAMILTON, "THE FEDERALIST, NO. 78," 1788

When Alexander Hamilton and his fellow founders crafted the exqui-sitely calibrated system of checks and balances in our Constitution, they knew that the freedoms it promised would be meaningless if there were not an independent judiciary to safeguard them. The Bill of Rights may have corrected for the terrible wrongs of King George's capricious and vindictive rule. But that document would have turned out to be just a bill of goods without judges and courts that were themselves free—from the political pressures and horse trading of the factional democracy the founders had created—to enforce the rule of law and protect the rights enumerated in the Constitution.

If Hamilton and company were alive today, they would be alternately incredulous and horrified at the perversely political turns that this particularly essential part of our democratic system has taken in recent years. They would see federal prosecutors morphing into political pawns, selectively pursuing cases to imprison political opponents or turn the tide in contested elections. They would see a U.S. attorney general and his top aides forced out of office for using political litmus tests to hire and fire U.S. attorneys, immigration judges, and even interns. They would see that the meanest, dirtiest, and most ruthless campaigns are no longer for the House or the Senate but for seats on state supreme courts.

In short, they would discover that the completely independent judiciary they so carefully crafted was on the verge of being completely compromised—by the same balance-busting forces that have broken our presidential selection and legislative processes.

This loss of independence is no accident. The partisanship in Washington is getting more poisonous, the stalemates more protracted, the pressure on ethical and legal boundaries more intense. It's little wonder that our judicial system, which was supposed to be the last line of defense for our democratic process, is more and more becoming the first place partisans go to settle the fights they can't resolve or win on the campaign trail or Capitol Hill. If you can't beat 'em, sue 'em!

The consequences here may not be as obvious as the breakdowns in the other two branches, but they are every bit as damaging, if not more so. Indeed, a justice system overrun by partisanship and influence peddling leads to things far worse than a nasty, unproductive political environment. It leads to public corruption, preferential treatment, selective law enforcement, and wrongful imprisonment. Moreover, it undermines the confidence that every American should have in our justice system. When you walk into a courtroom in America you need to know that justice is going to be served and the rights of individuals respected. But litigants and defendants no longer have that full faith and trust today, due to the growing political infection of our judiciary system.

That infection undeniably spread and reached feverish new levels under the George W. Bush administration. But if we are going to talk fairly here, we must acknowledge that the politicization of the judiciary has truly been bipartisan. The fact is, the spate of scandals involving Attorney General Alberto Gonzales were not exceptions to Bush's rule, but the natural evolution of an aisle-crossing boil that's been festering for years. Starting with the divisive judicial confirmation hearings in the 1980s, on through the independent prosecutors on rampage in the 1990s, both parties have been increasingly using our judicial system as another tool of partisan warfare.

This trend won't recede on its own, regardless of who is president and who is attorney general. That's partly because the habits of encroachment and partisanship run too deep at all levels of our government. But it's more because this is ultimately not a personal problem or a political problem but a structural one, which is not going to fade away on its own now that George W. Bush has left office.

So how do we fix this mess and re-declare the independence of our judiciary? I have a unique perspective on this count, as a lawyer by training and a pollster by avocation, who has worked in the highest reaches of politics for the last generation. And one thing I can tell you for sure is that the predominant conventional wisdom is wrong. The minimalists think we need only Band-Aid solutions, such as more special prosecutors, to weed out the bad actors. The maximalists think we need to go nuclear and change the Constitution to bring about reform. And the cautious types, mostly scholars, call for more study and more commissions to do so—or, rather, to maintain the status quo.

The truth is, this is not rocket science. It's not even political science, frankly. All we need to restore the equilibrium to our system of legal checks and balances are a handful of practical, hardheaded reforms that together will seamlessly, effectively, and quickly repair and reclaim our teetering justice system.

The good news is that the bad news is fomenting a demand for change. The scandals and abuses in our judiciary this past decade have been so outrageous and unprecedented that they have created a very receptive environment for reform. The climate is ripe for change—not just at the Justice Department, as President Obama has pledged, but throughout our legal system.

First and foremost, we must get politics out of the federal justice system from top to bottom. We need a nonpolitical attorney general who is independent from and not responsible to the political dictates of the president—much in the same way that the chairman of the Federal Reserve performs a vital function in any administration but is not part of the cabinet. U.S. attorneys themselves should be nonpolitical appointees who serve fixed terms, instead of at the pleasure and direction of a partisan president. And because the Justice Department is within the purview of the executive branch, we can achieve all of the necessary reforms quickly and unambiguously, without the need for massive legislative initiatives or five-hundred-page reports from think tanks and bipartisan commissions.

It's not just the potentially serious political prosecutions that lead to the need for oversight of Justice. It's how the Justice Department has operated in cases involving sensitive political information. Take the prosecution of Alaska senator Ted Stevens, which Attorney General Eric Holder was forced to drop because of outrageous and repeated examples of prosecutorial misconduct. Or the case of the two American Israel Public Affairs Committee (AIPAC) officers who were initially charged with espionage when it appeared that they had received information that was, in fact, very similar to the type of information that journalists get every day. There are enough questions about how the Justice Department operates, how it makes decisions, and how procedures are implemented, and plenty of examples that make it seem like they are not strictly based on the need to do justice, that oversight is required.

But it's not enough to take politics out of federal law enforcement. We need to remove the politics that is poisoning our courtrooms as well. My blueprint for doing so is straightforward and practical: eliminate special interest influence at the state level and political litmus tests at the federal level through independent, nonpartisan commissions that create an impenetrable firewall between our justice and politics.

As Hamilton reminds us, partial impartiality isn't good enough. We need full-time, nonstop, unquestioned independence. That's the only way to guard Americans against abuses of power and uphold the promise of equal protection under the law. And that's just what the common-sense structural reforms I am proposing will deliver.

POLITICAL WITCH HUNTS

The beauty of our political system as designed by our framers is its simplicity. Today, when Congress passes a spending bill or other legislation, there's a good chance that it is several hundred pages long, if not more. Our Constitution, on the other hand, isn't more than a few dozen paragraphs. And in those paragraphs, the founders' intentions are plain: a symmetrical arrangement of checks and balances that distributes power among the executive, legislative, and judicial branches.

Nowhere is that more evident than in the judiciary. The founders gave the president the power to appoint federal judges. They gave Congress the power to confirm them, as well as to remove them for misconduct. And once judges were put in place, the founders gave them unfettered authority to interpret the law and mete out justice without meddling from the other branches or special interests. Independence, fairness, and balance: these are the hallmarks of America's system of justice.

But the system started to unravel in the late 1980s, when the Democratic-controlled Senate and liberal interest groups initiated an unprecedented campaign to block President Ronald Reagan's nomination of conservative judge Robert Bork to the Supreme Court. The tenor of the Senate confirmation hearings was set early on with this astounding statement from Senator Ted Kennedy of Massachusetts, who took to the Senate floor within forty-five minutes of the announcement of Bork's nomination to denounce him: "Robert Bork's America is a land in which women would be forced into back-alley abortions, blacks would sit at segregated lunch counters, rogue police could break down citizens' doors in midnight raids, schoolchildren could not be taught about evolution, writers and artists would be censored at the whim of government, and the doors of the Federal courts would be shut on the fingers of millions of citizens for whom the judiciary is often the only protector of the individual rights that are the heart of our democracy."[1]

It only got worse from there. Eventually, liberal groups vehemently opposed to Bork's conservative judicial philosophy engaged in numerous personal attacks, at one point even suggesting that he was a pornography-loving sexual deviant. Bork was happily cleared of this charge, when his video rental records were leaked to the press. (That list, by the way, included the Marx Brothers' classic *A Day at the Races*, which served as an ironic grace note to this farce of a process.) But Bork's reputation and nomination were in tatters, and the Senate rejected his appointment to the Supreme Court.

Not surprisingly, the Bork rejection gave birth to the modern age of judicial politicization. Both political parties, realizing that the third branch could be a useful tool of partisan point scoring, started to use the courts, the Justice Department, special prosecutors, and eventually federal prosecutors to one-up or embarrass their opponents. Democrats engaged in blatant attacks on Clarence Thomas during his confirmation for the Supreme Court in 1991. Republicans ruthlessly and relentlessly used the courts to go after the Clintons, forcing the appointment of a special prosecutor to investigate the failed land deal known as White-water, which over time morphed into an investigation of Bill Clinton's relationship to Paula Jones, and ultimately culminated in the conservative witch hunt led by independent prosecutor Ken Starr and the impeachment of the president.

Tit for tat, of course, rules politics, and while Republicans used the courts to exact political vendettas, Democrats used the Justice Department to block their efforts. Clinton's attorney general, Janet Reno, drew the ire of Republicans for refusing to appoint an independent counsel to investigate the president's alleged fund-raising irregularities. The House ethics committee eventually voted to hold Reno in contempt for refusing to hand over White House documents in a related scandal.

If the judicial crisis was simmering throughout the 1990s, it boiled over in 2000 with the Supreme Court's decision in *Bush v. Gore* that ended the recount in Florida and handed the presidency to George W. Bush. This was something of a watershed moment in the history of our justice system. Many Americans, and not just partisan supporters of Al Gore, believed that the Supreme Court had crossed a bright legal line and let its political leanings shade its decision. They openly questioned the legitimacy of the court's action as well as the new president the court had installed. Did the Supreme Court choose the president or merely settle a legal dispute?

Faced with a divided nation and a crisis of confidence in our legal system, other presidents might have acted decisively to restore the trust of the American people in our courts and the balance of our separation of powers. Instead, from day one, the Bush administration went in the exact opposite direction and accelerated the judicial deterioration at both the federal and state levels.

EQUAL INJUSTICE UNDER LAW

It's hard to describe just how far the Bush administration went in compromising the independence of the judiciary without sounding partisan. But the facts—the long list of boundary-erasing, precedent-breaking actions that occurred in those eight years—speak for themselves. Forcing federal prosecutors to go after Democratic opponents. Putting political cronies in civil service positions at the Justice Department. Creating political litmus tests for immigration judges and assistant U.S. attorneys. Even dismissing candidates for entry-level positions in the department because they disagreed with the White House line on abortion and gay rights. And the coup de grâce, which as of this writing is just beginning to come to light: the likely involvement of Karl Rove in the firings of the U.S. attorneys who refused to go after Democrats targeted for judicial and political assassination by the White House.

What's truly shocking—and most relevant for the purposes of this discussion—is that it was all *illegal*. None of the abuses in question were permitted under the law. So how did the Justice Department become a political arm of the White House? Perhaps more important, how did the administration manage to escape accountability for its actions until it was too late?

To answer those questions, a little context is in order. Every executive agency in the federal government is made up primarily of civil service professionals and overseen by a handful of political appointees. From the Department of Transportation to the Food and Drug Administration, the president appoints political loyalists who run each agency and pursue the administration's policies and priorities, but career professionals carry out the work itself. It's a good system that's worked for decades and makes sense. We want skilled engineers, not campaign donors, designing and maintaining our highway infrastructure. Likewise, no one would argue that administration apparatchiks should make decisions about the safety of prescription drugs. That's a job for scientists, not political hacks.

In the Bush Justice Department, however, this model was flipped on its head. Scores of underqualified partisans were put in charge of enforcing and administering federal law, and the best and the brightest were turned away—or dismissed—if they didn't meet indefensible and unlawful political litmus tests.

Immigration indignation. It may be hard to believe from this vantage point in history, but back in 2005, Republicans thought they could build a permanent political majority in part by capturing an increasing share of the Hispanic vote and, at the same time, solidifying its base of non-Hispanic white voters. They were emboldened by a stronger-than-expected showing among Hispanics for George W. Bush. And in the wake of their sweeping victory in 2004, Republicans tried to play to both sides of the immigration issue, inciting their base with anti-immigration rhetoric and pandering to the Hispanic community by promising a new guest-worker program. Not even the shrewd brilliance of Karl Rove could pull off this mission impossible, and, ultimately, Republicans fell victim to their base.

I saw this firsthand from my vantage point as a FOX News contributor. After 2004, FOX News ran story after story about immigration, the need for a fence on the border, and the Minuteman Civil Defense Corps, a group I had barely heard of but who were a big deal to those on the right. Right-wing congressmen spoke eloquently and compellingly about the need to protect the border first and argued that we needed to keep America largely free of immigrants.

People like me who spoke of the need to have a balanced policy—which promoted border security but gave the twelve million immigrants a path to citizenship—were not well received. And I realized when I heard my colleagues at FOX News going off about immigration that the gains made in 2004 were almost certainly going to be lost in 2008. I said on television a number of times that the Republicans were costing themselves the election by pushing an extreme position on immigration.

My point here is that immigration was a vital political issue during the second term of the Bush administration. Indeed, few issues were more important. And as such, it's highly disturbing but not at all surprising that Attorney General Alberto Gonzales and his team at Justice politicized the implementation of our immigration laws and procedures to an unprecedented extent.

In 2004, Gonzales and a top aide, Kyle Sampson, took the job of hiring immigration judges and Board of Immigration Appeals members away from a three-member expert panel. Instead, they put in place a system to hand these sensitive positions to political loyalists with no background whatsoever in immigration law.

These are not trivial posts. Immigration judges oversee proceedings for deportation and asylum cases for the entire nation. The law requires that the Department of Justice select qualified jurists and professionals for these critically important civil service jobs. But in 2005, the White House handed down a directive that executive branch agencies were to find appointments for 108 partisans—campaign donors, prominent political supporters, and others—who had been particularly loyal to President Bush. And while many agencies followed suit and found a home for them in political positions, the Justice Department went haywire.

In response to a White House e-mail that outlined the placements to be made, Jan Williams, the White House liaison to the Justice Department, replied: "We pledge 7 slots within 40 days and 40 nights. Let the games begin!"[2] The "games" eventually involved giving a Bush campaign legal adviser for the Florida recount and a Texas state library commissioner positions as immigration judges—just the tip of the iceberg of unqualified political appointees who are frighteningly still on the bench, making decisions with incredibly serious legal, moral, and national security implications.[3]

Unequal opportunity employer. Williams left the Justice Department in 2006 and was succeeded as White House liaison by Monica Goodling. As a parting gift to Goodling, Williams e-mailed her a list of Internet research criteria she developed to weed out Democrats and liberals from being hired at the department, which included terms such as "NAFTA," "Florida recount," "Iran-Contra," "Clinton," and "homosexual." According to an internal investigation by the Justice Department's Office of the Inspector General and Office of Professional Responsibility, Goodling had a political checklist that she worked from as she screened potential candidates for positions as immigration judges, assistant U.S. attorneys, and other civil service positions within the department. In interviews, she would blatantly ask candidates about their political views.[4]

While conservative credentials landed you a job at the Justice Department under Gonzales and company, prestigious legal and professional credentials landed many stellar résumés in the shredder. In one instance, Goodling turned away a highly respected federal prosecutor who had received the attorney general's own Award for Exceptional Service for winning an important antiterrorism case. Despite this extraordinary record of accomplishment, Goodling turned down his bid for a job in the Executive Office of U.S. Attorneys because his wife was active in local Democratic politics.[5]

In fact, political litmus tests were so pervasive that the Department of Justice even screened its *summer interns*. The department's honors program participants and summer law interns were illegally vetted for their political views, and scores of candidates were rejected because they had worked for Democrats such as Hillary Clinton or liberal organizations such as Planned Parenthood. One stellar Harvard student was even tossed out of the running because he was a member of the Council on American-Islamic relations.[6]

"Performance issues." The more this story unravels, the more people lose their jobs—and hopefully, one day, they'll answer for their actions. The illegitimate firing of eight U.S. attorneys led to the resignation of Attorney General Gonzales and several of his top deputies. The public reason given for these dubious dismissals of U.S. attorneys was "performance issues." But the real reason was failure to cook up cases the White House was hungry to bring against Democrats before the midterm elections in 2006.

David Iglesias was a U.S. attorney in New Mexico and a rising star of the Republican Party who was pressured by two Republican members of Congress from his home state to bring charges against local Democrats in a heated political corruption case before the midterm election. Several weeks later, Gonzales asked for his resignation. Iglesias later wrote: "I will never forget John Ashcroft, then the attorney general, telling me during the summer of 2001 that politics should play no role during my tenure. I took that message to heart. Little did I know that I could be fired for *not* being political."[7]

Happy hunting. It wasn't just hiring and firing of staff that was determined by politics. There is abundant anecdotal evidence of a concerted effort by Republicans to use the justice system to go after Democratic opponents when they couldn't win at the ballot box. And if Iglesias and seven of his colleagues refused to pursue politically motivated convictions, other Bush-appointed prosecutors were more than willing to be good soldiers in partisan battles.

- In 2006, Chris Christie, a federal prosecutor in New Jersey and at the time of this writing a Republican candidate for governor of that state, issued subpoenas connected to a corruption investigation of Democratic senator Bob Menendez. Sounds aboveboard, until you consider that Christie was a top fund-raiser for George W. Bush, the subpoenas were issued just sixty-one days before Menendez was up for reelection, and Christie was a contributor to the campaign of Menendez's opponent, Tom Kean Jr., whose main campaign theme was trying to paint Menendez as a crook. With Menendez's seat critical for both parties in deciding the balance of power in the U.S. Senate—and with Christie's own well-known political ambitions—it all adds up to a scenario that's a little more than suspect.[8]

- In Wisconsin, a U.S. attorney prosecuted a civil servant who allegedly steered state contracts to supporters of Democratic governor Jim Doyle. Again, the indictment and conviction came during an election in which Doyle's Republican opponent attempted to portray him as the leader of a corrupt administration. An appeals court eventually threw out an earlier conviction based on shoddy evidence.[9]

- Even more disturbing is the prosecution and conviction of Alabama's former Democratic governor Don Siegelman, a political witch hunt that Republican sources say was orchestrated by Bush adviser Karl Rove and which Rove refuses to testify about before Congress.

These are far from the only examples, and there's hard empirical evidence to show there was a bigger pattern at work. A study by Columbia University professors Donald C. Shields and John F. Cragan shows that between 2001 and 2006, U.S. attorneys were seven times as likely to investigate Democratic officials, "a number that exceeds even the racial profiling of African Americans in traffic stops."[10]

The U.S. attorneys should be nonpolitical posts. If they truly were, they would be competent to prosecute alleged wrongdoing of other federal officials. As David B. Rivkin Jr. and Lee A. Casey, former Justice Department officials under Reagan and George H. W. Bush, argue, "In the future, the investigation of high-level misconduct should not be removed from the normal processes of the Justice Department. The U.S. attorneys, and the department's Criminal Division, are fully capable of investigating and prosecuting alleged wrongdoing by important government officials, and can do it with proper perspective. Almost all federal prosecutors are, in fact, career lawyers quite capable of balking if their political supervisors abuse their authority."[11]

Impact far beyond our courts. In a campaign year when candidates are exchanging infantile barbs or waxing patriotic on television, politics seems all too trivial. But when our system of justice becomes an extension of political campaigns, the consequences are disastrous. There is disturbing evidence that the placement of political pawns in important law enforcement positions has meant that critical laws have gone unenforced. In fact, the politicization of the Justice Department resulted in a Civil Rights Division that all but abandoned civil rights cases during the Bush administration.

In 2002, then attorney general John Ashcroft reversed decades of justice policy and tradition under administrations of all political and ideological stripes by abolishing the expert committees that hired the department's civil rights attorneys. Instead, the process was turned over to partisans the administration installed to run the Justice Department, and the result is that the Civil Rights Division was composed of dozens of lawyers who have no civil rights background or credentials and no interest in pursuing civil rights cases.

An investigative report by the *Boston Globe* found that while 77 percent of civil rights lawyers hired before Ashcroft's change in hiring practices had civil rights credentials, only 42 percent of those hired from 2003 to 2006 had any civil rights experience. These hires include protégés of conservative standard-bearers Ken Starr, former senator Trent Lott (D-Miss.), and Judge Charles Pickering, who as a Republican Party operative had chaired a subcommittee calling for a constitutional amendment to overrule *Roe v. Wade*. Not surprisingly, the *Globe* found that the Civil Rights Division prosecuted significantly fewer cases on traditional civil rights issues, namely discrimination against minorities. And longtime employees in the division have reacted accordingly. In 2005, sixty-three civil rights lawyers left the division, which the *Globe* found to be twice the rate of departure experienced during the Clinton years.[12]

In addition, political hiring in the Justice Department has impacted our national security, with unqualified immigration judges serving as the new gatekeepers to our borders. Only in a system of justice overwhelmed by politics would it be acceptable to demote a decorated veteran of the legal war on terrorism because his wife was a member of the wrong political party. You wouldn't think that in the world's greatest democracy it would be possible for a government to take political prisoners, but recent political prosecutions have, in fact, ended careers, ruined lives, and imprisoned innocent people.

Of course, in addition to these very tangible consequences, the politicization of the Justice Department has damaged our broken system in a few fundamental ways. It's further conflagrated the hyperpartisan environment that has contributed to a stalemated Congress. The balance of power between the executive and an independent judiciary has been totally compromised. An air of illegitimacy now enshrouds the nation's law enforcement efforts, and it will take years to dispel. But we can do much to restore justice by taking corrective measures to prevent politicization this poisonous from ever again infecting the Justice Department, and by restoring the separation of powers that is the core of our democracy.

Many of the problems we've analyzed so far have been decades in the making and have been the targets of failed reform efforts. But when it comes to the federal justice system, we're in uncharted waters. The fact is that *nothing like this has ever happened before.*

To be fair, the Justice Department during the Clinton administration was the subject of much political controversy. As an adviser to the White House during Travelgate, Chinagate, and other scandals, I remember vividly the accusations that Attorney General Janet Reno played politics at Justice. And any student of history knows that other administrations had ideologically aggressive justice departments, Ronald Reagan's being the oft-cited example. In fact, according to political scientist Nancy V. Baker, attorneys general have been accused of "manipulating legal advice to serve political ends" from the days of George Washington and ever since.[13] But career attorneys with decades of experience at the Department of Justice under more than four presidents say that there's never been anything like what the country experienced under George W. Bush's watch.

William R. Yeomans served in the department from 1981 until he resigned out of sheer frustration in 2005, and was a veteran of the Civil

Rights Division. Of the Bush administration's approach to the dismantling of the division, Yeomans wrote, "Despite the commitment of the Reagan era political leadership to change civil rights law in fundamental ways, there was no comparable effort to exclude career attorneys and replace them based on ideology."[14] Joseph D. Rich, who resigned as head of the Civil Rights Division after a distinguished thirty-seven-year career at Justice, testified before the House Judiciary Committee in 2007 that "since this administration took office, that professionalism and nonpartisan commitment to the historic mission of the division has been replaced by unprecedented political decision-making."[15] The point isn't that Republicans are more guilty or untrustworthy than Democrats. This testimony comes from two men who are far from ideologues, and both of whom served under more Republican than Democratic presidents. What they are telling us is that the system no longer works as it should in insulating the administration of justice from political pressures and partisan excesses.

This was one of the most telling findings of the Justice Department's own internal review of the Bush administration's personnel policies. The laws on the books were simply not a deterrent to the wholesale loss of independence.

> The evidence detailed above demonstrates that Kyle Sampson, Jan Williams, and Monica Goodling each violated Department of Justice policy and federal law by considering political or ideological affiliations in soliciting and evaluating candidates for [immigration judges], which are Schedule A career positions, not political appointments. Further, the evidence demonstrates that their violations were not isolated instances but were systematic in nature. The evidence demonstrates further that Goodling violated Department policy and federal law by considering political or ideological affiliations in selecting candidates for the BIA.[16]

So how do we fix something that no one thought possible, that has never before happened, and that is already illegal? The Department of Justice's Office of Inspector General and Office of Professional Responsibility proposed a number of fixes. I was glad that Attorney General Michael Mukasey implemented all of these. For instance, the process for hiring career positions, such as immigration judges and assistant U.S. attorneys, is now handled by career lawyers instead of political appointees. New training sessions and briefing materials are now given for the Justice Department's political staff as well. And after repeated calls from Congress, Mukasey appointed an independent prosecutor to investigate if there was any criminal wrongdoing in the Bush administration's firing of eight U.S. attorneys for political or personal reasons.

That's all well and good, but it's hardly going to prevent a future administration from revisiting the same unethical and illegal tactics down the road. Just because it's against the law doesn't mean it won't happen. And especially in politics, where there's a will, there's a way. Independent prosecutors are the equivalent of chicken soup for a cold. They make us feel better, but they don't get at the root problem. It's not enough to weed out bad actors after they've had a chance to wreak havoc. This is clearly a systemic problem that demands systemic solutions.

BUILDING TRULY INDEPENDENT JUSTICE

It's all too clear that the fundamental checks and balances in our system have gone awry. Nonpartisanship has been eviscerated. Independence has been compromised. The only workable solutions to these problems are structural changes that get to the bottom of the issue—structural solutions that should be a rallying point for individuals on the left and the right who are concerned with the fairness of our system of justice.

Remove the attorney general from the cabinet

Cool heads and sharp intellects have determined over the years that when it comes to the business of government, there are a few positions so essential to our common well-being and security that they must be wholly insulated from politics. As the nation's chief law enforcement officer, the attorney general should be one of those positions. And this is a fix we can implement without a complicated constitutional amendment. All that's needed is an act of Congress.

Today, the attorney general is a political appointee who plays the dual role of the people's lawyer and the president's lawyer. It's time to put the

Department of Justice in the hands of a nonpolitical steward who will have no interest, desire, or need to consider politics in enforcing federal law. And the best way to do this is by removing the attorney general from the cabinet, removing the Justice Department from executive oversight, and appointing the attorney general to a term of ten years or more.

While there's no precedent for removing executive-level agencies from the cabinet, there's plenty of precedent in keeping certain federal officials above the political fray. For instance, members of the board of governors of the Federal Reserve serve fourteen-year terms, and the chairman of the Fed serves four-year terms that continue even after the president who made the appointment leaves office. Likewise, the president appoints the FBI director to a ten-year term, subject to the advice and consent of the Senate. That way, any given FBI director serves under at least two presidents. It's beyond befuddling that while the FBI director is a nonpolitical appointee, the bureau itself technically falls within the institutional bounds of the Justice Department. If the FBI director is a nonpolitical appointee, it follows that the attorney general should be as well. And like the FBI director, instead of serving at the pleasure of the president, once the appointment is made and confirmed by the Senate, the only way to remove an attorney general should be by trial in Congress for malfeasance, not the political prerogative of the executive.

Granted, I'm not the first to propose this idea. In fact, it's been shot down several times in the past, including immediately after Watergate and during the Carter administration. For reasons that escape me, this attitude is still pervasive. After all, legal scholars and lawmakers are sticklers for tradition, and some argue that removing the attorney general from the cabinet would alter the separation of powers intended by our framers. Too late—thanks to the political carnage wreaked by the likes of Ashcroft and Gonzales, that separation no longer exists. In fact, the only way to restore the proper distribution of power between the executive and the judiciary is to put up a firewall between justice and politics. Removing the attorney general from the cabinet is a move that not only would give the entire Justice Department badly needed independence; it would also restore credibility to an institution badly damaged by partisanship.

End the practice of appointing special counsels

Like so many failed policies that I've noted throughout this work, special counsel investigations were once a good idea that unfortunately over time have resulted in more grief than they were instituted to solve in the first place. Initiated under President Carter in the wake of Watergate, the Independent Counsel Act of 1978 was created to enable investigations of wrongdoing by public officials untainted by politics.

Unfortunately, they had the exact opposite effect. Independent counsel investigations resulted in some of the nastiest, unadulterated political battles of recent decades, including Iran-Contra, Whitewater, and the Monica Lewinsky investigation. Mercifully, the Office of the Independent Counsel, which reached its inquisitorial apotheosis under Ken Starr, finally lost its statutory authorization in 1999. Since then, the attorney general has appointed independent counsels.

I'm one of those who thought independent counsels are and were an unaccountable, unconstitutional fourth branch of government. But even before Starr began his career as the Texas Torquemada, seeking to destroy a presidency, his predecessor Larry Walsh had managed to nudge an election to that very same president. In 1992, just weeks before voters went to the polls to decide the contest between Bill Clinton and George H. W. Bush, Walsh indicted Caspar Weinberger, a Bush supporter and the secretary of defense under Ronald Reagan, for his involvement in the Iran-Contra affair. This "October Surprise," which landed just before the general election, is thought by many to have helped Clinton to his upset victory against a sitting president. (Walsh was widely known as an old GOP warhorse, but even Clinton himself is said to have acknowledged that he benefited.)

More recently, we've seen Special Counsel Patrick Fitzgerald spend millions to find out that several uncoordinated and unrelated officials gossiped about the same CIA operative to several reporters, convicting Lewis "Scooter" Libby, the assistant to Vice President Dick Cheney, for perjury related to the investigation but not for any underlying crime (and jailing a reporter, Judith Miller of the New York Times, for eighty-five days, to boot).

What Libby did to Valerie Plame wasn't nice, but his conviction—on a technicality—represents a criminalization of politics that could harm any administration and could certainly give pause to honest, qualified individuals contemplating public service. The whole point of a special prosecutor is to see if there is a substantial crime that has been committed. Perjury traps give special counsels the ability to run amok.

The notion of ending special counsels—which have no constitutional authority and technically report to nobody and no single governmental entity—has appealed to both conservatives and liberals. The special counsel has a history of exacerbating the inherent politics and prejudices of already volatile issues.

Create a new joint chiefs of justice to administer the Department of Justice and keep our law enforcement in the hands of professionals

We can't afford to have legal novices running our justice system any more than we can afford untested commanders in charge of our military. Unfortunately, the Justice Department under George W. Bush demonstrated just how easy it is under our current system to install civil rights lawyers with no civil rights experience and immigration judges with no background in immigration law.

The Department of Defense is a good analogue for an alternative structure for Justice. Whatever you think of the wars in Iraq and Afghanistan, no one can argue that the men and women we send overseas are not professionals of the highest degree. Sadly, the same is far from true at the Justice Department. The secretary of defense—a civilian political appointee—runs the Defense Department, but the military is managed by professionals and overseen by the Joint Chiefs of Staff. And while the Joint Chiefs are technically political appointees as well, they're also heavily decorated and highly experienced veterans of the military branches they chair. This means that while the administration sets our foreign policy goals and objectives, professionals of the highest caliber are ultimately responsible for protecting the nation.

That's a good thing, and the same should be true of the agency that enforces federal law. Even though Donald Rumsfeld was a disaster at the post of defense secretary, at least he wasn't able to make Paul Wolfowitz a brigadier general or anoint George W. Bush's high school buddies as battalion commanders. On the other hand, Ashcroft and Gonzales *were* able to put unqualified ideologues in positions of incredible authority.

There is an easy and effective fix that would require no new legislation and no constitutional changes and could be implemented immediately. Here's how it would work. A nonpolitical attorney general would appoint the joint chiefs from the ranks of career Justice Department attorneys, and candidates for joint chiefs positions would need to have a minimum level of experience within their area of responsibility. There would be a chief for every major division of the Justice Department— Civil Rights, Criminal, Antitrust, and so on.

It's already illegal to politicize civil service positions that enforce federal law—but as I noted above, illegal doesn't cut it. We need a joint chiefs of justice composed of trusted veterans, which would make it practically impossible for politics to pervert the essential functions of law enforcement at the federal level.

Make federal prosecutors nonpolitical positions appointed to five-year terms and give them the independence they need to enforce the law

Many Americans would be shocked to know that the nation's ninety-three U.S. attorneys—in charge of investigating and prosecuting violations of federal law and putting away the worst of the worst—are equal parts political operatives and law enforcement officers. This setup opens the doors wide to abuse, by enabling the executive to manipulate our system of justice to achieve political ends. We need to prevent even the *possibility* of abuse of this sort by making our federal prosecutors nonpolitical appointees, giving them fixed five-year terms, and making them accountable to the law and to Congress, instead of to political overlords in the White House.

There are two extraordinary problems with the current system. First, as we saw during the scandal that led to the downfall of Gonzales and his cronies, U.S. attorneys can be fired at any time and for any reason.

Case in point, one of the eight U.S. attorneys fired by the Bush administration now believes that she was dismissed over false rumors of a same-
sex relationship with a career prosecutor in her office.[17]

Second, federal prosecutors that are political appointees can all too
easily pursue political witch hunts at the direction of the White House.
Grand juries are supposed to provide a safeguard against political
persecution by prosecution. But it's clear that this system has broken down.

One popular solution to these problems is simply to mandate that
half of the nation's prosecutors are Democrats and half are Republicans.
This is how the Federal Communications Commission is structured,
and having an equal partisan mix would balance out any perceived or
actual political considerations. Or so the argument goes. It's hard to
imagine this setup doing any good. If politics are part of getting the job,
they'll be part of doing the job.

My solution, again, is to make it impossible. Today, U.S. attorneys are
handpicked by the White House, in consultation with political appointees at the Department of Justice. Instead, candidates should be vetted
and recommended to the White House by the new joint chiefs of justice,
with input from apolitical state bar associations and retired judges and
with confirmation by the Senate. Instead of serving at the pleasure of
the president, which makes them prone to political pressure, prosecutors should serve five-year fixed terms, and the Senate alone should have
the power to remove prosecutors before their term is up.

Make the political hiring of career justice officials a criminal offense—and prosecute it

Why on earth aren't Monica Goodling, Jan Williams, and Kyle Sampson
in prison? It's clear they broke the law. But it turns out the *right* law isn't
yet on the books.

As I noted earlier, an internal Justice Department investigation
determined that Gonzales's top political deputies were guilty of misconduct for violating federal civil service laws. But the punishment for this
violation is disciplinary action by the department, not a prison sentence.
The worst that Goodling, Williams, and Sampson face today is being

stripped of their bar licenses. Even that hasn't yet happened—and at this point, it's rather unlikely.

You might think I'm being unduly harsh. After all, Goodling, Williams, and Sampson have each said they didn't know they were breaking the law when they made hiring decisions based on party affiliation and ideological litmus tests. I say, tell it to a jury. I certainly don't buy it, and I doubt you could find twelve people anywhere that would.

It's bad enough that there was a political choke hold on the Justice Department in the first place. The fact that the people responsible for breaking the law got away with a slap on the wrist is a crime in and of itself. We need tough new penalties on the books that send a clear message. Playing politics with our justice system will get you a prison sentence, not a book deal.

8

SHAKE UP OUR MEDIA
Creating Real Citizen Checks on Power

> This instrument can teach, it can illuminate; yes, and it can even inspire.
> But it can do so only to the extent that humans are determined to use it to
> those ends. Otherwise it is merely wires and lights in a box. There is a great
> and perhaps decisive battle to be fought against ignorance, intolerance and
> indifference. This weapon of television could be useful.
> —EDWARD R. MURROW, 1958

In 2005, George Clooney's Oscar-winning film *Good Night, and Good Luck* dramatized one of the most compelling—and lesser-known—speeches in American history. It was given in 1958 by Edward R. Murrow, then the nation's most respected, celebrated, and famous journalist, to an annual gathering of the Radio-Television News Directors Association in Chicago. Murrow took his compatriot audience to task. He said he was "seized with an abiding fear regarding what these two instruments are doing to our society, our culture and our heritage." Murrow saw a world confronted with myriad problems and a news media that consistently ignored them to the nation's detriment. He was troubled by the fleeting focus on real issues and the persistent appeal to society's lowest common denominator—the desire to be entertained instead of the need to be informed.[1]

Murrow would have been both deeply fascinated and profoundly distressed by the 2008 presidential campaign. On the one hand, today's news coverage is a mile wide and half an inch deep—a phenomenon that Elizabeth Edwards, the health care advocate and wife of former senator John Edwards, brilliantly coined "strobe light journalism." Our pundits only play reporters on television, entertaining the public while failing to inform. There's not enough accountability, not enough diversity of opinions and perspectives, and far too little credit given to the American public's intelligence and desire for hard news and real analysis. To make matters worse, the advent of twenty-four-hour cable news and the rise of the blogosphere have created a news vacuum that must continually be fed, oftentimes by trivia, hearsay, and manufactured content that masquerades as news. In this way, technology has amplified many of the deficiencies at which Murrow despaired a half century ago. The result is an out-of-touch news media, an uninformed citizenry, and the perpetuation of systemic problems we've previously discussed.

On the other hand, Murrow would have been astounded by the changes that have taken place at every level of the media—from the business of news to the technology that disseminates it to the way the public consumes it. The Internet has dramatically improved citizen access to information and enabled candidates to directly engage the public without the distorting filter of the mass media. Everyday citizens, through blogs, social networking sites, and YouTube, are now able to reach just as many people through their personal computers as the major broadcasters can through cable boxes. From Internet sites that monitor and report on media bias and misinformed punditry to investigative bloggers picking up where the mainstream media leave off, the Web is a powerful tool to give citizens more and better information. That's exactly what we need to reinvigorate the mass media in America today.

Murrow called on his fellow journalists to take a hard look at their profession, and he outlined a series of principles as a guide to reform: illumination, accountability, and diversity. Five decades later, this prescription is perfectly apt. We need to marry the principles of Murrow's generation with today's technological innovations to create a new media model for the twenty-first century.

What should that new model look like? In short, we need media by the people, of the people, and for the people. We need to create incentives for more alternative news outlets, more citizen journalism, and more interactive journalism. We need to encourage more perspectives from the left, right, and center. We need to protect the neutrality of Internet access and demand accountability from the big networks. We need to leverage the technology available to us to finally achieve Murrow's vision of a mass media that strengthens the fabric of our democracy and our civic institutions.

MEDIA MADNESS

It's more than symbolic that the Bill of Rights guarantees the freedom of public speech before anything else. Unencumbered and responsible media are so essential to our democracy as to be virtually indistinguishable from it. Our framers' view on the matter is best summed up by this memorable passage, penned by Thomas Jefferson in 1787: "The basis of our governments being the opinion of the people, the very first object should be to keep that right; and were it left to me to decide whether we should have a government without newspapers or newspapers without a government, I should not hesitate a moment to prefer the latter."[2]

For the past two hundred years and change, this has been the prevailing view of both liberals and conservatives. In fact, many scholars consider the press a "fourth branch" of government. As Supreme Court associate justice Potter Stewart succinctly put it to an audience at Yale University some forty years ago, "The primary purpose of the constitutional guarantee of a free press was . . . to create a fourth institution outside the Government as an additional check on the three official branches."[3]

We've previously discussed and analyzed the partisanship and dysfunction that has brought the three branches of our federal government to a grinding halt. The media, our "fourth branch" of government, have been similarly infected. Today, like Congress and our system of campaigns and elections, our mainstream media are simply not doing what they were designed to do: give our citizens the critically important information they need to make intelligent, informed, and responsible decisions at the ballot box.

This failure is both no one's fault and everyone's fault. Quality journalism is decreasing. Partisan bias in the media is increasing. The real issues we face have taken a backseat to celebrity and "gotcha" journalism. The result is that a frighteningly large number of Americans are uninformed, misinformed, or both, which contributes to the further degradation of our democratic government and traditions.

But we need to follow the example that Murrow set more than fifty years ago by avoiding the blame game. Murrow noted in his famous speech that he had "no grounds for personal complaint . . . no feud, either with my employers, any sponsors, or with the professional critics of radio and television." There was no personal or partisan filter to his critique. And while I often cringe when I open up the newspaper or turn on the nightly news, the purpose of this chapter is not to criticize those individuals with whom I disagree or dislike. Rather, my purpose here is simply to examine what's wrong and how we can strengthen the fabric of our democracy by improving the mass media in America.

Quality journalism decreasing. I've had the privilege to work with a lot of political journalists over the years, and I've nearly always been impressed by their collective intelligence and their good humor in doing a difficult job that requires very late nights, exhausting travel, and lots of caffeine. But something larger than any one reporter has led to a precipitous decline in the quality of journalism in America. Let me provide two quick case studies—one macro and one micro—that demonstrate this point.

The first example needs little explication. We all know now that most media were asleep at the switch during the run-up to the Iraq war. But a recent report shows just how deep that slumber was. According to an in-depth study by the Center for Public Integrity and the Fund for Independence in Journalism, the Bush administration made an astounding 935 false statements during the two-year period before the first bombs fell on Baghdad. More than half of these proclamations stated with certainty that Iraq had both weapons of mass destruction and links to al-Qaida, despite intelligence reports that were much less certain—or even contrary to—both suppositions. The study concluded, "Some journalists—indeed, even some entire news organizations—have since acknowledged that their coverage during those prewar months was far too deferential and uncritical. These mea culpas notwithstanding, much of the wall-to-wall media coverage provided additional, 'independent' validation of the Bush administration's false statements about Iraq."[4]

The financial crisis of 2008 provides the backdrop for another key example of the media dropping the ball and the country paying a heavy price as a result. According to the conservative media watchdog NewsBusters, in the five years leading up to the meltdown at Fannie

Mae and Freddie Mac that precipitated the global financial crisis, the
major networks aired *only ten stories* on the two mortgage lenders.
This, despite serious troubles at both institutions during that time,
including congressional hearings on bogus accounting practices and a
bonus scandal involving its top leadership. According to the News-
Busters study, "A review of the three networks' morning and evening
news programs from January 1, 2003, through December 31, 2007,
found nine anchor-read items or brief references to the companies'
troubles, plus one in-depth report by CBS's Anthony Mason on the May
23, 2006, *Evening News*, after Fannie Mae was fined $400 million for
accounting fraud."[5]

These aren't small-potato issues. We're talking about war and peace
and economic life and death. I think that reporters are by and large a
pretty smart bunch. So how do we account for the decline in quality
journalism? There are a few important trend lines to consider.

First of all, the simultaneous rise of cable news and the Internet has
forever altered the nature of the news. For decades, there were two
news cycles: one in the morning that determined the coverage of late-
edition papers and the evening news, and one in the afternoon that dic-
tated the morning papers and broadcast news programming. Today,
those two distinct news cycles are now a single, perpetual twenty-four-
hour news cycle. The reason? Cable outlets such as CNN, FOX News,
and MSNBC, as well as blogs such as the Drudge Report and the Huffington Post, offer news content all hours of the day and night. These
operations are constantly competing for and searching for breaking
news. As such, the standards for what qualifies as both "breaking" and
"news" have diminished substantially. Suddenly, Joe Biden mistaking
Teddy Roosevelt for FDR in a campaign speech or Sarah Palin bum-
bling the name of a foreign dignitary in an interview become the stuff
of major network headlines.

Another important trend line is that newspaper profits have dramatically shrunk. The industry today is contending with a combination
of declining advertising revenue and increasing costs that together have
whittled earnings at the nation's major publishers. In the third quarter
of 2008, the Washington Post Company saw a stunning 86 percent de-

cline in profits from the previous year.[6] By the end of the year, the venerable Tribune Company, owner of the *Chicago Tribune* and other media assets, had fallen into bankruptcy. By early 2009, the *New York Times* was in such financial straits that columnists debated whether the company would survive. Although the picture has stabilized somewhat, questions about the long-term viability of many print properties remain.

There's a connection between the decline in profits and the decline in quality. According to the Pew Research Center's Project for Excellence in Journalism, print journalism in America has been hit hard by across-the-board cuts in resources and staff.

> Meet the American daily newspaper of 2008.
>
> It has fewer pages than three years ago, the paper stock is thinner, and the stories are shorter. There is less foreign and national news, less space devoted to science, the arts, features and a range of specialized subjects. Business coverage is either packaged in an increasingly thin stand-alone section or collapsed into another part of the paper. . . .
>
> The newsroom staff producing the paper is also smaller, younger. . . . The staff is also under greater pressure, has less institutional memory, less knowledge of the community, of how to gather news and the history of individual beats. There are fewer editors to catch mistakes.[7]

This isn't just conjecture; it's empirical. According to Pew's in-depth survey of nearly three hundred newspapers across the nation:

- Eighty-five percent of large-circulation newspapers surveyed by Pew cut their newsroom staff between 2005 and 2008.
- Sixty-one percent have reduced the physical size of their papers, and therefore the space available for coverage.
- Forty-two percent of newspapers surveyed—and 67 percent of large newspapers—cut their copyediting staff.
- Thirty percent have cut the number of general editors.
- Sixty-four percent of newspapers reported cutting the amount of international coverage.
- Fifty-nine percent have cut their coverage of national news.

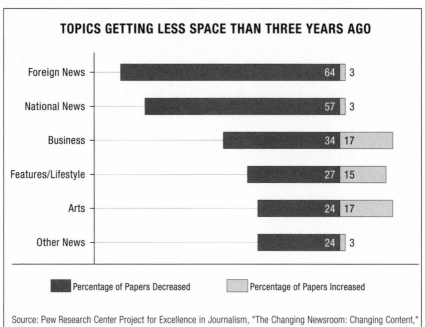

TOPICS GETTING LESS SPACE THAN THREE YEARS AGO

Foreign News	64	3
National News	57	3
Business	34	17
Features/Lifestyle	27	15
Arts	24	17
Other News	24	3

■ Percentage of Papers Decreased   □ Percentage of Papers Increased

Source: Pew Research Center Project for Excellence in Journalism, "The Changing Newsroom: Changing Content," July 21, 2008, http://www.journalism.org/node/11963.

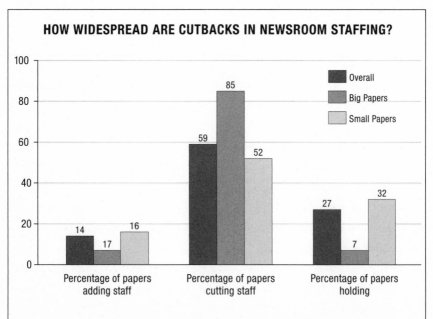

HOW WIDESPREAD ARE CUTBACKS IN NEWSROOM STAFFING?

Legend: ■ Overall   ■ Big Papers   □ Small Papers

	Overall	Big Papers	Small Papers
Percentage of papers adding staff	14	17	16
Percentage of papers cutting staff	59	85	52
Percentage of papers holding	27	7	32

Source: Pew Research Center Project for Excellence in Journalism, "The Changing Newsroom: Staff Cutbacks," July 21, 2008, http://www.journalism.org/node/11962.

When taken together, an insatiable news cycle, declining profits, and shrinking newsrooms have increased competitive pressures to under-report hard news and sensationalize the trivial. It's impossible to know if better reporting could have prevented an unnecessary war or a difficult recession. What's for certain, however, is that American democracy depends on an unfettered press holding our elected officials' feet to the fire and unearthing the kernels of fact from the mountains of spin. When the press fails to do its job—whatever the reason—it paves the path for our elected officials and our government to fail right alongside.

Coverage that ignores the issues. In the run-up to the 1860 Republican convention, Abraham Lincoln went on a barnstorming tour, speaking to audiences from Illinois to New York, much as candidates barnstorm across the early primary states today. Yet more than a century ago, the press essentially distributed the candidate's message. Speeches were reprinted verbatim in newspapers and handed out in pamphlet form. Lincoln's ideas, not his rustic and somewhat shabby clothes or his slightly odd appearance (which would later cause Washington society to sneeringly liken him to a baboon), were what commanded the public's attention.

Compare that with the 2008 campaign, which focused at length on John Edwards's $400 haircut, Sarah Palin's $150,000 wardrobe, Barack Obama's swimsuit, Joe Biden's gaffes, and—the coup de grâce—Hillary Clinton's décolletage. From the coverage of the campaign, you might not have known that the country was in the midst of the worst financial crisis since the Great Depression, fighting two wars, contending with a failed health care system, and anticipating an impending entitlement disaster.

According to one accounting of campaign coverage in the *New York Times*—the nation's venerable paper of record—*only 10 percent* of stories focused on real issues during the critical time frame of August to early October. The rest of the *Times*'s coverage focused on the presidential horse race, the money chase, what the candidates wore, and how they spoke—instead of what they were actually saying. The same was true of coverage on the major networks and cable outlets. As the nonprofit watchdog Media Matters for America reported: "From 9 a.m. to 5 p.m. ET on July 30,

MSNBC devoted a total of 23 minutes and 42 seconds to segments discussing Sen. Hillary Rodham Clinton's (D-NY) 'cleavage.' MSNBC broadcast separate segments on this topic during the hours of 9 a.m., 10 a.m., 11
a.m., 1 p.m., 2 p.m., and 3 p.m. ET, skipping only the noon and 4 p.m.
hours. During the same period, CNN devoted 3 minutes and 54 seconds
to coverage of Clinton's cleavage, while Fox News devoted none."[8]

Elizabeth Edwards has been a sharp-witted critic of the media's
obsessive focus on meaningless details from the campaign trail. She
has effectively argued that "every analysis that is shortened, every corner that is cut, moves us further away from the truth until what is left
is the Cliffs Notes of the news, or what I call strobe-light journalism,
in which the outlines are accurate enough but we cannot really see the
whole picture." In the *New York Times*, she lamented that voters likely
knew not a thing about then presidential contender Joe Biden's health
care plan, but they likely could cite Barack Obama's unimpressive bowling score from a well-covered campaign event in the heartland. And
Edwards argues that the lack of focus on real issues creates a democracy deficit: "The news media cut candidates like Joe Biden out of the
process even before they got started. Just to be clear: I'm not talking
about my husband. I'm referring to other worthy Democratic contenders. Few people even had the chance to find out about Joe Biden's
health care plan before he was literally forced from the race by the
news blackout that depressed his poll numbers, which in turn depressed his fund-raising."[9]

This strobe-light journalism has the added effect of obscuring the
coverage of important issues. For example, according to research by the
Center for Excellence in Journalism, during the height of the 2008
presidential campaign, coverage of the Iraq war all but ceased. While
Iraq accounted for 23 percent of network TV news during the first
months of 2007, it plummeted to 3 percent during the peak of the primary campaign frenzy in 2008. On cable, Iraq war coverage dropped
from 24 percent to a paltry 1 percent during the same time frame.[10]

This isn't just about coverage of the war. It's about coverage of *everything*. That is, everything that's not horse-race journalism or celebrity-
oriented political coverage. According to the Pew Research Center's

"News Coverage Index"—an ongoing tabulation of media focus—presidential campaign coverage accounted for 69 percent of all news stories during the week of August 25 to 31, 2008, when the major parties held their conventions and the presidential nominees picked their running mates. During this height of campaign coverage, the issues all but vanished from newspapers and TVs across the country. According to Pew, "Stories about the candidates' policy positions filled only 2 percent of the campaign newshole . . . the smallest amount of attention paid to the policy debate since the general election began in June. Half of that coverage was focused on the economy (1 percent). Other subjects on which McCain and Obama disagree—such as energy and Iraq—generated negligible coverage."[11]

There's nothing inherently wrong with lighthearted stories from the campaign trail or horse-race coverage of elections. It would be disingenuous for me to say I didn't read or enjoy this brand of journalism. But campaign coverage is something of a weed that has choked out other flora from the topography of our public affairs. And when journalists fail to give the public information on issues, the public is unable to make informed decisions at the ballot box.

Trapped in the World Wide Web. In the early summer of 2007, well before the presidential primary campaign was in full swing, I had the chance to sit down for lunch with Bill and Hillary Clinton. Hillary was the presumed Democratic nominee, her campaign still in great shape and gaining momentum. Yet the Clintons were both mindful of the unpredictable nature of politics in our Internet age and wary of what could—and ultimately would—happen.

President Clinton told me, "Look, I was walking around Chicago the other day campaigning, getting to see people I had seen before. And all I saw were cameras, cell phones, and tape recorders pointed in my face. Anything I said, any exchange of words would be recorded. I could not even say hello to people without fear that what I would say would be potentially used against me."

Hillary added, "As a candidate, you want to try different lines, see how people react and test notions on the campaign trail. You can't do that; it does not work. It doesn't work because every word is parsed, every emotion analyzed, and you simply cannot do what you'd like to do because of the all-pervasive scrutiny."

As it turned out, they were right.

In the spring of 2008, during the heated and protracted primary battle between Hillary Clinton and Barack Obama, an intrepid "citizen journalist" with admittedly no training in journalism changed the course of the campaign coverage with two blog posts. The blogger, Mayhill Fowler, first posted comments that Senator Obama had made at a private fund-raiser closed to reporters in San Francisco, during which he posited that the lack of economic opportunity has led many in small-town America to become "bitter" and to "cling to guns and religion." A few months later, Fowler caught Bill Clinton greeting supporters at a rope line in South Dakota. Without introducing herself as a blogger, Fowler asked Clinton about a particularly vituperative story in *Vanity Fair*, prompting the former president to call the story's author a "scumbag." Obama and Clinton spent days trying to quiet the furor over their respective gaffes.[12]

To be sure, media sensationalism is nothing new. This has always existed to some degree in American politics. But what we're dealing with today is far more pernicious than what Murrow's generation had to contend with. What's different? In short, incentive, access, and amplification.

- The proliferation of cable news channels, in which anyone can access news on live TV at any time of day or night, has created the *incentive* to seek out breaking news, however vapid.
- The proliferation of YouTube, cell phone cameras, and the blogosphere has created unprecedented *access* to new sources of "news." So-called citizen journalists such as Fowler can go where other reporters can't and capture news that otherwise wouldn't be reported. In this way, bloggers can be just as powerful as Tom Brokaw or Charlie Gibson. Anyone with a digital recorder and a little luck can change the focus of the national media.
- To top it all off, Web sites *amplify* the focus on nonissues by aggregating sensationalist stories for one-stop shopping. Overworked and under-resourced reporters turn to these sites to get *their* news, perpetuating the coverage of nonissues.

As they say, nature hates a vacuum. In the absence of substantive reporting on real issues—and with increased incentive to generate inane "breaking news" and new means of obtaining it—our media today constantly turn to the latest scandal, gaffe, or hearsay, however insignificant or irrelevant to the challenges we face as a nation.

A frighteningly uninformed public. As Lee Hamilton, vice chair of the 9/11 commission and a respected former member of Congress, wrote, "In a democracy, public misperceptions carry an enormous cost." He's absolutely right. For self-government to work, and to work well, we need to get certain basic facts straight. And when we don't get them straight, things can go very badly, very quickly.

Hamilton cites the disturbing statistic that 69 percent of Americans at one time thought that Saddam Hussein was linked to the 9/11 terrorist attacks, although no evidence of such a link has ever existed.[13] That's right: two-thirds of the entire nation believed fervently in something that was repeatedly disproven, including by the 9/11 commission.

Here's another statistic that drives home the impact of our tuned-out news media. According to the Pew Research Center for the People and the Press, in July 2007, 54 percent of Americans knew the casualty rate of American troops in Iraq. By March 2008, as the national media virtually dropped Iraq coverage to focus on the presidential primary, that figure plummeted to 28 percent.[14]

As Hamilton noted, "Voters' misperceptions . . . can become formidable obstacles to the functioning of our representative democracy." The American public is too often misinformed or uniformed about critical issues that face the nation. For all of its merits, our free press is falling down on the job, and the implications of this failure are deadly serious.

CONTEXT IS KING

It's important to acknowledge that despite the problems I've catalogued above, our mainstream media are vastly superior to the means by which most—if not all—of the world is fed their news. As Murrow told his audience in Chicago, his concern about the state of journalism was born out of his great respect for America's free press. He believed that "potentially the commercial system of broadcasting as practiced in this country is the best and freest yet devised." I couldn't agree more. And that's exactly why we have to take a hard look at specific and realistic ways to strengthen it.

My own approach differs somewhat from the typical calls for reform. To that end, astute readers will note a couple conspicuous omissions from the above accounting of problems facing our media. Almost without fail, most critics who think and write about the deficiencies of our media cite two pressing issues: worsening media bias and increasing media conglomeration. Indeed, others typically focus on these two issues as *the* fundamental and underlying problems we must contend with. And while I heartily agree, I've chosen not to give them in-depth analysis for very specific reasons that speak to my overall philosophy when it comes to reforming our mass media. Let me address these problems by way of introducing my own solutions.

Media bias. A 2008 Rasmussen poll found that a whopping 55 percent of Americans believed that media bias was the biggest problem facing our political system, compared to 36 percent who pegged the biggest problem as campaign finance.[15] It's easy to understand why. Anyone who turns on cable television knows that there's no shortage of talking heads espousing their deeply biased political views and prognosticating in favor of their favorite horse in the race. *I'm one of them.* As a commentator on FOX News, a regular blogger on the Huffington Post, and a frequent contributor to several national newspapers, I'm the first to admit that punditry in America is out of control. Media bias exists beyond a reasonable doubt, and we have to do something about it.

In fact, there's such ample evidence that both liberal and conservative biases exist across the spectrum, there's little to debate on this point. Take, for instance, the Pew Research Center's finding that press coverage in 2008 from the party conventions through the end of the presidential debates was empirically more negative toward John McCain. "For Obama during this period, just over a third of the stories were clearly positive in tone (36 percent), while a similar number (35 percent) were neutral or mixed. A smaller number (29 percent) were negative," the center reported. "For McCain, by comparison, nearly six-in-ten stories studied were decidedly negative in nature (57 percent), while fewer than two-in-ten (14 percent) were positive."[16]

Before you feel too sorry for McCain, however, consider a separate study by the staff at Media Matters. They analyzed seven thousand guest appearances on the Sunday morning political talk shows between 1997 and 2005, and it turns out that McCain was the most frequent guest over those nine years, with 124 separate appearances. In fact, conservative guests in general were heavily favored on these all-important shows, which are watched obsessively by political journalists and often influence the direction of a particular candidacy or the national debate on a given issue. Between 2001 and 2005, 69 percent of journalists invited to these shows as guest pundits were identifiably conservative, and 61 percent of elected and administration officials who appeared on Sunday morning were Republicans.[17]

In response to the overwhelming evidence of media bias on both the right and the left, several nationally prominent Democrats in 2007 posited reinstating the Fairness Doctrine, an FCC rule first implemented in 1949 that required broadcasters to address both sides of the debate when covering an issue. The rule was struck back in 1987 on the grounds that the doctrine might, in fact, have done more to stifle debate than enhance it by giving broadcasters a negative incentive to raise politically sensitive issues in the first place.[18]

Frankly, these calls to revive the Fairness Doctrine are overwrought. I'm sympathetic to those cable critics who think that there's too much "FOX" and not enough "News." FOX, CNN, and MSNBC are all guilty of trying to pass off politically biased punditry as "fair and balanced" news coverage. But reinstating the Fairness Doctrine would be a twentieth-century fix for a twenty-first-century problem. We don't need new restrictions. *We need more viewpoints and perspectives.* We don't need more objectivity. *We need more transparency.* We don't need to forcibly change the programming on FOX or CNN. We need these networks to be more transparent about their viewpoints and more accountable to their audiences.

The fact is that we can't prevent or control biased coverage of our politics. It would run foul of the Constitution, not to mention common sense, to sanitize our airwaves in this way. What we need, instead, is to create incentives and outlets to dramatically increase the volume of balanced and substantive coverage, the diversity of political perspectives, and the ability of viewers to distinguish political *views* from political *news*.

Media conglomeration. In *The New Media Monopoly*, veteran journalist, academic, and Pulitzer Prize winner Ben H. Bagdikian writes with a degree of humor about the decidedly unfunny state of media conglomeration in America. "In 1983, the men and women who headed the fifty mass media corporations that dominated American audiences could have fit comfortably in a modest hotel ballroom," he notes. "By 2003, five men controlled all these media once run by the fifty corporations of twenty years earlier. These five, owners of additional digital corporations, could fit in a generous phone booth."[19] These five conglomerates— Time Warner, the Walt Disney Company, News Corporation, Viacom, and Bertelsmann AG—own virtually every means by which you consume

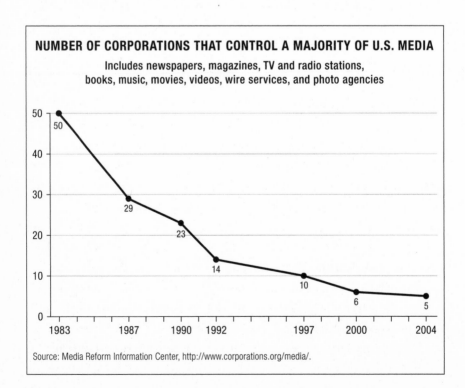

NUMBER OF CORPORATIONS THAT CONTROL A MAJORITY OF U.S. MEDIA

Includes newspapers, magazines, TV and radio stations, books, music, movies, videos, wire services, and photo agencies

Source: Media Reform Information Center, http://www.corporations.org/media/.

information and entertainment. TV and radio stations, newspapers and magazines, music and movies—all of these are in the hands (and the pockets) of a select few people who oversee billion-dollar enterprises and are responsible *only* to their shareholders.[20]

The history of this consolidation and the reasons for it are less interesting for our purposes than the effect it has had on journalism and the information available to the public, and its impact on our national discourse. And the situation is largely closed to debate. As media conglomeration has increased, the quality of journalism has decreased proportionately. As media commentators Robert McChesney and John Nichols reported in the *Nation* in 2008:

> Veteran reporters like Walter Cronkite are appalled by the merger-mania that has swept the industry, diluting standards, dumbing down the news and gutting newsrooms. Rapid consolidation, evidenced most recently by the breakup of the once-venerable Knight-Ridder newspapers, the sale of the Tribune Company and its media properties and the swallowing of the *Wall Street Journal* by Murdoch's News Corp continues the steady replacement of civic and democratic values by commercial and entertainment priorities. But responsible journalists have less and less to say about newsroom agendas these days. The calls are being made by consultants and bean counters, who increasingly rely on official sources and talking-head pundits rather than newsgathering or serious debate.[21]

Perhaps the most damning testimony has come from Lawrence K. Grossman, the former president of NBC News and PBS. Grossman has described the devastating fallout in newsroom operations when General Electric, under the stewardship of CEO Jack Welch, acquired NBC in 1988.

> In his book, Jack complains that I operated "under the theory that networks should lose money while covering the news in the name of journalistic integrity." The two of us, he said, "were on different planets." I take his complaint as a compliment. Under the law, broadcasters, who hold valuable licenses to use the public's airwaves, are considered public trustees. I thought, and still do, that responsible worldwide network

news coverage, which is costly, is an obligation to be borne by the network broadcasters as a loss leader if need be. Welch's priorities were entirely different. He made it clear that he would judge NBC News no differently than any other GE division. News would be expected to make the same profit margins they did. Welch was disdainful of any other approach. The news division, he said, had no greater obligation to provide public service than those GE lines that manufacture refrigerators, light bulbs, or jet engines. For Welch, as one critic put it, the financial perspective was the only one that mattered. That tunnel vision helped produce an era of network news that focused more on nonfiction entertainment than on the information citizens need about a dangerous and vulnerable world.[22]

The direction of today's mass media is determined not by the public interest but by corporate interests. These media empires are concerned solely with profits, not with public policy. Journalism in America has faltered as a result.

The solution, however, is less obvious. We can't wave a magic wand to make hard news coverage profitable. It never has been and likely never will be. Many reformers have called for new FCC regulations that would force these conglomerates to sell some of their news assets and relinquish their ever-increasing control over the mass media. I'm not opposed to tighter government regulation—but, at the same time, I'm not convinced it would do much good.

It seems to me that this isn't a problem that we can regulate our way out of. We need to *grow* our way out of it. The solutions I identify below leverage technology to offer more news, more sources, more perspectives, more independent oversight, and *much more* focus on issues. Right now, in today's confused media environment, more is definitely better. That's just what we need to change the journalistic landscape in America today: more, better, now.

BREAKING THE MEDIA MONOPOLY

As they say, the more things change, the more they stay the same. I noted above that Murrow wouldn't recognize the way Americans consume news today, but he would recognize the problems plaguing our mass media, from the competitive pressures that have tainted the quality of coverage to underreporting on the existential threats facing the nation. Murrow's perspective is extremely useful today as we contemplate how best to reform our media. Were he alive today, he might wryly note that for all our digital gadgetry we still haven't gotten the basics down.

In 1958, Murrow delivered a straightforward, three-part critique. First, he called on the media to illuminate the real issues of the day. Second, he called on broadcasters and journalists to act responsibly and to be accountable to the public. And, finally, he called for diverse broadcasting that stimulated public debate instead of an "endless outpouring of tranquilizers."

This framework for reform applies equally well today, and below I outline a number of solutions that are informed by Murrow's timeless critique of our mass media. In short, my recommendations use Murrow as a guide—and technology as a means—to move us beyond the problems that have plagued us for years.

Create public affairs trust funds at the major networks to dramatically increase hard news programming on air and online

As Lawrence Grossman noted, with newsrooms driven and shaped by corporate profit margins, the quantity and quality of public affairs programming has continued to decline in our age of corporate news conglomeration. That's why we should create public affairs trust funds at the major networks, a creative idea that would increase hard news offerings on the networks and online.

I wish I could claim this as my own idea. In fact, Edward R. Murrow proposed something similar in his famous 1958 speech: "Let us have a little competition. Not only in selling soap, cigarettes and automobiles, but also in informing a troubled, apprehensive but receptive public. Why should not each of the twenty or thirty big corporations which dominate radio and television decide that they will give up one or two of their regularly scheduled programs each year, turn the time over to the networks and say in effect: 'This is a tiny tithe, just a little bit of our profits. On this particular night we aren't going to try to sell cigarettes or automobiles; this is merely a gesture to indicate our belief in the importance of ideas."

It's a fifty-year-old idea that's as relevant today as ever. Murrow's basic premise is to have advertisers "donate" airtime purchased on the big networks, so that the networks could air commercial-free issues-oriented programming. The advertisers would get credit for helping to sponsor the program but would have nothing to do with the content. Murrow couldn't have foreseen the Internet, but it seems to me that the trust fund could enable this programming to be seen for free online, as well as in prime time. It's a novel idea that could help generate needed attention to pressing issues that today get short shrift thanks to corporate profit motives. For a few days each month, a public affairs trust fund at the major networks would help change that motive from private profit to public good.

Create a fund for online journalism to increase the quantity and quality of citizen journalism and blog content that focuses on real issues

The best way to combat the disturbing trend of media conglomeration is to dramatically grow the competition: the ranks of online journalists who are increasingly beating the mainstream media to the punch on important stories. We ought to encourage more of this brand of serious, investigative reporting by creating a fund for online journalism to help support independent Web-based journalists.

I noted above that bloggers and citizen journalists can help feed our twenty-four-hour news cycle and are sometimes complicit in giving the mainstream media the political drivel it loves instead of the real coverage of real issues that the American people need. But citizen journalism isn't always a bad thing. In fact, done right, bloggers can influence mass media for the better, by breaking stories that the major news outlets are ignoring, and shaping our national discourse on important political and policy-oriented issues.

Of the many unprecedented happenings in the rather eventful year of 2008 was a relatively little-noticed tectonic shift in the world of journalism. For the first time, a prestigious George Polk Award for excellence in journalism was given to a blogger, Joshua Micah Marshall. In the previous chapter, I discussed the revelation that the Bush administration fired U.S. attorneys for overtly political reasons. Josh Marshall and his Talking Points Memo are the reason we know about these firings, and he is largely credited with raising the furor that led to the resignation of Alberto Gonzales.[23]

As Pat Flannery noted in the *Arizona Republic*, real reporting by bloggers is on the rise and has indeed shaped the national debate on a number of occasions in recent years.

> Recent episodes dramatize how swiftly and powerfully [bloggers] may react, sometimes rivaling mainstream media in their ability to track events and connect the dots in real time, and influencing traditional news coverage. Consider: Blogs applied the pressure that led to Trent Lott's 2002 resignation from the U.S. Senate after making what some construed as racist remarks. It was a blogger dubbed "Buckhead" who in 2004 exposed forged documents used by CBS News and Dan Rather in stories about President Bush's National Guard service. Former Sen. Tom Daschle, D-S.D., was unseated two years ago after conservative bloggers attacked him and forced the state's largest newspaper to modify its coverage of the race.[24]

There's nothing new about independent journalism having an outsized impact on our national discourse. In fact, an independent investigative journalist named Seymour Hersh broke the story about the My Lai massacre and cover-up during the Vietnam War. The ensuing controversy bolstered the outrage and determination of antiwar activists and helped cement public opinion against the war. Interestingly, Hersh's reporting was made possible by a grant from the Fund for Investigative Journalism (FIJ), which for forty years has made small grants to independent journalists, enabling them to pursue their craft outside of the mainstream media.

We need a similar philanthropic fund for our digital age. A fund for online journalism could be financed by a number of philanthropies or corporations and overseen by one of the nation's prominent journalism schools—such as the Grady College of Journalism and Mass Communication at the University of Georgia, which also administers the Peabody Awards. Even a small fund could have a huge impact. In 1969, Hersh's grant from FIJ was a paltry $250. Even adjusting for inflation, that's not a lot of money. Imagine a $1 million fund, which could make a thousand grants of $1,000. A fund for online journalism could enable and inspire the next Josh Marshall and marginalize uninteresting gotcha bloggers like Mayhill Fowler.

There is a not-for-profit journalism outfit that's similar in ways to both a fund for online journalism and a public affairs trust fund. ProPublica, launched in 2008, describes itself as "an independent, nonprofit newsroom that produces investigative journalism in the public interest." It's led by former *Wall Street Journal* managing editor Paul Steiger and Stephen Engelberg, and now employs twenty-eight reporters who follow business, justice, energy and the environment, government and politics, health and science, media and technology, and national security. Its Web site, http://www.ProPublica.org, features its own work and aggregates the best of what's on the Internet. It has already partnered with a number of media outlets on investigations.

The Kaiser Family Foundation has set up a health policy news service, Kaiser Health News, "to produce in-depth coverage of health care policy for an independent Web site and in collaboration with mainstream media outlets." Even though Kaiser is a player in the health care debate, it appears to have built a firewall between its for-profit health services and its not-for-profit news source. Laurie McGinley, former deputy bureau chief for global economics at the *Wall Street Journal*, and Peggy Girshman, a top editor of *Congressional Quarterly* and previously at National Public Radio, were tapped to launch it.

These news services could be models for other policy-area-specific outlets that could beef up coverage in service to the general public. We could use public trusts that sponsor reporting on Social Security, entitlement reform, national security, education, and any number of neglected areas.

Create a coalition for excellence in journalism, a new professional organization for members of the media

Let me be perfectly clear. I'm against any kind of government oversight that would impinge on free speech. But I do think that journalists as a profession could do a much better job of policing their own. Standards have continued to decline, and journalists themselves are really the only ones who can do anything to right their ship. It's time for members of the media to come together and collectively raise the bar for what's expected of their trade. And the best way to do this is by creating a co- alition for excellence in journalism—a new, voluntary organization that would enforce a basic code of ethics among its members. Journalists no doubt shudder at hearing the words "enforce" and "standards." But we badly need both, and, done right, a new professional organization would enhance free speech, not stifle it.

Today, the Society of Professional Journalists (SPJ) has a decent code of ethics that is "voluntarily embraced" by its membership. A better way to put it might be selectively adhered to. SPJ also has an ethics commit- tee that "encourages" the use of the group's code. However, SPJ is staunchly against enforcing the code or sanctioning members who vio- late it, because they fear such a step would, in turn, violate the very idea of freedom of speech.

I get the concern, but I respectfully disagree that setting a minimum standard of professional conduct would harm free speech in America. After all, the SPJ already has a very good—and very basic—code of eth- ics. Among its clauses:

- "Journalists should be honest, fair and courageous in gathering, reporting and interpreting information."
- Journalists should "test the accuracy of information from all sources and exercise care to avoid inadvertent error. Deliberate distortion is never permissible."
- Journalists should "make certain that headlines, news teases and promo- tional material, photos, video, audio, graphics, sound bites and quotations do not misrepresent."

- "Ethical journalists treat sources, subjects and colleagues as human beings deserving of respect."
- "Journalists should be free of obligation to any interest other than the public's right to know."[25]

It's a little curious to me how an organization could have a membership that doesn't abide by its basic tenets. That defeats the purpose of having an organization in the first place. But that's exactly how the SPJ operates today.

A new coalition for excellence in journalism could move us in the right direction. It would be run by journalists, for journalists, and would offer membership only to individual journalists who agree to abide by its very basic and unobtrusive code of conduct. It would help enforce important journalistic tenets, such as *accuracy in reporting* and full disclosure of financial or political conflicts. It would help preserve a bright line between *reporting* and *espousing* and help the public distinguish between political opinion and objective fact. Repeated violations or complaints from the public would trigger peer review that, with cause, could lead to expulsion from the coalition.

Basically, what we're talking about is peer pressure. The coalition would be a badge of honor worn by self-respecting professionals, and it would be stripped from those who violate basic standards. The result would be that journalists have a peer-driven incentive to raise the standard of their craft. To my mind, that can only enhance freedom of speech in America.

A blogger code of ethics to guide responsible reporting on the Web

There's no question that blogs have become an important and even indispensable component of our mass media. Even though bloggers aren't traditional journalists, there's a good argument to be made that they have a responsibility to their readers to abide by a basic standard of honest and ethical reporting. I wouldn't want to tell bloggers how to act— and I'm strongly against any effort to censor Web content or compromise Net neutrality. But I strongly believe that bloggers should collectively decide upon a minimal code of ethics to guide their actions on the Web.

Should responsible bloggers post news content anonymously? Should they be obligated, like traditional journalists, to protect the identity of their sources? Should they post the confidential e-mails of a candidate for vice president that have been hacked into by an anonymous cyber thief?

These are just some of the questions that confront the blogosphere, and a movement to address these and other issues is already under way. In 2007, several prominent online advocates, including Jimmy Wales, the cofounder of Wikipedia, began working together on the dos and don'ts of the blogosphere.[26] The online resource CyberJournalist.net created a Bloggers Code of Ethics that's based loosely on the SPJ's professional code.[27]

For my part, a voluntary code that models the guidelines that traditional journalists are expected to follow makes tremendous sense. That means bloggers shouldn't sneak into private political fund-raisers by pretending to be supporters, and self-respecting partisans should do some due diligence before repeating bogus claims about, say, Barack Obama's religious beliefs. A digital dialogue on these issues is essential as the blogosphere continues to grow in size and influence.

Use the aggregating power of the Web to root out political bias in the mainstream media

The Internet is a compelling aggregator of public opinion. As business guru James Surowiecki brilliantly argues in *The Wisdom of Crowds*, the collective intelligence of millions of networked people can be a powerful tool. Consumer protection watchdogs have been using that power for years to help people make smart purchases online and in stores. You can go to any number of Web sites that rate various consumer products, from vacuum cleaners to microwave ovens, based on the reviews of thousands of people from across the country. It's time to employ this easy, market-oriented fix for another consumer product: the news.

Angie's List is one of those little miracles of the Internet. It's a Web site, http://www.angieslist.com, that collects hundreds of thousands of reviews of service companies and health care professions to help you weed out the bad ones before you hire a shoddy plumber or visit a sadistic dentist. I think it's high time to create a new site—say, http://www .murrowslist.org—to aggregate public opinion on reporters and pundits. In other words, to help consumers of news weed out biased and unethical journalists.

Like Angie's List, this new site would be intuitive and uncomplicated. After logging on, you could look up a particular reporter—local, national, on-air, or in print—and rate him or her on a simple one-to-ten scale of partisanship. And like Angie's List, with a lot of entries, a picture would emerge of the partisan bent of a particular media personality or an entire network. Murrow's List could be an incredibly useful and easy tool to help Americans who are interested in unbiased reporting find it quickly.

Enact Net neutrality

Earlier in the chapter, I said that we need to protect the neutrality of the Internet and demand accountability from the big networks. This in part speaks to a looming controversy about whether telecoms can create a tiered Internet and practice data-pricing and data-carrying discrimination.

I believe that the Internet is a public trust and that telecoms and other service providers should be regulated to reflect that trust—that is, that they should submit to some other discipline than the free market. Congress will likely soon take up this issue.

Of the legislation out there, the Snowe-Dorgan bill for Internet freedom preservation seems to be a reasonable compromise among the competing interests. This bill, if enacted, would ensure that all content, applications, and services be treated uniformly and fairly on the Internet by barring broadband network operators from blocking, degrading, or prioritizing service on their networks, while still allowing Internet providers to prioritize content that originates from their own networks. The act would further amend the Telecommunications Act of 1996 so that online businesses and consumers can use the Internet without interference or bias from broadband service providers. Broadband service providers are limited in how they can manage the network to, for example, protecting the network's security and allowing users to choose between different levels of broadband connections.

Web-based resources to fight misinformation and sloppy reporting

As I noted above, misinformation in today's media has had serious consequences for public opinion and public policy. Fortunately, the Internet is a phenomenal way to correct the record quickly and efficiently. There are a number of excellent Web-based resources that enable individuals and members of the media to get the facts straight on sensitive and important issues. There's no need to reinvent the wheel here, but I think it's worth pointing out a few of these sites and the service they provide.

- The Annenberg Political Fact Check (http://www.FactCheck.org) is a great resource if you want to get the real story on politics. True to its name, it vets the statements of political candidates, their ads and their speeches, which are too often taken at face value by reporters who lack the time, resources, or inclination to get to the bottom of things. Run by the Annenberg Public Policy Center at the University of Pennsylvania, the site is entirely nonpartisan. The Annenberg Foundation is its major backer, so you can rest assured that business and political organizations have no influence over its analysis.
- While FactCheck.org is becoming a well-known resource, there's no reason why mainstream media outlets can't provide the same function. Indeed, some already do. The *St. Petersburg Times* was a finalist for the Pulitzer Prize in public service for its "PolitiFact" initiative, which operated much like FactCheck.org. Other local papers and broadcast stations could easily implement similar fact-checking services for local markets, which would provide a much-needed service for citizens who want to avoid the mudslinging and just get the facts of a local mayoral or city council race.
- As I stated earlier, there's plenty of biased reporting on the right and the left that results in the proliferation of incorrect information in our media. There are two Web sites that have very different perspectives, but both do an excellent job of rebutting bias and bad information. Media Matters for

America (http://MediaMatters.org), which I've cited a number of times, is a nonprofit that posts information about media coverage that it feels is unfairly skewed to the right. While it makes no bones about the fact that its purpose is to combat a perceived conservative bias in the media, its staffers are very evenhanded in their analysis. The same goes for NewsBusters (http://www.NewsBusters.org), which is run by the very conservative Media Research Center. I've drawn upon its research repeatedly, and while the perspective is considerably right of center, the analysis is generally very fair.

• One of the most exciting and technology-driven resources I've found to date is a free download called SpinSpotter (http://spinspotter.com). It works with your Web browser to proactively spot spin in online news articles. The developers are still working on perfecting their admittedly flawed software, which relies on the analysis of experts, the input of public opinion, and proprietary spin-spotting formulas. But the idea of using existing technology to help solve the age-old problem of spin is certainly intriguing.[28]

To some extent, the public will always have to do its part to keep the press honest. Many blogs were born of this need and desire. We have more access to information than ever before. We also have a responsibility now to seek out that information, and with it the truth. After all, our democracy is only as strong as we make it—a subject I explore in-depth in chapter 9.

9

WAKE UP, AMERICA
Reviving Self-Government

> Public sentiment is everything. With public sentiment,
> nothing can fail; without it nothing can succeed.
> —ABRAHAM LINCOLN, 1858

Most political reformers and observers tend to have a narrow view of things. They blame our problems entirely on the politicians or the press, on bad legislation in Congress or ethically bankrupt lobbyists on Capitol Hill. As I've discussed throughout this book, these are certainly part of the equation we must solve if American democracy is to recover and rebound. But there is another contributing factor that most analysts discount or disregard: our disengaged citizenry, which is to blame for our dysfunctional democracy as much as anything else.

Self-government doesn't work with a checked-out citizenry. As Barack Obama reminded Americans in his inaugural address, the problems we face aren't the fault of recalcitrant Republicans or do-nothing Democrats. Instead, the root of our predicament is "our collective failure to make hard choices and prepare the nation for a new age." Obama called on Americans to usher in a new era of responsibility. Doing so will require us to reimagine what American citizenship means in the twenty-first century.

It's not enough to fix our institutions without new ways to involve our citizens in the exercise and the function of our democracy. America badly needs a new concept of citizenship to make our democracy work again. We need to redefine the demands and habits of citizenship in a way that will reengage our people and reinvigorate our civic institutions.

A new definition of responsible citizenship means two things.

First, it means a new way of thinking about politics. Instead of sitting back while our leaders attempt to divide and conquer the voting public, a new concept of citizenship would enable and demand each of us to actively participate in shaping our local and national politics.

Second, it means a new commitment to service. A new definition of citizenship recognizes that living in a democracy demands our active engagement—not just at the ballot box, but also in our schools, our community centers, our public libraries, and our public parks.

With respect to politics, Obama's unprecedented campaign for the presidency—which clearly struck a chord in the body politic—is a terrific model. Obama asked Americans to be a part of something larger than themselves, and millions responded to his call. The way in which he achieved victory—by building a people-powered campaign, by recruiting a bottom-up army of small-dollar donors, and by creatively using social networking technology to recruit millions of volunteers—suggests a new politics for the future. It's a bottom-up model driven by the engagement of everyday citizens and sustained by politicians and campaigns that seek citizen involvement through social networking, online fund-raising, and virtual campaigning. It has the potential to revolutionize the political dimensions of American citizenship.

But redefining citizenship in America is about more than politics. It's about a sense of connection to our neighbors and a sense of duty to our country. It's about serving our communities and valuing the greater good. It's about a citizenship that is dedicated to service—from faith-based organizations and church groups to new opportunities and rewards for national service. It's about a bottom-up model for improving and enhancing civic life in America, where the Internet is an effective tool not only for political organizing but for community organizing and service learning as well. It's a new citizenship for all members of society, irrespective of social status or age.

Detractors derided Obama during the presidential campaign for his nonprofit background as a community organizer on Chicago's South

Side. But that's precisely what America needs more of today. Not just citizens who are willing to contribute to political campaigns, attend political rallies, and knock on doors. But also citizens who are willing to get involved as organizers, teachers, civil servants, and social workers—citizens who are eager to volunteer their time and contribute to their communities. We need fewer financial analysts trying to make a quick buck selling credit default swaps on Wall Street and more community workers trying to make a real difference on our city streets.

This is the new era of responsibility that President Obama challenged Americans to build. And I argue in this chapter that it must be rooted in a redefinition of American citizenship—one in which Americans don't just challenge our elected representatives to reshape government but also reshape our very relationship to politics and politicians. We must change the way we think about service. And we must take bold steps to ensure these changes take hold.

To that end, I offer a number of solutions, and each is part and parcel of a deeper, broader idea. If we want to increase civic engagement in America, if we want our people to give their time and effort to better our nation through political action and community service, our nation has to give something back. That means creating more than just a series of new programs, new initiatives, and new spending. It means creating an entirely new dynamic in the United States and a "new deal" between Americans and their government—a mutual reinvestment in our civic infrastructure and institutions, based on this new concept of citizenship. By reinventing citizenship in America, we can reinvigorate our politics and our communities and send a message to the world that American democracy is stronger than ever.

THE ENTROPY OF ENGAGEMENT

In recent years, we've seen flashes of America's civic spirit. After 9/11, millions of Americans rushed to local hospitals to give blood. After the tsunamis in Southeast Asia in 2004, everyday Americans responded with tremendous generosity, donating more than $902 million to the relief effort. We all remember the outpouring of support nationwide when Hurricanes Katrina and Rita decimated New Orleans and the Gulf Coast—from those who opened their wallets to those who opened their homes for victims of the storms.

And yet, despite these magnanimous moments of the past decade, by nearly every measure civic engagement in America is on the decline. Despite the excitement of the 2008 elections, we are less politically engaged and less interested in current events than previous generations. Despite our digitally interconnected world and the explosion of the Internet, we are less connected to our communities and our neighbors. And despite the incredible proliferation of social networking Web sites such as MySpace, YouTube, Facebook, and Twitter, our tangible social networks themselves are less robust than ever before. While these virtual networks are sprawling online, they're not necessarily sprawling in our everyday lives or in our civic institutions.

No one has captured the decline in American civic life quite like Harvard political scientist Robert Putnam. In his groundbreaking book *Bowling Alone*, Putnam mines reams of data to demonstrate the many ways in which "social capital"—a measure of connectedness and trust among social networks and communities—has declined in recent decades. Putnam now heads the Saguaro Seminar at Harvard's John F. Kennedy School of Government, the nation's premier forum for research on social capital and trends in civic engagement.

He has uncovered some stunning trends that illustrate this decline in stark terms. As the title of his book suggests, more Americans today *are* bowling alone. Participation in communal activities (including bowling leagues) is today *half* of what it was twenty-five years ago. A similar decline has occurred in other aspects of American social life. In the past quarter century, according to research compiled by Putnam:

- Socializing with friends at one's home has declined by 45 percent.
- Attending public meetings has declined by 35 percent.
- Attending church has declined by more than 30 percent.
- Philanthropy has declined by more than 30 percent.

What has increased: the number of people in America who are "socially isolated." According to the Saguaro Seminar, this figure has climbed from 10 percent of Americans in 1984 to a whopping 25 percent in 2004.[1]

Of course, there are a number of additional indicators that suggest the social fabric in America is deteriorating.

- **Decline in voting:** While pundits predicted record-breaking turnout for the historic 2008 elections, those projections didn't pan out. In the election that was billed as a renewal of civic life in America, half of eligible voters stayed home. Such esteemed democracies as Somalia and Uzbekistan have higher turnout than the United States in nationwide elections.[2]

- **Disengagement from the political process:** There's no doubt that Obama's supporters were highly engaged during the 2008 campaign. But according to surveys by the Pew Research Center—and despite the hype from pundits—*the percentage of voters who personally volunteered for a presidential campaign actually declined during the 2008 cycle.* Only 7 percent of the public volunteered in 2008, compared to 9 percent during the 2006 and 2004 election cycles. One reason: While Democrats were particularly engaged in all three cycles, Republicans became disengaged in 2008. Obama supporters out-volunteered McCain supporters by 11 percent to 3 percent.[3]

- **Decline in the consumption of hard news:** According to the Center for Information and Research on Civic Learning and Engagement (CIRCLE), fewer Americans take part in what has historically been a daily ritual of civic engagement since our nation's founding—that is, reading the newspaper. In 1972, 72.9 percent of adult Americans—nearly three quarters of the country—read the newspaper each day. In the last three decades, that figure has plummeted. In 2004, only 42.9 percent of adults said that reading a newspaper was part of their daily routine. Likewise, in 1972, 44.4 percent of young Americans aged eighteen to twenty-five read the paper. In 2004, that figure has dropped off considerably, to only 27.9 percent. You might attribute these statistics to the rise of the Internet as a source of daily news. But according to CIRCLE, "regardless of age, people prefer to get their news from magazines rather than any other source on a regular basis."[4]

- **Community service not a priority:** One of the best measures of a civically engaged public is the percentage of people who volunteer their time to improve their communities. Across the country, levels of volunteerism remain largely unchanged from previous decades. In 1972, 23.6 percent of Americans reported volunteering in their communities, compared to 26.2 percent thirty-five years later, in 2007. That's a slight improvement but not one to write home about—especially as the volunteer rate actually decreased during the 2000s, from a high of 28.8 percent from 2003 to 2005.[5]

- *Decline in military service:* America's military prowess depends not on a conscripted force, like many armies throughout the world, but on an all-volunteer force. Yet during the past decade, recruitment declined in the midst of two unpopular wars, and Americans for some years seemed less willing to serve. In 2005, the U.S. Army missed its recruiting target by the largest margin since 1979.[6] In 2007, according to the military, only 16 percent of young Americans planned to join the military—the lowest percentage ever reported.[7] To compensate for the decline, the armed forces relaxed rules on accepting recruits with drug convictions and criminal records, and it even considered starting a "fat farm" in order not to turn away overweight recruits.[8] It also spent more than *$1 billion* on recruitment incentives, only to continue to struggle to fill its ranks. When in 2008 the deepest recession since the Great Depression hit, the decline in recruitment mitigated and the military began meeting—and even beating—its recruitment goals. Even so, the future of the all-volunteer force needs to be addressed when the economy rebounds.

It's hard to separate this overall decline in the quantity and quality of our civic life from the mirror decline in our politics. After all, a democracy is nothing more than the sum of its parts. When you add a disaffected citizenry to declining democratic institutions, the end result is a nation whose government is cut off from the people it serves, by the people it serves. In other words, a nation that is trapped in a vicious cycle of apathy, cynicism, and decline.

THE DEMOCRATIC (SMALL D) FUTURE

In 2008 we caught a small glimpse of what American citizenship could look like in the future.

First, we saw millions of everyday Americans contributing small-dollar donations that drowned out the influence of special interests. We saw young people excited to vote, to volunteer, and to learn about the political system. Powerful party machines have traditionally monopolized politics. But in 2008, the Internet connected communities of Obama supporters from across the nation into arguably the most potent political machine ever—powered by online social networking technology. The campaign used technology to interact with its donors and create a dialogue with its supporters. On the Web, regular people set the political dialogue for the 2008 presidential campaign.

In the weeks and months following Election Day, New York City nonprofit coordinators reported a tremendous surge in volunteerism. Volunteer attendance was up markedly. New York City's volunteer clearinghouse, New York Cares, saw a huge increase in Web site traffic. In fact, they reported that all of the one thousand not-for-profit organizations and school volunteer programs that are part of their volunteer network were full.[9]

It's an exciting thought that political activism can lead to social activism—and that a political process that engages voters can help repair some of the holes that have been exposed in our social fabric. But given the volunteerism statistics cited above, it is very much an open question whether this sort of politics takes permanent root or withers, whether the uptick in political activism and volunteerism is sustained or short-lived.

Frankly, I'm not as giddy as some political observers. I believe the 2008 election was an important indicator that America's civic pulse has not flatlined. But I do not believe that the nature of Obama's campaign and the fact of his election prove that politics and society have meaningfully changed. Especially in light of Putnam's research and the statistics above, I'm convinced that 2008 proves only that change is possible—not that it is here to stay. The future very much depends on how we respond over the coming years, and the recent past should both give us hope and give us pause.

On the one hand, we can find hope in the long, bipartisan tradition of American presidents championing community service and engagement. George H. W. Bush spoke of "a thousand points of light," representing the vast network of activists in America serving the public good, and he called for an increase in service. Bill Clinton created AmeriCorps, a national community service program, and laid the groundwork for federal support of faith-based institutions. George W. Bush, though widely pilloried for failing to call the nation to make meaningful sacrifices after 9/11, was, in fact, quite progressive on service initiatives. He doubled the size of AmeriCorps, created USA Freedom Corps, which promotes volunteerism across the nation, and increased funding for faith-based and community organizations—so many of which depend on volunteers to provide services to communities in need. On the other hand, while all of these efforts are laudable, thus far, collectively, they haven't captured the imagination of Americans to create a sustained ethic of national service.

During the 2008 campaign, Obama championed the idea of changing the way we think about politics and about service. In addition to the political reforms his campaign itself embodied, he also campaigned on a platform of "universal voluntary public service," which included a number of interesting and worthwhile proposals to increase civic engagement in America. Obama called for dramatically expanding AmeriCorps, from 75,000 volunteers to 250,000; doubling the size of the Peace Corps, from 8,000 to 16,000 positions by 2011; engaging retirees in service projects; and setting a goal that all high school students complete fifty hours of community service a year and all college students volunteer one hundred hours each year. Soon after the inauguration, Congress overwhelmingly passed the Edward M. Kennedy Serve America Act, a $6 billion measure that increased the size of AmeriCorps and created new opportunities for Americans to serve their country through work in areas such as sustainability and health care.

But we need more than a bigger, better version of what we've done in the past. For two decades, our political leaders on the right and the left have done much to increase the opportunities for Americans to give back to their communities. None of these efforts, however, have brought about the sea change we desperately need. None of these efforts fundamentally changed citizenship in America.

If we are going to truly transform the culture of civic engagement in America—and reinvigorate our democracy in the process—we need to do more than simply expand on programs that already exist today. And if we're going to capitalize on this moment of hope and change engen-

dered by the 2008 elections, we need more than just a shift in resources. It's time for a paradigm shift and a new dynamic in America—a
dynamic that says *if you invest in America, America will invest in you.*

This dual bargain is desperately needed to bring about a new concept of American citizenship. The future of our democracy depends on
the engagement of our citizens. And the engagement of our citizens
depends on Washington's willingness to seize this moment of potential
renewal, encourage and enable that increased engagement, and help
sustain it.

FIXING THE PUBLIC'S INTEREST

At this time, when Americans are more receptive to the concept of service than at any time in the recent past, we need game-changing measures that will fundamentally alter the way Americans think about
service and the way they act—and live—in their communities.

To inspire a call to volunteerism among Americans, we first need to
make service a priority—and not just a priority in spirit. Service needs
to become a priority *in the federal budget*, with funding allocations that
are far greater than today's merely perfunctory appropriations. If we can
spend hundreds of billions to bail out our financial institutions, let alone
hundreds of billions to build a democracy in Iraq, we should be willing
to spend serious money on bailing out our civic institutions and our
democracy at home. Done right, this effort will cost billions—not
millions—and we should be willing to take on that level of investment.

In order to change the culture of civic engagement, we also must
leverage technology. As I noted earlier, it's ironic that during this time of
unprecedented technological advancement—especially in social networking technology—we are less connected than at any time in our
past. The Obama campaign's online efforts proved that we can successfully use existing technologies to better connect people to one another,
to their communities, and to their government.

What follows is a continuum of civic engagement. On one end of the
spectrum is a new kind of individual engagement, enabled by new technologies. On the other end of the spectrum is more meaningful communal engagement, enabled by a paradigm shift—a "new deal"—in the

way we think about, encourage, and reward service in America. It's a tall order, but we have the winds of change at our back, and we have technology on our side.

Convene technology-based "fireside" chats and citizen videoconferences to connect the powerful directly to the people, without the media as middle man

It's not an overstatement to say that the rise of the Internet has been *the* most important development in politics in the past two decades. It's changed the way candidates raise money. It's changed the way reporters cover campaigns and elections. And it's continuing to change the way candidates interact with voters. The president and other national political figures should continue this positive development by leveraging technology to bypass the mainstream media and engage directly with the public.

One of the most interesting moments of the 2008 presidential race was when the Obama campaign decided to buck decades of tradition in announcing the selection of running mate Joe Biden. Instead of giving the leak to a reporter—standard operating procedure for political campaigns—Obama notified his supporters and journalists at the same time *by text message.*

In my opinion, the more our elected officials are able to interact directly with the public through the medium of the Web—instead of the medium of cable news and television pundits—the better. Just as FDR took advantage of the relatively new technology of radio to go directly to the public with his fireside chats, the Internet presents an unprecedented opportunity for the president and congressional leaders to have a direct dialogue with the public. It makes new and creative ways for our elected officials to engage voters possible.

For instance, imagine that in three or four years' time, instead of a typical West Wing press conference, the president could hold a videoconference with the public, and regular citizens could ask questions directly of the president. Or instead of fireside chats, why not fireside blogs? Like any other blog, the public could post comments to the president's posts, and the president could reply to those comments. You-Tube also offers our officeholders the ability to cheaply and efficiently record and broadcast their meetings with citizens groups, their public appearances, and their floor speeches.

From my perspective, the more the better. The more interaction we have and the more information we have, the more democracy we have. It's an equation made possible by the Internet revolution, and we should seize it to reinvigorate our national discourse.

Deliver government and community services via the Internet

If you've ever tried to get service from a government agency over the Internet, you've likely found it to be a frustrating experience. That's because the government continues to use the Web as simply an add-on—a "bells and whistles" feature—instead of an integral part of its mission. Go to the Web site of any federal agency, and you'll see that the Internet is used almost exclusively as a means of transmitting information out. But grassroots organizing efforts like the ones organized by the Obama campaign and MoveOn.org understand that the Web is not just a special feature; it's the *central* feature. It offers much more than the power of dissemination—it enables *conversation, participation,* and *self-determination.*

The federal government can dramatically transform the way that citizens interact with government—indeed, the way they think about citizenship—by giving every single American their own "citizen home page." It's an idea first floated by Micah Sifry and Andrew Rasiej, founders of the online magazine and conference Personal Democracy Forum.

Sifry and Rasiej have brilliantly suggested the creation of a "Citizen.gov" site, which would connect Americans to their government and to one another. Every American would have an online profile, similar to accounts that you might create on Facebook or MySpace. It would allow individuals to access personal information, from taxes to Medicaid to the contact information for their state, local, and federal elected officials. And it would also help people find volunteer opportunities in their local communities and connect them to like-minded activists and advocates.[10]

These "online citizenship accounts" would help change the way people think about citizenship. Instead of an estranged relationship with government—centered around infrequent interactions such as paying taxes, contesting a parking ticket, showing up for jury duty, and other unpleasantries—a Citizen.gov portal would create a virtual two-way dialogue that recent political campaigns have successfully used to engage and excite voters.

Tax-free income for those who work to serve the public good

We need to make service in America as attractive a career path as lucrative vocations in banking, finance, and law. If we're going to create a nation in which service is valued and revered, we need to reward it properly. There is perhaps no better way to underscore the importance of those who work for the benefit of our nation than to waive their tax liabilities in honor of their service.

A new, service-oriented tax code could exempt a number of workers from income taxes: teachers, nonprofit workers, community organizers, and others who sacrifice the promise of a high-paying job in order to serve the greater good. After all, those who work in these highly consequential positions make salaries that are far below the compensation they would receive for similar work in the private sector. In fact, in many ways there is an inverse correlation between the importance of these positions to our society and the monetary benefits associated with them. Jobs that are indispensable—such as educating our children and caring for the needy—typically come with salaries that are laughable.

Eliminating income taxes for those who work hard to better our communities would rectify this inequity—and it would also change the way this type of work is perceived by the public, sought after by our young people, and honored by our nation.

A tax code that rewards service and volunteerism

There is arguably no clearer window into the soul of a nation than its tax code. And if you look hard at America's tax code, it's painfully obvious that we place little value on community service and those who work for the greater good. It's time to change our tax code to reward volunteerism and civic engagement.

Since 1917, the federal government has provided a tax deduction to those who make charitable contributions to nonprofit organizations. For the past ninety years, the idea has been the same—if you give money to a charitable organization, you get a tax break. But if you give your time, energy, services, and sweat to an organization that contributes to the public good, all you get is thanks.

Today, our tax code subsidizes the contributions of wealthy Americans who should be giving to charity anyhow. We need to update laws that have distorted our values and changed the purpose of giving. In addition to giving tax deductions for charitable contributions, we should provide a $1,000 tax credit to every American who volunteers one hundred hours each year in their community.

Free college tuition in exchange for two years of national community service

Creating a new ethic of service in America must start with our youth. But today, many college graduates seek out high-paying jobs instead of life-enriching service opportunities. The reason isn't greed or self-involvement. It's a direct result of the message that we send our young people today: If you want to give back, you have to give up. We reward selfishness and discourage selflessness. We should change the message and strike a new bargain with America's youth: If you commit to two years of community service after college, we'll pay for your education. This "two-by-four" law would dramatically alter the priorities of undergraduates approaching graduation.

There are numerous opportunities for young people and students to engage in service during school and after graduation. But many are forced to use their free time to work in order to offset the cost of tuition, which has skyrocketed in recent years. Not surprisingly, many students seek high-paying jobs after graduation in order to pay off hefty college loans they acquired in order to earn their degrees.

At the same time, the financial incentives for young Americans to dedicate themselves to service projects such as the Peace Corps and

AmeriCorps are paltry, to say the least. In AmeriCorps, for instance, members who serve full-time over a ten- to twelve-month period receive an AmeriCorps Education Award of up to $4,725 to pay for college or graduate school, or to pay back qualified student loan deferments. That would barely buy a years' worth of books and board at today's colleges and universities.

Offering free college tuition in exchange for two years of community service in AmeriCorps or the Peace Corps would dramatically shift the civic culture in America. Young people would be encouraged to pursue a career in service much in the same way they are currently encouraged to pursue a career in finance or law. Today, a handful of states offer free in-state tuition to students who attain and maintain a certain threshold of academic achievement. A new bargain with our students would put the emphasis on service as well as academics, and it could alter our civic culture, benefit our economy, and transform our nation.

Reorganize, reenergize, and reinvent national service programs

Over the past decade, there have been repeated calls—and successful initiatives—to expand the nation's most popular service programs, including AmeriCorps and the Peace Corps. It's now time for us to reinvent the way we define government and community service.

Reinvent the Peace Corps to meet the demand at home and abroad. The Peace Corps is one of the most symbolically important efforts of the federal government. Yet adjusted for inflation, the federal government today spends significantly less on the corps that it did in the 1960s, despite huge demand among Americans to serve and from developing nations for volunteers. While only four thousand volunteers are selected each year, the inquiries about serving in the corps usually run to more than one hundred thousand per year. Additionally, while the Peace Corps currently operates in seventy-four nations, as many as twenty additional countries have asked for volunteers.[11]

The demand to serve is great, and the need is great. But so, too, is the strategic benefit of reinventing the size and scope of the Peace Corps. In considering how to prevent the growth of terrorism, the 9/11 commission stated the U.S. government should "communicate and defend American ideals in the Islamic world, through much stronger public diplomacy to reach more people, including students and leaders outside of government."[12]

Reorganize service programming and administration in Washington. Today there is no central organization to coordinate the nation's many domestic and international service efforts, and there are many separate departments that potentially duplicate efforts and waste resources. The Peace Corps is an independent federal agency. Freedom Corps and the Office for Faith-Based and Community Initiatives are both executive office divisions in the White House. President Clinton spearheaded and signed the National Community Service Trust Act of 1993, creating the Corporation for National and Community Service, which today oversees AmeriCorps and perhaps a dozen additional national service programs. It seems that all of these efforts should be organized into a new cabinet-level agency, which reports directly to the president.

Reenergize volunteerism in America by creating a democracy czar. A "democracy czar" would do for citizen engagement what the surgeon general does for public health—act as a national spokesperson and chief advocate for community service in America. However, unlike the surgeon general, a democracy czar would have the important function of overseeing all of the nation's domestic and international service programs. Interestingly, George W. Bush set the precedent for elevating national service to the level of the White House. In 2003, he created the President's Council on Service and Civic Participation, which coordinates the President's Volunteer Service Award program. As Rick Stengel of *Time* magazine has smartly noted, "Don't appoint a gray bureaucrat to this job; make it someone like Arnold Schwarzenegger or Mike Bloomberg, who would capture the imagination of the public."[13] Stengel is right, and the nation badly needs a full-time cheerleader for strengthening our democracy—someone who can engage and excite Americans of all ages in the promise and rewards of service.

10

THE INCUBATORS
Lessons from the States

> It is this same republican spirit, it is these manners and customs of a free people, which are engendered and nurtured in the different States, to be afterwards applied to the country at large.
> —ALEXIS DE TOCQUEVILLE, 1835

Politics in America is in many ways the tale of two states: New York and California. Throughout this volume, the systemic problems I've described at each level of our government—unfair and uncompetitive elections, unresponsive government, courtrooms degraded by politics—are rampant in both places. These large states bookend the continental United States, and they represent the broad spectrum of political pitfalls we face at the local, state, and federal levels.

New York represents government at its most oligarchic. The state is a bastion of corruption, disenfranchisement, and political patronage. Not to mention dysfunction. As Rudy Giuliani put it, "There is a mound of evidence that something is terribly wrong with the political system in New York."[1] And to give you a sense of just how bad things are, the former mayor gave this quote to the *New York Times* in 1987, *more than twenty years ago*. Very little has changed since then. Political contributions from corporations are all but unchecked.[2] Trial court judges are handpicked by political bosses. And citizens, as a result of these and many other political anachronisms, are locked out of the system.

In New York, one only has to open up one of the daily tabloids for the latest revelation of abuse, fraud, or neglect as a result of the utter

lack of transparent and accountable politics and government. Most recently, partisan bickering and maneuvering among the leadership in the
state senate brought government to a halt, as they couldn't figure out
which cabal of insiders was calling the shots. Back-room negotiating finally brought about a solution that citizens were powerless to influence.
Or take the shocking report that two deputies to the state comptroller,
who oversees a $120 billion pension fund, were being indicted on 123
counts of receiving millions in kickbacks. Of course, the comptroller is
the only official who oversees the fund, making it a ripe and obvious
target for exactly this kind of abuse. And whether it's pension funds or
judicial primary elections, the closed-door nature of New York politics
and government enables gross violations of the public trust.

California represents government at its most unresponsive. The
state's ongoing experiment with direct democracy run amok has put Sac-
ramento into a perpetual tailspin. Reform-minded progressives implemented the ballot initiative and referendum at the beginning of the
twentieth century. But a hundred years later, these tools of citizen
empowerment have been co-opted by special interests. State law makes
it relatively easy to collect signatures for ballot measures. Today, interest
groups can make an end run around the state legislature by simply paying a vendor to collect the signatures they need. As a result, Californians have voted on an astounding 107 ballot initiatives since 2000.[3]
Wealthy financiers and special interests have manipulated the ballot for
any number of purposes, from recalling a governor for political payback
(Gray Davis was ousted in 2003) to changing the state constitution (gay
marriage was banned in 2008).

By some accounts, the political environment has never been worse.
In the midst of the national downturn in the spring of 2009, a Public
Policy Institute of California poll found that 77 percent of voters believe
the state was on the wrong track, only 33 percent approved of Governor
Schwarzenegger's performance in office, and just 11 percent approved
of the state legislature.[4]

This data underscore political failure that has arguably reached an
unprecedented level. Scott Plotkin, the executive director of the California School Boards Association, penned "Welcome to California, the
State of Dysfunction," in which he notes that the political devolution in

the state—combined with the global downturn—led to the proposal of a state budget that decreases funds for public schools for the first time since the Great Depression.[5] But political dysfunction is just part of the equation. In recent years, citizens have approved several ballot measures that have been struck down by courts as unconstitutional, wasting untold millions of tax dollars in the process.

The result of this stymied system is that real people with real lives are going to be in real pain. California's recent budget slashed billions in services to those who rely on the government for everything from quality education to affordable health care. As the *New York Times* noted:

> The California dream is, for now, delayed, as demonstrated by the budget state lawmakers and the governor agreed upon late Monday. At no point in modern history has the state dealt with its fiscal issues by retreating so deeply in its services, beginning this spring with a round of multibillion-dollar budget cuts and continuing with, in total, some $30 billion in cuts over two fiscal years to schools, colleges, health care, welfare, corrections, recreation and more.[6]

Of course, New York and California aren't alone. There are a thousand examples of other state and municipal governments that fall somewhere in between the extreme oligarchy of New York and the dysfunctional discord of California. Indeed, there are too many to summarize or analyze here.

But if these coastal calamities represent the worst extremes of our politics, a number of states in Middle America represent the best of American democracy. Our decentralized federal constitution, which empowers states to make their own laws and forge their own paths, has enabled many states to overcome systemic political challenges by implementing extremely innovative solutions. And many of these local innovations have national implications that warrant our serious attention and consideration.

That's the purpose of this chapter. Instead of dissecting the disparate problems faced by states, below I take note of the interesting and innovative reforms that have been adopted from the bayou to the heartland. They're uniquely American solutions to uniquely American challenges. From opening up government to engaging citizens in the political process, they represent avenues of reform that legislators in Washington and reformers around the country should take a hard look at implementing nationally.

THE REFORMED DEMOCRACY LABORATORIES

America faces vast systemic problems that plague our political system. There's no question that we have to confront them head-on. But there's little doubt in my mind that as a nation we can and will forge ahead. Why the overwhelming confidence? After all, I've painted a rather dire picture of American politics in this volume. The reason, as I hinted at above, is simple: federalism.

In researching and writing this book of solutions, I've confirmed a long presumed notion of mine that our federal system of government, over time, has uniquely enabled American citizens to bring about reform. Our Constitution gives states considerable autonomy and power to pursue their own experimentations in government. With the exception of interstate commerce, national security, and international relations, states are more or less on their own. It's one of our country's fundamental strengths that each state can serve as a laboratory of reform and innovation in this way.

And it's nothing new.

When Alexis de Tocqueville came to America in 1831, he was impressed—perhaps above all else—by American federalism. Tocqueville considered America's Constitution unique in the history of self-government and a triumph of the American colonial and frontier experience. He saw the citizens of different states as the drivers of progress, each forging solutions to problems in their home cities and neighborhoods. Ultimately, he noted how this decentralized system creates a unique symbiosis that benefits the entire nation as much as it does individual states and their citizens: "The public spirit of the Union is, so to speak, nothing more than an abstract of the patriotic zeal of the provinces. Every citizen of the United States transfuses his attachment to his little republic in the common store of American patriotism. In defending the Union he defends the increasing prosperity of his own district, the right of conducting its affairs, and the hope of causing measures of improvement to be adopted which may be favorable to his own interest; and these are motives which are wont to stir men more readily than the general interests of the country and the glory of the nation."[7]

In other words, for Tocqueville, it was all about the primacy of the states.

Nearly two hundred years after Tocqueville wrote *Democracy in America*, the "public spirit of the Union" is alive and well. Indeed, you could read the history of progress in America as that of states acting in their own interest and, in doing so, furthering the national interest. Throughout this book, in fact, there are numerous examples of states paving the way for reform: Florida became the first state to open the primary selection process to voters. Wisconsin and North Carolina are leading the charge to provide for publicly financed judicial campaigns. Iowa is on the cutting edge of redistricting reform.

Granted, there are numerous instances in our history of federalism reinforcing repression instead of enabling progress. States' rights entrenched Jim Crow laws in the segregated South. In 2008, several states changed their constitutions to ban gay marriage. Federalism engenders reform, but the path is oftentimes a long and winding road.

But by and large, there are exciting things happening today in state capitals across the nation. Reformers at the state level are leading the way in crafting new means to eliminate special interest influence from elections, enhance judicial independence, and increase civic engagement.

LOCAL INNOVATIONS, NATIONAL SOLUTIONS

As I've discussed previously, different states have different systems for selecting their judges, drawing their congressional districts, and ensuring that government is open and responsive. But all states—and the federal government, for that matter—face the same set of problems endemic to American democracy.

- How do we ensure transparency, openness, and responsiveness in our civic institutions?

- How do we prevent conflicts of interest and corruption in our campaigns and our government?
- How do we enhance civic participation and ensure that citizens are engaged and informed?

Opening up government. I've discussed before the chronic problem of citizen mistrust of government. It's something I saw reflected in poll after poll during my work on dozens of political campaigns over more than thirty years in politics. In fact, there has been a 20 to 30 percent drop in trust in government since I started polling. It's a sentiment I share with the vast majority of Americans. And in many ways, it's the reason I decided to write this book.

In part, we can restore the confidence of the public in our civic institutions by strengthening the laws that keep government officials on the straight and narrow. But we also need a concerted effort to open up the corridors of power to public scrutiny.

Citizens are distrustful of government in part because they don't have enough information about what it's doing, where their tax dollars are going, and why. They say sunshine is the best disinfectant, but it's also an important way to fortify public trust. Forward-thinking governors and legislatures across the country are using the Web and information technology in innovative ways to open up government. The following solutions are excellent attempts by states to improve citizen access to the workings of government by leveraging existing technology.

Kansas: The first state "Google for Government" Web site that allows citizens to search state spending online

While it doesn't happen often, every now and again Congress is on the cutting edge of reform.

In chapter 5, I mentioned the failed attempt by Senators Ted Stevens and Robert Byrd to place a secret hold on legislation creating a searchable Internet database of federal spending. The measure was popular with the blogosphere, which ultimately rooted out the senatorial roadblock. Sponsored by both John McCain and Barack Obama, the bill ultimately passed in 2006, creating for the first time a "Google for

Government" Web site—http://www.USAspending.gov—where Americans can track federal spending and congressional earmarks online.

In 2007, Kansas became the first state to follow the federal government's lead. According to the conservative Commonwealth Foundation, the state's "KanView" Web site sets the national standard for government transparency: "Kansas . . . boasts one of the most comprehensive online databases for government expenditure." The online database "posts bond indebtedness, annual revenue, and expenditures (including individual grants, contracts, and transactions). The database is hosted as a single, searchable Web site accessible to the public and organized by categories including agency, fund, and vendor."[8]

According to an analysis by Grover Norquist's watchdog group Americans for Tax Reform, since 2006, twelve states have passed "Google for Government" legislation and five governors have issued executive orders to post state spending online for public inspection.[9] In fact, in the wake of the historic federal stimulus bill, Arizona and other states are making the process of allocating stimulus money transparent, posting a record of state stimulus spending online. In California, Governor Arnold Schwarzenegger has taken the additional step of creating an inspector general to monitor the distribution of stimulus money. This movement toward accountability and transparency using the Web is an enormously positive trend that began in Washington, is catching on in select states, and deserves to be implemented nationwide.

Alaska: Posting the state checkbook on the Web

Governor Sarah Palin might have been a lightning rod for criticism during the 2008 presidential campaign, but it's hard to complain about her efforts to give Alaskans more information about the workings of their government. Similar to "Google for Government" projects in others states, Palin opted for a folksy fix that's characteristic of her frontier style: posting the state's check register online.

There's a subtle but important difference between Palin's effort and that of Kansas. While the KanView searchable database is comprehensive and intuitive, you have to know what you're looking for. Alaska's Web site, on the other hand, lets you play state treasurer. You can download Microsoft Excel or PDF spreadsheets that show much more than what the legislature appropriated. They show what the state actually *paid* to specific vendors, where those vendors are located (in or out of state), when the payment was made, and the category of service provided (travel, consulting, equipment, etc.).

For instance, I downloaded the state's vendor report for fiscal year 2008 and found that the governor's office paid $10,462.90 to a company called Alaska Executive Search, Inc., for program management and consulting services. Alaska's "Checkbook Online" site takes the additional step of listing departmental contacts at different state agencies. So if you have questions about a specific expenditure—like the above consulting fee paid by Palin's office—all you have to do is pick up the phone.

Palin's style might strike some as a politics at its worst, but her efforts to open up Alaska's ledgers strike me as government at its best.

Arizona: Using the Web to solicit input from the public and exchange best practices among government agencies

As the economic crisis worsened in 2008, governors across the country realized their states were in for a bumpy ride. The slumping economy led to a sharp decline in projected tax revenues, which meant huge budget deficits for the majority of state governments. There are only two ways to deal with a shortfall: raise taxes or cut spending. Neither solution is a popular one, but in many states both were necessary.

In confronting her state's economic crisis, Arizona governor Janet Napolitano, now the secretary of homeland security, had a novel idea. She decided to use the power of the Internet to help state agencies share and implement cost-saving measures and enable citizens to participate in the budget-balancing process. The Web site, Arizona Openness and Savings Strategies, is a statewide, intra-agency exchange for identifying areas for budget trimming. It allows state officials to swap ideas for cutting expenses, and it gives members of the public a bully pulpit to share their thoughts as well. The site offers department administrators a number of best practices and guides to implement them, including Web conferencing to cut back on business travel, digital imaging of documents to save space and office supplies, and other cost-cutting ideas from across state government. There are tips for state employees to help their agencies cut back and a feature that allows workers to submit their own ideas. The site also asks Arizona business owners to contribute solutions from the private sector, and it offers up-to-date information for citizens on the budgeting process and the governor's deficit-reduction efforts.[10]

During a difficult time, Napolitano erred on the side of giving the public more information and access. She opened up the process to public input and inspection, and she empowered officials at state agencies to collaborate on cost savings instead of bicker over limited resources.

Virginia: An online "Ideas Forum" for improving government and quality of life in the commonwealth

In chapters 8 and 9, I discussed how the Internet and online communities are changing the way Americans get their news and get involved in their communities. In Virginia, Governor Tim Kaine has used the blogosphere to change the way he manages state government.

In 2008, Kaine launched the Virginia Ideas Forum (http://www.ideasvirginia.gov), a Web site that allows Virginians to engage in a free-form virtual conversation about issues impacting the state and how best to solve them. The function of the site itself would be familiar to anyone who has a Facebook or MySpace page or who has read a blog on the Huffington Post. It allows users to create an account and an alias, and then participate in any number of online discussions on a range of issues, from state taxes to public transportation to the state's university system. Users can rate various ideas, sort ideas by subject, search previous posts, and make comments—just like on an ordinary blog. Of course, what makes this blog different is that the governor's office is monitoring the site for creative thinking and new ideas that might just become public policy.[11]

Kaine is on to something. Building on the Google model of government, the Virginia Ideas Forum is an exciting experiment in "Wiki-government." Just as the Wikipedia online encyclopedia is an open-source site that allows any user to edit its content, the Virginia Ideas Forum invites anyone and everyone to contribute. The idea is that the "wisdom of crowds"—millions of users clicking through the site—will help some great new ideas bubble to the surface.

It's unclear if Kaine's concept will catch on in Virginia or elsewhere or eventually lead to new policy solutions. But the concept is intriguing, and using technology to promote new energy and new ideas in state government is certainly a model for other administrations to follow.

New York City: A toll-free hotline to access important government services

Washington may have been ahead of the curve on its transparency efforts to make federal spending available to the public online. But municipal governments—New York City in particular—have been leaders in using technology to dramatically improve both public services and the confidence of citizens in their local government.

I've always admired New York City mayor Michael Bloomberg for being one of the best innovators in the nation. He made his billions by taking existing technology and putting it to use in ways no one else had previously thought to do. As Bloomberg's chief strategist during his run for mayor in 2001, I always clicked with him over the idea of leveraging technology in polling and politics. And ever since, I've been impressed by how he translated not just his management expertise but also his technological savvy into the most effective and efficient administration of a major American city.

One of the many campaign pledges that the mayor has made good on since 2001 was implementing a citywide 3-1-1 nonemergency hotline for New Yorkers. Baltimore was the first city in the nation to create a hotline for citizens to access city services in 1996. Chicago followed suit in 1999. But today, New York City's 3-1-1 system is by far the best in the nation. It's a twenty-four-hours-a-day, seven-days-a-week, 365-days-a-year telephone and Internet nerve center that fields some *forty thousand requests a day* from New Yorkers. From noise complaints to permits to garbage collection, 3-1-1 is a one-stop shop that has significantly improved service delivery in the city. And the Bloomberg administration is now expanding 3-1-1 services through its Web portal, http://www.NYC.gov.

As an adviser, I remember telling the mayor that this particular idea didn't test all that well. But it was a project that he wanted to push,

based on his experience developing and delivering information resources for companies and news organizations. In my view, the 3-1-1
system has made New York City's government more responsive, but it
has done more than improve city service delivery. It has also dramatically improved citizen confidence in their government. In fact, the city
council voted in 2008 to suspend a law that would have confined Mayor
Bloomberg to two terms, forcing him to leave office in 2009 without a
chance for the voters to speak their minds. That decision, I think, is
thanks to his deserved popularity in expertly managing city affairs.

This type of innovation—and leadership—is needed at all levels of
governance today. Officials from around the nation and the world have
taken note of Mayor Bloomberg's efforts to make it as easy as possible
for the public to ask for government service and receive it. According to
Paul J. Cosgrave, head of New York City's Department of Information
Technology and Telecommunications (aptly nicknamed DOITT), government representatives from thirty different countries on six continents
have visited the city's 3-1-1 call center to study how it works.[12]

UPROOTING CONFLICTS OF INTEREST

It's been a consistent theme throughout this book: our system of government and politics too often encourages and enables elected officials
to abuse their power, collude with lobbyists, and personally benefit from
the trust placed in them by voters. I've previously addressed many systemic solutions that will make it much more difficult for legislators,
judges, and others to pad their pockets or campaign coffers. The solutions below, enacted by reform-minded legislatures from Alaska to New
Mexico, are creative measures that draw an especially bright line distinguishing right behavior from wrong and create stiff penalties for those
who would violate ethics laws.

There's no question that punitive measures cannot and will not fix
the systemic problems we face. However, we have to restore the public's
faith in government, which has steadily eroded over the years. Everyday
Americans need to know that abuse won't be tolerated. These sensible,
meaningful, and serious reforms send the right message to members of
the public and public servants alike.

Connecticut: State officials convicted of ethics violations lose their pensions

In the last decade, several members of Congress have been convicted for ethics violations that range from political corruption to tax evasion. Former Alaska senator Ted Stevens is the most recent member to be tried and sentenced, after he was found guilty of covering up massive gifts that he received from an oil company. (Stevens's conviction was thrown out in the spring of 2009.) Stevens and his former colleagues will continue to receive generous federal pensions for the rest of their lives.

There's no reason that taxpayers should foot the bill for the pensions of crooked ex-lawmakers. It sends the wrong message to both members of Congress and the public. Washington should follow the lead of several states that have stripped state pensions from officials convicted of ethics transgressions.

Connecticut is the latest state to take this decisive step. Several years ago, the state was in the midst of a serious ethics crisis. Republican governor John G. Rowland resigned from office after pleading guilty to charges of corruption for accepting gifts and bribes and even having state workers make home improvements free of charge to his private property.[13] Several of his aides were also convicted, and state senator Ernest Newton was imprisoned in a separate bribery and corruption incident.

While Rowland served time in federal prison, his lieutenant governor, Jodi Rell, was left to pick up the pieces in the scandal-ridden state. She called for tough new ethics laws to turn the state around. Today, much to her credit and the bipartisan cooperation of the state's legislature, Connecticut has some of the toughest ethics laws in the nation.

In 2008, Governor Rell signed into law comprehensive ethics reform that implemented tough new measures. It makes it a crime for a state official to fail to report a bribe, and it puts new restrictions on political activity of aides to the state's top executives. It also allows a judge to revoke or reduce the pensions of state and local officials who are found guilty of abusing their elected or appointed government positions.[14]

According to the Connecticut Office of Legislative Research, only thirteen states have laws that strip state pensions from public servants who are convicted of certain crimes.[15] This should be a national standard. Washington, and the majority of states that lack this creative fix, should follow Connecticut's lead.

Alaska, New Mexico, and South Dakota: Tough laws that stop former lawmakers from using their positions and access for personal profit

Incumbency means not only a substantial federal pension but also the promise of certain rewards when members retire from Congress. A shocking number of former officeholders join the ranks of lobbying firms when they step down from elected office. Indeed, former members earn top dollar for the access they provide interest group clients to the corridors of power and to their former colleagues. According to an analysis by Public Citizen, a whopping 43 percent of members of Congress who retired between 1998 and 2004 became lobbyists—including one of every two retiring senators and a total of sixty-eight representatives.[16]

This is an obvious source of conflicts of interest. Members of Congress planning to retire can negotiate sweet deals with lobbying firms in exchange for doing the firm's bidding while still in office. Federal law currently mandates "cooling-off" periods for retiring members. Former representatives are banned from lobbying their former colleagues for a year after they leave office. Senators are required to abide by a two-year cooling-off period. But Washington could take a page from several states that have enacted tougher preventive and punitive measures.

- *Alaska* doesn't confine its cooling-off period to lobbying. The Frontier State's constitution bars former lawmakers from taking any elected or appointed roles that were created during their time in the legislature that would allow them to profit personally.[17]
- According to the National Conference of State Legislatures, *New Mexico* "permanently prohibits former public officers from representing a person in dealings with the government on a matter in which they participated personally and substantially while in office."[18] This guarantees that a powerful former legislator or political appointee can't go to bat for an industry or a corporation that he or she used to help regulate.

- **South Dakota** has taken the tough but appropriate measure of criminal-izing violations of its one-year ban on lobbying. Former lawmakers who ignore this ban could be convicted of a Class 1 misdemeanor.[19]

Louisiana: An ethics overhaul for the twenty-first century

A longtime Louisiana congressman, Billy Tauzin (who switched from being a Democrat to being a Republican after fifteen years in the House), once famously said, "Half of Louisiana is under water, and the other half is under indictment."[20] The state has never quite been able to shake the famously corrupt image cultivated by its notorious Depression-era gover-nor Huey Long. That is, until now.

For years, Louisiana has consistently ranked at the bottom of ethics lists compiled by good-government watchdogs. It had some of the lowest standards for financial disclosure in the nation and incredibly lax laws governing the conduct of state officials. In 2006, the Center for Public Integrity's analysis of state ethics laws ranked Louisiana at forty-fourth in the nation.[21] In 2002, the Better Government Association's Alper Integrity Index ranked the state forty-sixth.[22]

All that changed in 2008, when Governor Bobby Jindal called the legislature into special session to deal specifically with the ethics issue. Jindal called for and ultimately signed a series of bills that provide the toughest ethics oversight in the state's history. Among the reforms, Louisiana closed loopholes that allowed elected officials to receive free tickets to sporting events and unlimited food and drinks from lobbyists. The new laws require officials to recuse themselves in the case of a con-flict of interest, and it requires nearly all state and local officials to post detailed financial disclosure information online.[23] The net result is that Louisiana today likely has the toughest ethics laws in the nation.

My point here is less about a specific reform that Louisiana insti-tuted and more about the *idea* of reform. If a Republican governor in a southern, traditionally Democratic, and famously corrupt state can make ethics reform a reality, so, too, can Congress, as well as the many states around the nation that badly need to restore dignity to their state capitals and confidence in the minds of their constituents.

Louisiana summoned the bipartisan willpower to give Baton Rouge a face-lift. Other states should muster similar courage and follow Governor Jindal's example.

GROWING GOVERNMENT, FROM THE GRASS ROOTS UP

An unresponsive Congress and uncompetitive elections have forced many Americans to simply tune out of civic life. But democracy—and especially our federal democracy—depends on an engaged public to make informed decisions and participate fully in our democratic institutions. Citizen groups and public officials in several states are pursuing initiatives that they hope will improve dialogue and participation at the state and local levels.

Kentucky: The Civic Literacy Initiative of Kentucky, a state-sponsored effort to invest in an informed citizenry

According to a 2006 study by the National Center for Education, only 27 percent of the nation's twelfth graders were proficient in civics. An American Bar Association poll in 2005 found that only 55 percent of Americans could name the three branches of government.[24] Declining civic literacy is a highly disturbing trend. And it's one that deserves a multipronged approach. On the one hand, citizens groups and the grass roots can do their part to enhance public dialogue and increase involvement in community affairs. But there's a role for government, too.

State officials in Kentucky have smartly identified civic literacy as a policy priority. In 2004, the Kentucky General Assembly created the nonpartisan Civic Literacy Initiative of Kentucky (CLIK) to identify an action plan that would improve basic knowledge about government and enhance citizen participation throughout the state. Over the following two years, Secretary of State Trey Grayson convened summits throughout Kentucky and in other southern states to solicit input from public officials, community advocates, and students. The result of this successful outreach was a 2006 report, "Rediscovering Democracy," which outlined a series of steps for the state to dramatically improve civic literacy.

Not surprisingly, Kentucky is now focusing on improving civic education in schools and is supporting teachers in this regard. CLIK created a Kentucky Teacher Network for Excellence in Civic Education, "to provide civic educators across the Commonwealth with a collaborative environment where the expansion of civic knowledge and effective teaching methods are paramount."[25]

Kentucky's approach to the civic literacy crisis is forward thinking, collaborative, and could be a model for a national initiative. After all, this isn't a state or regional problem.

Connecticut: The Connecticut Community Conversations Project, a grassroots effort to enhance citizen engagement

Far too many communities and states in America follow the oligarchic model of government perfected in New York. I remember the first time I went to Albany, when I was still a teenager, having worked on a successful state assembly campaign in 1970. I quickly realized that the coinage of "three men in a room" running the state—the governor, the speaker of the assembly, and the state senate majority leader—very accurately described the structure of decision making in New York State. Even today, individual members of the state legislature have little to no influence. See the recent stalemate in the state senate, where the absence of a leader for the chamber effectively shut down state government in the summer of 2009. There is rarely public debate; no public record is kept of votes cast. Indeed, as long as a legislator shows up in Albany one day, he or she can effectively give a proxy to the leadership, and the "three men" can cast votes on the legislator's behalf, legally or not.

This kind of centralized decision making is contrary to the very concept of government of the people, by the people, and for the people. Many citizens groups have launched efforts to combat this democratic degradation over the years. One of the most successful has been the Connecticut Community Conversations Project.

Public Agenda, a good-government group in Connecticut, partnered with several other nonprofits in 1997 to improve public dialogue in the state on education quality and the public school environment. The model is relatively simple: create a nonpartisan space where a diverse group of people can solve problems and build consensus around issues, first in small groups, then in larger coalitions. Those coalitions then provide a feedback mechanism for local government officials and policy makers. They also provide citizens with a new avenue of engagement in the civic process and a greater sense of ownership and investment in their communities.

The Connecticut Community Conversations Project has since been implemented by eighty cities and towns, which have together held more than forty community conversations involving thousands of citizens. Bridgeport, Connecticut, has particularly embraced this model, which is now being applied to issues other than public education. Researchers found that as a result of the community conversations, politics in Bridgeport is more collaborative, business leaders are more engaged in community affairs, leadership is more inclusive, and city policies have been more sustainable thanks to a citizenry active in developing those policies. The researchers noted that "public engagement has become embedded in the life of the community" and "it is by all accounts relatively rare to find behind-the-scenes decision-making by a small group of elites."[26]

It's hard to imagine a community conversation at the national level. But improved dialogue at the local level would certainly percolate up to improve the discourse on issues that confront the nation as a whole.

CONCLUSION
Democracy, Reborn

This book is about more than making our political process more responsive. And it's about more than American democracy. To be sure, I very much hope the ideas and arguments I have put forth will contribute to the essential cause of strengthening our civic institutions. But there's another issue—perhaps a larger issue—at stake.

In two of my earlier books, *The Power of the Vote* and *Declaring Independence*, I offered my perspective on how we must make our system more open and more inclusive. I also wrote about the core values of democracy, liberty, and freedom and about how an expansive and flexible democratic system makes us a stronger country and makes others around the world look to us, and our system of government, as a source of inspiration and emulation. As I write this, protesters in Iran continue to take to the street in mass demonstrations against their government's fraudulent election on June 12, 2009. While the long-term outcome of the street demonstrations is not yet known, we must acknowledge that these Iranians who yearn for a more open society most likely look to the United States as a representation of their aspirations for the country. This is not because the United States has actively tried to convince Iran's citizens that American-style democracy is their best hope. Quite the contrary;

Iranians came to that conclusion on their own, which speaks to the power of our system of government in and of itself to inspire democratic reform across the globe.

If America is to continue to be a democratic beacon for the rest of the world, we must have a democratic system that really works. But let's be honest. Today, we don't.

When you read the wiretap transcripts of Illinois governor Rod Blagojevich discussing his plans to award Barack Obama's vacated Senate seat to the highest bidder—among other alleged activities—it's hard not to shake your head in disbelief. Amazingly, Blagojevich refused to step down while pleading his case. Could this really be happening in the Land of Lincoln? As that story, as well as breaking news of financial fraud, was plastered across headlines at the end of 2008, Thomas Friedman, the Pulitzer Prize–winning *New York Times* columnist, noted that a foreigner asked him, "How corrupt is America?" The person, a respected businessman from Hong Kong, told Friedman that American democracy "itself is in trouble. . . . It is hard for America to take its own medicine that it prescribed successfully for others. There is no doctor anymore. The doctor himself is sick."[1]

The nation was reportedly suffering from a political scandal, the largest Ponzi scheme ever perpetuated, the potential bankruptcy of the Big Three auto companies, and the wavering spirits of once-prestigious capital markets—simultaneously. How high could unemployment—already at the highest levels in three decades—go? Could General Motors go under? How could a governor brazenly extort payment for a political appointment? How could Bernie Madoff, a man who had earned the trust of legions of savvy financiers, expert investors, and hedge fund managers, bilk so many for so long? Were they stupid or greedy or lazy or complacent, or some combination thereof? What's more chilling than the answers to the questions is that the questions even had to be raised at all. They are indicative of our current malaise. They ultimately reveal our utter failure to understand our own behavior. America has indeed grown ill.

When communism fell and the Berlin Wall was torn down, the United States appeared to be the leading light toward a world with a better understanding of what was right. We were the pacesetters for freedom and the envy of aspiring democracies. Our standing through-out the world has been reduced because of our continual bad judgment— not just bad judgment in unpopular policies such as the war in Iraq or our refusal to participate in discussions about world climate change, but because of the devaluation and degradation of our most precious asset, our democracy. It seems like the very pillars of our brilliantly conceived form of government have been wobbling on a shaky foundation. How can we call ourselves a beacon to the world if we don't have a fair, democratic system? How can we influence better governance on a global scale if our own system is so flawed? The crucial element of American democracy is that it was started with the idea of "imperfection." And that's the prime reason it was designed to be flexible, to be organic, and to embrace change. Lately, the system has been stuck, entrenched in the interests of incumbent politicians, lobbying special interests, lazy media, and an uninspired citizenry. Our weaknesses have become self-evident. We will be an even weaker nation if our democratic system becomes less responsive to new notions about governance and progressive change.

Chris Patten, the last British governor of Hong Kong and a former politician, has an uncanny feel for America's current stasis in today's world. Yet he, like me, sees there is reason for hope: "Fixing what happens at home should be the easy part of the agenda. To promote freedom and democracy abroad, it is essential to recognize that this is not a 'pick and mix' policy."[2] The first step is to fix how we practice democracy at home.

How we govern ourselves, how we implement the tenets of our Constitution, speaks volumes not just about our current mood but also about our national character. We need to have a democracy that works and solves our difficult issues. We also need a centrist coalition that can come to agreement on the major issues affecting Americans.

That said, having a model democracy doesn't mean much if it doesn't confront head-on our country's most pressing problems. We could have a great democratic system but if our country is falling apart, what country will look to us as a standard? Liberal and conservative columnists have debated the current fiscal crisis, and the causes and culprits are many. But the bottom line is that we've been fiscally irresponsible, using the system to plunge ourselves deeper into debt. It's as if our Treasury Department treated the world's credit markets as a giant ATM. Tax cuts? No problem. Billions for war in Iraq and Afghanistan? No problem. Who's going to pay for all this? Our children and grandchildren and our great-grandchildren?

Let me explain how dire the situation is. We've experienced a precipitous decline that makes it difficult to calculate our real obligations. As of October 2008, the total outstanding debt was $10.5 trillion, which is approximately 73 percent of our gross domestic product. This amounts to a share of more than $35,000 per citizen. You can look at those digital debt clocks and snicker. But it's rising every day. According to the nonpartisan Concord Coalition, "Budget deficits are back for as far as the eye can see. This alone is a very serious development. Of more concern, however, is that politicians in Washington are not even working on a plan to bring the deficit under control. Instead, they have indiscriminately cut taxes, increased spending, allowed budget enforcement rules to expire and ignored the long-term dangers of large chronic deficits."[3]

Peter G. Peterson, the former commerce secretary, set up a foundation in 2008 with $1 billion in seed money to spread the alarm about our growing fiscal crisis. The Peterson Foundation indicated that we were far worse off than even the Concord Coalition calculated, largely because of future obligations. The foundation reported, "The financial statements show approximately $56.4 trillion in debts, liabilities, and unfunded promises for Medicare and Social Security versus the Federal Reserve's estimate of a total household net worth of $56.5 trillion, both as of September 30, 2008."[4] The figures were not indicative of the year's fourth quarter, where there was an additional toll taken by more market declines, bailout packages, and record deficits. Foundation president and CEO David M. Walker concluded, "Given more recent developments, it's clear that America now owes more than its citizens are worth." Warren Buffett put it succinctly: "This country is consuming more than it is producing." We are a nation of spenders, not savers, and we are now beginning what economists are predicting to be a long, dark nightmare.

The spillover effect of too much borrowing and too many obligations to bond holders here and in other countries is that our credit standing is devalued. Hence, we have less money to fund and sustain defense and our most sacred entitlements, including Social Security, Medicare, and Medicaid. These are third-rail items, issues that Republicans and Democrats alike will not touch. But soon, they will be forced to do so. Michael Leavitt, the former secretary of health and human services who finished his term at the end of 2008, said that health care could be "a nation-ruining issue." Without fundamental reforms, the average American household's health care spending, including the portion of its taxes that pays for Medicaid and Medicare, will go from 23 percent to 41 percent over the next two decades. Further, the current recession (and thus the decrease in the average person's income) will make the Medicare Part A trust fund deplete several years sooner than previously expected. Leavitt says it is "predictable" that the traumatizing economic turbulence we face, by increasing Americans' insecurity, will make reforming entitlements more challenging.[5]

At the end of the day, Congress approves and appropriates spending, and the evidence shows that there is a shared responsibility on both sides of the aisle for all of our ill-conceived policies. The American public largely agrees with my view. The two-party system has become basically meaningless to those folks who want to see problems solved. In 2007, I conducted a series of polls for the Aspen Institute that examined the public's opinion of the current two-party system. The results were shocking: 60 percent said that our country was headed in the wrong direction, and 80 percent said that U.S. relations with the world had worsened over the past five years. While more than half of voters thought bipartisanship was very important, 70 percent believed that the two major parties disagreed on most issues and hardly ever worked together. And this was a year before our congressional leadership bitterly disagreed on whether to advance funds to save General Motors, Chrysler, and Ford—and a new poll in 2009 found that opinion had not changed much.

Ever since 9/11, the nation has used its own fear of terrorism as an excuse to essentially give the military a blank check. We fund new technology and advanced weapons programs, many of which are necessary, but some of which are not. Much of this part of the budget goes to prop up the defense industry, and some of it is pure pork, doled out to contractors who supply jobs or contributions to sitting members of Congress. We do need a strong defense, and this is never an inexpensive proposition. But the bottom line is that our fighting forces are under-staffed and underfunded while pricey, high-tech contracts have re-mained in the budget. Why would a congressman or senator be more concerned about building a new bomber than about getting adequate protective gear to constituent-soldiers stationed in Baghdad?

It's not simply that money corrupts; a disengaged citizenry corrupts, too. As a nation, we have endured the misconduct of leaders who approved torturing prisoners at the Abu Ghraib prison, near Baghdad. Whether the conduct was illegal or legal, the photos of the prisoners' treatment shifted international public opinion and put our soldiers at greater risk—but the vast majority of voters have not demanded a sig-nificant change in policy. Our government placed accused terrorists in the prison at Guantánamo Bay and detained them for years, without trial, but we are content to leave the politicians to decide when and how to suspend the writ of habeas corpus—and when to restore it. Besides that, the government disregarded the law prohibiting wiretaps without court orders, dismissing concerns about liberty based on politicians' claims that listening in on private conversations might lead to Osama bin Laden's cave in the hills of Pakistan, or some other supposed threat.

I don't think anyone really feels the methodology we have for choos-ing elected officials is fair. From the presidency on down to the least vis-ible congressional seats, we've seen how money and old-school backroom politics have tainted the system. Serious candidates must march in lock-step within a party's boundaries and platforms; worse, they must bow to the whims of political action committees and special interests. The judicial system—from the attorney general's office through the federal courts—reeks of political partisanship, where ideology is beginning to tip the scales of justice. If this continues to occur, fewer and fewer of our most talented people will want to go into public service. The media—the last critical link in our delicate chain of checks and balances—have lost much of their independence and clout, and have shirked many of their responsibilities in calling attention to wrongdoing. The American press is no longer the standard-bearer it once was. Solid investigative reporting is giving way to indiscriminant, unqualified columnists and bloggers more interested in gossip than real news.

As the system has broken down, as our institutions have become compromised, we've seen how it has affected our ability to serve the public. Regulatory agencies are weakened; congressional oversight falls short; and we find ourselves worrying about many of the things we've taken for granted. Our food is more likely to be tainted, drugs are recalled, health care is unavailable to the poor and elderly, educational standards are lax; indeed, there has been a breakdown of normalcy in our society. Our children have been polled, and they do not necessarily envision a living standard that is better than their forebears. Perhaps more alarming, researchers are predicting for the first time in a century that the next generation may be the first to see life expectancies actually decrease.

Despite our faults—and there are many—in November 2008 there was a glimmer of the spirit that has made America a unique place. As Chris Patten put it, "The 2008 Democratic and presidential campaigns kindled enthusiasm on every continent. . . . It is what lifted the spirits of so many people outside the United States—observing democracy in action—wholly irrelevant to government in their own lands, at best no more than its equal, at worst an inferior article."[6]

Three organizations have done much to spread America's model of democracy, maintaining outposts and doing work in as many as a hundred foreign venues. The National Endowment for Democracy was created in 1983 to strengthen democratic institutions around the world through nongovernmental efforts. Led by an independent board of directors, it makes hundreds of grants each year to support pro-democracy groups in Africa, Asia, central and eastern Europe, Latin America, the Middle East, and the former Soviet Union. Both U.S. political parties have also set up international democracy-promotion initiatives. The National Democratic Institute works to support and strengthen democratic institutions worldwide by promoting citizen participation, openness, and accountability in government. The International Republican Institute advances freedom and democracy worldwide by developing political parties and civic institutions and promoting open elections, good governance, and the rule of law. It is critical that these three efforts continue and are expanded, but as useful and as important as they are, we need to invest just as much in reinvigorating the process of democracy at home.

Throughout this book, I've tried to provide an inside look at American democracy at a crossroads. At this point in our history, I am occasionally in despair, but I remain an optimist. I do not believe that our system is fractured beyond repair. So I've described our system of electoral democracy and the functions of government, that is, how the political system was conceived by the founders and how it should serve the public good. I've explained how this system was twisted into a game to be played for personal profit, and why past, narrow attempts at reform have failed to reengage citizens in the process. Finally, and most important, I've proposed real, politically feasible fixes to these problems that I believe will appeal to people with a wide range of political perspectives. That's where you come in.

Lawyers—and lots of politicians start life as lawyers—are taught the meaning and importance of pro bono publico, in the public good, to take on cases and causes without personal profit because there are greater stakes involved. For the most part, the people I have met and know in government care deeply about the nation's future; they have the fundamental desire to improve the lives of their constituents; they want to do the right thing. I've shared in these pages the solutions that I think any politician, of any party, could support for the public good. Elected officials need you—America's citizens—to put these solutions and the full power of American democracy into action.

If I have learned anything as a consultant and as an adviser, it is that people around the world are desperately interested in who we are and what we do. If I leave one lesson from this book, it is that our democracy is the most important and yet most fragile one on earth. Unless we seek to restore, enhance, and revitalize it every day, we are jeopardizing the cause of freedom and liberty, which we all hopefully believe is most precious. I certainly do.

NOTES

INTRODUCTION

1. *"This Week* Transcript: Brown, Corker, Gibbs," ABC News, December 28, 2008, http://www.abcnews.go.com/print?id=6537109.

1. SHOW THE MONEY

1. Sam Stein, "Mark Penn's Firm Paid $4.3 Million by Clinton Campaign," Huffington Post, February 6, 2008, http://www.huffingtonpost.com/2008/02/06/mark-penns-firm-paid-4_n_85192.html.

2. Matthew Mosk, "McCain Got Loan by Pledging to Seek Federal Funds," *Washington Post*, February 16, 2008, http://www.washingtonpost.com/wp-dyn/content/article/2008/02/15/AR2008021503639.html.

3. Brian Stelter, "The Facebooker Who Friended Obama," *New York Times*, July 7, 2008, http://www.nytimes.com/2008/07/07/technology/07hughes.html?pagewanted=1&partner=permalink&exprod=permalink.

4. Jeff Zeleny and Patrick Healy, "Obama Shows His Strength in a Fund-Raising Feat on Par with Clinton," *New York Times*, April 5, 2007, http://www.nytimes.com/2007/04/05/us/politics/05obama.html.

5. Carla Marinucci, "Obama's Savvy Internet Campaign," *San Francisco*

Chronicle, April 5, 2007, http://www.sfgate.com/cgi-bin/article.cgi?f=/c/a/2007/
04/05/OBAMA.TMP.

6. Center for Responsive Politics, "Donor Demographics: Contribution
Size," Open Secrets, February 9, 2009, http://www.opensecrets.org/pres08/
donordems.php?sortby=N.

7. Anthony Corrado, "Money in Politics: A History of Federal Campaign
Finance Law," *The New Campaign Finance Sourcebook* (Washington, D.C.:
Brookings Institution, 2005), 7.

8. Mark Memmott and Jim Drinkard, "Election Ad Battle Smashes Record
in 2004," *USA Today*, November 25, 2004, http://www.usatoday.com/news/
washington/2004-11-25-election-ads_x.htm.

9. Federal Election Campaign (FEC), Presidential Campaign Finance,
http://www.fec.gov/DisclosureSearch/mapApp.do?cand_id=P00000001&
searchType=&searchSQLType=&searchKeyword=; Evan Tracey, TNS Media
Intelligence/Campaign Media Analysis Group, "Role of Advertising in the 2008
U.S. Presidential Campaigns," http://s3.amazonaws.com/thearf-org-aux-assets/
downloads/cnc/ad-effectiveness/2008-11-06_ARF_AE_TNS.pdf.

10. Marketing Trees 2008, *Advertising Age*, http://adage.com/marketer
trees08/, by subscription only.

11. Statement of Senator Dianne Feinstein before the Rules and Administration Committee, U.S. Senate, June 20, 2007, http://rules.senate.gov/hear
ings/2007/062007FeinsteinOpen.pdf.

13. Statement of Senator Dick Durbin before the Rules and Administration
Committee, U.S. Senate, June 20, 2007, http://rules.senate.gov/hearings/2007/
Durbin062007.pdf.

13. Andrei Scheinkman, G. V. Xaquin, and Stephan Weitberg, "The Ad
Wars," *New York Times*, December 1, 2008, http://elections.nytimes.com/2008/
president/advertising/index.html.

14. Stephen J. Farnsworth and S. Robert Lichter, *The Nightly News Night-
mare: Network Television's Coverage of U.S. Presidential Elections 1988–2004*
(Lanham, Conn.: Rowman and Littlefield Publishers, 2007), p. 44.

15. "Dean: Special Interests Have Hold over Kerry," CNN.com, February
1, 2004, http://www.cnn.com/2004/ALLPOLITICS/01/31/elec04.prez.main/
index.html.

16. Center for Responsive Politics, "Lawyers and Lobbyists Sector Totals to
Candidates," Open Secrets, January 5, 2009, http://www.opensecrets.org/pres08/
sectors.php?sector=K; Center for Responsive Politics, "Summary Data for John
McCain," Open Secrets, February 9, 2009, http://www.opensecrets.org/pres08/
summary.php?cycle=2008&cid=N00006424.

17. Center for Responsive Politics, "Lawyers and Lobbyists Sector Totals to Candidates"; Center for Responsive Politics, "Summary Data for Barack Obama," Open Secrets, February 9, 2009, http://www.opensecrets.org/pres08/summary.php?cycle=2008&cid=N00009638.

18. ABC News, "Clinton to Return Hsu-Linked Cash," September 10, 2007, http://blogs.abcnews.com/theblotter/2007/09/clinton-to-retu.html.

19. Brody Mullins, "Donor Bundling Emerges as Major Ill in '08 Race," *Wall Street Journal*, October 18, 2007, http://online.wsj.com/article/SB119267248520862997.html.

20. Ibid.

21. Ibid.

22. Center for Responsive Politics, "Bundlers, Barack Obama," Open Secrets, February 9, 2009, http://www.opensecrets.org/pres08/bundlers.php?id=N00009638.

23. Center for Responsive Politics, "Bundlers, John McCain," Open Secrets, February 9, 2009, http://www.opensecrets.org/pres08/bundlers.php?id=N00006424&cycle2=2008&goButt2.x=10&goButt2.y=7&goButt2=Submit.

24. Thomas E. Mann, "A Collapse of the Campaign Finance Regime?" *Forum* 6, no. 1 (April 2008).

25. FEC, Presidential Campaign Finance.

26. Jose Antonio Vargas, "Ron Paul Beats Own Fundraising Record," *Washington Post*, Trail, December 17, 2007, http://blog.washingtonpost.com/the-trail/2007/12/17/ron_paul_beats_own_fundraising.html.

27. Robert H. Frank, "Untying a Knot in Campaign Finance," *New York Times*, July 6, 2008, http://www.nytimes.com/2008/07/06/business/06view.html.

28. Michael Luo and Griff Palmer, "In Fine Print, a Proliferation of Large Donors," *New York Times*, October 20, 2008, http://www.nytimes.com/2008/10/21/us/politics/21donate.html?hp.

29. Center for Responsive Politics, "Presidential: Joint Fundraising Committees," Open Secrets, http://www.opensecrets.org/pres08/jfc.php.

30. Sakura Saunders and Ben Clarke, "Media Money," Corpwatch, August 25, 2004, http://www.corpwatch.org/article.php?id=11504.

31. Gail Robinson, "The Ad Race," *Gotham Gazette*, September 10, 2000, http://www.gothamgazette.com/iotw/polads/.

2. BREAK UP THE PARTIES

1. Larry J. Sabato, "Why We Are Courting Disaster in Next Year's Presidential Primaries," University of Virginia Center for Politics, Crystal Ball, February 8, 2007, http://www.centerforpolitics.org/crystalball/print.php?article=LJS2007020801.

2. Peter Slevin, "Mich. Primary Move Splits Democrats," *Washington Post*, October 9, 2007, http://www.washingtonpost.com/wp-dyn/content/article/2007/10/08/AR2007100801511_pf.html.

3. Dan Balz, "At the Breaking Point?" *Washington Post*, Trail, August 9, 2007, http://blog.washingtonpost.com/the-trail/2007/08/09/now_what.html.

4. Hugh Gregg, "History of the New Hampshire Primary," *Nashua* (N.H.) *Telegraph*, December 8, 2003, http://www.nashuatelegraph.com/apps/pbcs.dll/article?AID=/20031208/NEWS0803/31208015.

5. Chris Nammour, "2004 Democratic Primaries: Overview of the Primary Process," *The NewsHour with Jim Lehrer*, December 15, 2003, http://www.pbs.org/newshour/vote2004/primaries/sr_primary_overview.html.

6. David S. Broder, "The Democrats' Dysfunctional Calendar," *Washington Post*, August 31, 2006, http://www.washingtonpost.com/wp-dyn/content/article/2006/08/30/AR2006083002732.html.

7. Iowa Caucus 2008, "About the Iowa Caucuses," http://www.iowacaucus.org/iacaucus.html.

8. Pew Center on the States, "2008 Primary in Review," July 2008, http://www.pewtrusts.org/uploadedFiles/wwwpewtrustsorg/Reports/Election_reform/Primary_2008_FINAL.pdf.

9. Rhodes Cook, "The 'Controversial' Caucuses," University of Virginia Center for Politics, Crystal Ball, May 29, 2008, http://www.centerforpolitics.org/crystalball/article.php?id=FRC2008052901.

10. "Rep. Levin Welcomes Senate Introduction of Presidential Primary Reform Bill," press release, Office of Representative Sandy Levin, September 6, 2007, http://www.house.gov/apps/list/press/mi12_levin/PR090607.shtml.

3. MAKE EVERYONE A SWING VOTER

1. Clifford Krauss, "Congressional Roundup," *New York Times*, May 13, 1992.

2. *New York Times* 2008 exit poll, http://elections.nytimes.com/2008/results/president/exit-polls.html.

3. CNN.com 2004 exit poll, http://www.cnn.com/ELECTION/2004/pages/results/states/US/P/00/epolls.0.html.

4. CNN.com 2008 exit poll, http://www.cnn.com/ELECTION/2008/results/polls/#USP00p1.

5. Andrew Kohut, "Post-Election Perspectives," Pew Research Center Publications, November 13, 2008, http://pewresearch.org/pubs/1039/post-election-perspectives.

6. Hendrik Hertzberg, "Pile Up," *New Yorker,* April 16, 2007, http://www.newyorker.com/talk/comment/2007/04/16/070416taco_talk_hertzberg.

7. Thomas Jefferson to George Hay, 1823, in Paul Leicester Ford, ed., *The Writings of Thomas Jefferson*, vol. 10, *1816–1826* (New York: G. P. Putnam's Sons, 1892–99), 264.

8. Frequently Asked Questions, National Archives and Records Administration, http://www.archives.gov/federal-register/electoral-college/faq.html.

9. Tom Brokaw, "Sip and Spin," op-ed, *New York Times,* August 17, 2007, http://www.nytimes.com/2007/08/17/opinion/17brokaw.html.

10. "Highest Rated Presidential Debates: 1960 to Present," Nielsen Wire, October 6, 2008, http://blog.nielsen.com/nielsenwire/media_entertainment/top-ten-presidential-debates-1960-to-present/; "63.2 Million Watched McCain and Obama's Second Debate," Nielsen Wire, October 8, 2008, http://blog.nielsen.com/nielsenwire/media_entertainment/632-million-watched-mccain-and-obamas-second-debate/.

11. "FEC Takes Final Action on Six Matters," press release, FEC, February 27, 2009, http://www.fec.gov/press/press2009/20090227MUR.shtml.

12. Project Vote, "Restrictive Voter Identification Requirements," *Issues in Election Administration*, Policy Brief No. 8, March 23, 2007, http://projectvote.org/fileadmin/ProjectVote/Policy_Briefs/Project_Vote_Policy_Brief_8_Voter_ID.pdf.

13. Myrna Pérez, "Voter Purges," Brennan Center for Justice, New York University School of Law, September 30, 2008, http://www.brennancenter.org/content/resource/voter_purges/.

14. Ian Urbina, "States' Actions to Block Voters Appear Illegal," *New York Times*, October 8, 2008, http://www.nytimes.com/2008/10/09/us/politics/09voting.html?hp.

15. Wendy R. Weiser, "Are HAVA's Provisional Ballots Working?" Brennan Center for Justice, New York University School of Law, March 29, 2006, http://www.brennancenter.org/page/-/d/download_file_39043.pdf.

16. Editorial, "New Standards for Elections," *New York Times,* November 7, 2004, http://people.csail.mit.edu/rivest/voting/press/nyt/2004-11-07%20NYT%20New%20Standards%20For%20Elections.pdf.

17. "Absentee and Early Voting Laws," Early Voting Education Center at Reed College, October 23, 2008, http://earlyvoting.net/states/abslaws.php.

18. Jill Lepore, "Rock, Paper, Scissors: How We Used to Vote," *New Yorker*, October 13, 2008, http://www.newyorker.com/reporting/2008/10/13/081013fa_fact_lepore.

19. National Popular Vote, http://www.nationalpopularvote.com.

20. Editorial, "Sidestepping the Electoral College: California Should Join the National Popular Vote Movement, Which Seeks to Reform the Presidential Election System," *Los Angeles Times*, August 18, 2008, http://articles.latimes.com/2008/aug/18/opinion/ed-elections18.

21. National Popular Vote.

22. Bruce Ackerman and Ian Ayres, "Campaign Reform's Worst Enemy," op-ed, *New York Times*, July 6, 2002, http://www.nytimes.com/2002/07/06/opinion/campaign-reform-s-worst-enemy.html.

23. Wendy Weiser, Michael Waldman, and Renée Paradis, "Universal Voter Registration: Policy Summary," Brennan Center for Justice, New York University School of Law, 2008, http://brennan.3cdn.net/27dfe0578eaa840369_glm6bne8d.pdf.

24. Project Vote, "Restrictive Voter Identification Requirements."

25. "Why Do We Vote on Tuesday?," Why Tuesday?, 2008, http://www.whytuesday.org/answer.

26. "Likely Rise in Voter Turnout Bodes Well for Democrats," Pew Research Center, July 10, 2008, http://people-press.org/report/?pageid=1336.

27. Oskar Garcia, "ACORN Office in Vegas Raided in Voter-fraud Probe," Associated Press, October 7, 2008, http://www.usatoday.com/news/politics/2008-10-07-3243380519_x.htm.

4. KILL THE SAFE SEATS

1. Lydia Saad, "Congress' Approval Rating Ties Lowest in Gallup Records," Gallup, May 14, 2008, http://www.gallup.com/poll/107242/Congress-Approval-Rating-Ties-Lowest-Gallup-Records.aspx.

2. Center for Responsive Politics, "Election Stats: Election Cycle 2004," Open Secrets, http://www.opensecrets.org/bigpicture/elec_stats.php?cycle=2004.

3. Center for Responsive Politics, "Election Stats: Election Cycle 2006," Open Secrets, http://www.opensecrets.org/bigpicture/elec_stats.php?cycle=2006.

4. Center for Responsive Politics, "Money Wins Presidency and 9 Out of 10 Congressional Races in Priciest U.S. Election Ever," Open Secrets, Novem-

ber 5, 2008, http://www.opensecrets.org/news/2008/11/money-wins-white-house-and.html.

5. Center for Responsive Politics, "Political Parties Overview," Open Secrets, 2008, http://www.opensecrets.org/parties/index.php.

6. Ian Urbina, "Popular Ohio Democrat Drops Out of Race, and Perhaps Politics," *New York Times*, February 14, 2006, http://www.nytimes.com/2006/02/14/politics/14ohio.html.

7. Jonathan E. Kaplan, "Cegelis Refuses to Endorse Duckworth after Primary," *Hill*, March 28, 2006, http://thehill.com/campaign-2008/cegelis-refuses-to-endorse-duckworth-after-primary-2006-03-28.html.

8. In 2004, the DSCC handpicked Oklahoma representative Brad Carson to run for his state's open Senate seat, making it one of the committee's top targets for that election cycle. The DSCC's nod of approval and promise of campaign cash instantly gave Carson national attention that he didn't necessarily deserve. Carson lost the race to Republican Tom Coburn by a whopping 12 percent.

9. Center for Responsive Politics, "Election Stats: Election Cycle 2006."

10. This section (as well as chapter 1) draws heavily on research compiled by the Center for Responsive Politics, an indispensable resource for data that demonstrates the influence of money in politics. Its Web site, Open Secrets (http://www.opensecrets.org), is an accessible, fascinating, and vast source for anyone who wishes to learn more about special interests and how they pervade our politics. While CRP has a legislative agenda that you may or may not agree with, its compilation and organization of information from thousands of campaign finance reports speaks for itself.

11. Center for Responsive Politics, "Different Races, Different Costs: Election Cycle 2006," Open Secrets, http://www.opensecrets.org/bigpicture/incad.php?cycle=2006.

12. Center for Responsive Politics, "Where the Money Came From: Election Cycle 2006," Open Secrets, http://www.opensecrets.org/bigpicture/wherefrom.php?cycle=2006.

13. Center for Responsive Politics, "Top In-State vs. Out-of-State," Open Secrets, http://www.opensecrets.org/bigpicture/instvsout.php.

14. Alan Fram, "Number of Political Action Committees Hits Record," Associated Press, March 14, 2009, published at http://www.huffingtonpost.com/2009/03/14/number-of-political-actio_n_174933.html.

15. National Conference of State Legislatures, http://www.ncsl.org/Default.aspx?TabID=746&tabs=1116,115,788#1116 (accessible to registered members only).

16. Editorial, "Angry Voters," *USA Today*, May 15, 2008, http://www.usato day.com/printedition/news/20080515/edtwo15.art.htm.

17. David D. Kirkpatrick, "Senate Measure Puts Spotlight on Fund-raising," *New York Times*, January 20, 2007, http://www.nytimes.com/2007/01/20/us/politics/20ethics.html?n=Top/Reference/Times%20Topics/People/L/Landrieu, %20Mary.

18. Conor Kenny, "Capital Crimes: How Our Current Campaign Finance System Breeds Political Corruption," *In These Times,* July 31, 2006, http://www.inthesetimes.com/article/2732/capital_crimes/.

5. SERVE THE PEOPLE

1. Richard S. Dunham, Eamon Javers, and Lorraine Woellert, "Shakedown on K Street," *BusinessWeek*, February 20, 2006, http://www.business week.com/magazine/content/06_08/b3972054.htm.

2. "House Dems Who Changed Their Vote to Support FISA Bill, Giving Immunity to Telcos, Received, on Average, $8,359 in PAC Contributions from Verizon, AT&T, and Sprint," press release, MapLight.org, June 24, 2008, http://www.maplight.org/FISA_June08.

3. Citizens Against Government Waste, "Pork-Barrel Report," 1991–2009, http://www.cagw.org/site/PageServer?pagename=reports_porkbarrelreport.

4. Lawrence M. Krauss, "McCain's Science Earmark Error: Millions to Study Grizzly Bear DNA Is a 'Waste of Money,' McCain Says. Wrong," *Los Angeles Times*, October 28, 2008, cited at http://www.climatesciencewatch.org/index .php/csw/details/mccain_palin_misrepresenting_science_projects.

5. Senate Republican Policy Committee, "Legislative Notice: S.1— Honest Leadership and Open Government Act of 2007," August 2, 2007, http://rpc.senate.gov/public/_files/L26S1HonestLeadershipOpen Govt080207CJ.pdf.

6. Thomas D. Elias, "Many Earmarks Are Beneficial," *Long Beach* (Calif.) *Press-Telegram*, March 21, 2009, http://www.presstelegram.com/opinions/ci_11967988.

7. Susan Crabtree, "Rangel to File Complaint Against Self—First Official Greivance Since 2004," *Hill*, July 22, 2008, http://thehill.com/leading-the-news/rangel-to-file-complaint-against-self–first-official-grievance-since-2004-2008-07-22.html.

8. Editorial, "Jack Abramoff, Jack Abramoff . . . ," *New York Times*, February 28, 2008, http://www.nytimes.com/2008/02/28/opinion/28thu2.html.

9. "Senator Says His Aide Wrote Terri Schiavo Memo: Florida Republican

Confirms Authenticity of GOP Talking Points, Obtained by ABC News," ABC News, March 2005, http://abcnews.go.com/Politics/Schiavo/Story?id=600937& page=2.

10. Lisa Lerer, "Fannie, Freddie spent $200M to Buy Influence," Politico, July 16, 2008, http://www.politico.com/news/stories/0708/11781.html.

11. Lindsay Renick Mayer, Center for Responsive Politics, "Fannie Mae and Freddie Mac Invest in Democrats," Open Secrets, July 16, 2008, http://www.opensecrets.org/news/2008/07/top-senate-recipients-of-fanni.html.

12. Bethany McLean, "Fannie Mae's Last Stand," *Vanity Fair*, February 2009, http://www.vanityfair.com/politics/features/2009/02/fannie-and-freddie 200902.

13. Albert B. Crenshaw, "High Pay at Fannie Mae for the Well-Connected: Many Former Officials Landed Jobs There," *Washington Post*, December 23, 2004, http://www.washingtonpost.com/wp-dyn/articles/A21138-2004Dec22.html.

14. Martin Wolf, "Is America the New Russia?" *Financial Times*, April 14, 2009, http://www.ft.com/cms/s/0/09f8c996-2930-11de-bc5e-00144feabdc0.html.

15. Eliot Spitzer, "The Regulatory Charade," Slate, April 1, 2009, http://www.slate.com/toolbar.aspx?action=print&id=2215055.

16. Statement by Senator Carl Levin before the Committee on Homeland Security and Governmental Affairs, U.S. Senate, January 21, 2009, http://hsgac.senate.gov/public/_files/012109Levin.pdf

17. Testimony of Chairman Christopher Cox, U.S. Securities and Exchange Commission, before the Committee on Oversight and Government Reform, U.S. House of Representatives, October 23, 2008, http://oversight.house.gov/documents/20081023100525.pdf.

18. John Samples, *The Fallacy of Campaign Finance Reform* (Chicago: University of Chicago Press, 2006), p. 254.

19. Public Citizen, "History of the Lobbying Disclosure Act," July 26, 2005, http://www.lobbyinginfo.org/laws/page.cfm?pageid=15.

20. Kate Phillips, "Revisiting the Heated Debate Exchange on Lobbying," *New York Times*, Caucus, August 4, 2007, http://thecaucus.blogs.nytimes.com/2007/08/04/revisiting-the-heated-debate-exchange-on-lobbying/.

21. Eliza Newlin Carney and Bara Vaida, "Shifting Ground," *National Journal*, March 30, 2007, http://www.nationaljournal.com/about/njweekly/stories/2007/0330nj1.htm.

22. Ibid.

23. Robins Air Force Base, http://www.robins.af.mil/.

24. Gretchen Morgenson, "He Doesn't Let Money Managers Off the

Hook," *New York Times*, April 11, 2009, http://www.nytimes.com/2009/04/12/business/12gret.html.

25. Testimony of Chairman Christopher Cox before the Committee on Oversight and Government Reform.

26. Brian M. Reidl, "The Stop Over-Spending Act: A Real Opportunity to Limit Spending," Heritage Foundation WebMemo no. 1132, June 19, 2006, http://www.heritage.org/Research/Budget/wm1132.cfm.

27. Andrew Taylor, "Senate's 'Holds' Are Secret Bill-Stoppers," Associated Press, September 18, 2006, as cited at Office of Representative Tom Coburn, U.S. House of Representatives, http://coburn.senate.gov/public/index.cfm?FuseAction=LatestNews.NewsStories&ContentRecord_id=c7d85c5f-802a-23ad-417d-f5008c710670&Issue_id=.

28. "Conference Committee," U.S. Senate Glossary, http://www.senate.gov/reference/glossary_term/conference_committee.htm.

29. Carl Hulse, "In Conference: Process Undone by Partisanship," *New York Times*, September 26, 2007, http://www.nytimes.com/2007/09/26/washington/26memo.html?scp=2&sq=%22conference%20committee%22&st=cse.

30. National Conference of State Legislatures, "Ethics Committees and Ethics Commissions: What's the Difference?" http://www.ncsl.org/programs/ethics/whats_the_difference.htm.

31. Thomas E. Mann and Norman J. Ornstein, *The Broken Branch: How Congress Is Failing America and How to Get It Back on Track* (New York: Oxford University Press, 2006), p. 236.

32. Ron Suskind, "Faith, Certainty and the Presidency of George W. Bush," *New York Times Magazine*, October 17, 2004, http://www.nytimes.com/2004/10/17/magazine/17BUSH.html?ex=1255665600&en=890a96189e162076&ei=5090&partner=rssuserland.

6. TAKE POLITICS OUT OF JUSTICE

1. Matthew J. Streb, ed., *Running for Judge: The Rising Political, Financial, and Legal Stakes of Judicial Elections* (New York: New York University Press, 2007), p. 7.

2. Hal A. Linde, quoted in Norman L. Greene, "Perspectives from the Rule of Law and International Economic Development: Are There Lessons for the Reform of Judicial Selection in the United Sates?," *Denver University Law Review,* vol. 86, no. 1 (2008), http://law.du.edu/documents/denver-university-law-review/Greene.pdf.

3. Ibid., p. 3.

4. Ibid., p. vii.

5. Stacy Forster, "Justices Decry Outside Campaign Ads," *Milwaukee Journal Sentinel*, March 9, 2008, http://www.jsonline.com/story/index.aspx?id=726161.

6. Editorial, *Los Angeles Times*, November, 26, 2004.

7. Ruth Marcus, "The Attack Ads Will Come to Order," *Washington Post*, May 30, 2007, http://www.washingtonpost.com/wp-dyn/content/article/2007/05/29/AR2007052901638.html.

8. Ibid.

9. Joel Connelly, "Attack Ads on Judges Paid for by Fake PACs," *Seattle Post Intelligencer*, September 11, 2006, http://seattlepi.nwsource.com/connelly/284607_joel11.html.

10. Streb, *Running for Judge*, p. vii.

11. Ibid.

12. Adam Liptak, "Looking Anew at Campaign Cash and Elected Judges," *New York Times*, January 29, 2009, http://www.nytimes.com/2008/01/29/us/29bar.html?_r=2&sq=liptak&st=nyt&oref=slogin.

13. Adam Liptak and Janet Roberts, "Campaign Cash Mirrors a High Court's Rulings," *New York Times*, October 1, 2006, http://www.nytimes.com/2006/10/01/us/01judges.html?_r=1&oref=slogin.

14. "Caperton v. Massey," Brennan Center for Justice, New York University School of Law, January 5, 2009, http://www.brennancenter.org/content/resource/caperton_v_massey/.

15. James Sample, "Justice for Sale," *Wall Street Journal*, March 22, 2008, http://online.wsj.com/article/SB120614225489456227.html.

16. Ibid.

17. "Wisconsin Supreme Court Election Raises New Questions About Judicial Election Reform," press release, Brennan Center for Justice, New York University School of Law, April 2, 2008, http://www.brennancenter.org/content/resource/wisconsin_supreme_court_election_raises_new_questions_about_judicial_electi/.

18. "First in the Nation: NC's Judicial Public Financing Program," North Carolina Voters for Clean Elections, http://www.ncvce.org/index.php?page=ncjudicialprogram.

19. William Fortune and Penny J. White, "Judicial Campaign Oversight Committees' Complaint Handling in the 2006 Elections: Survey and Recommendations," *Judicature*, March–April 2008, 235, http://www.ajs.org/ajs/publications/Judicature_PDFs/915/White_915.pdf.

20. Michael J. Gerhardt, *The Federal Appointments Process: A Constitutional and Historical Analysis* (Durham, N.C.: Duke University Press, 2003), p. xv.

21. Jerry Markon, "The Politics of the Federal Bench," *Washington Post*, December 8, 2008, http://www.washingtonpost.com/wp-dyn/content/article/2008/12/07/AR2008120702703.html.

22. Charlie Savage, "Liberal Legal Group Is Following New Administration's Path to Power," *New York Times*, December 10, 2008, http://www.nytimes.com/2008/12/11/us/politics/11network.html.

23. Gerhardt, *Federal Appointment Process*, p. 140.

24. "Gary Bauer Claimed Republicans Too 'Gentlemanly' to Block Judicial Nominees," Media Matters for America, March 1, 2005, http://mediamatters.org/items/200503010003.

25. George J. Mitchell, "The Not-So-Secret History of Filibusters," *New York Times*, May 10, 2005, http://www.nytimes.com/2005/05/10/opinion/10Mitchell.html?_r=1&scp=1&sq=George%20J.%20Mitchell%20%20Not-so-Secret&st=cse&oref=slogin.

26. Betsy Palmer, "Evolution of the Senate's Role in the Nomination and Confirmation Process: A Brief History," CRS Report for Congress, Congressional Research Service, March 29, 2005, http://digital.library.unt.edu/govdocs/crs/permalink/meta-crs-6156:1.

27. Ibid.

28. Ibid.

7. TAKE JUSTICE OUT OF POLITICS

1. Ted Kennedy, quoted in Suzanne Fields, "No Slouching Toward Confirmation," Real Clear Politics, June 5, 2009, http://www.realclearpolitics.com/articles/2009/06/05/no_slouching_toward_confirmation_96849.html.

2. U.S. Department of Justice, "An Investigation of Allegations of Politicized Hiring by Monica Goodling and Other Staff in the Office of the Attorney General," July 28, 2008, http://www.usdoj.gov/oig/special/s0807/final.pdf.

3. "Immigration Judges Lack Apt Backgrounds," *Los Angeles Times*, May 26, 2007, http://articles.latimes.com/2007/may/26/nation/na-usattys26.

4. U.S. Department of Justice, "Investigation of Allegations of Politicized Hiring."

5. Joe Palazzolo, "Political Test Applied to Hiring, Justice Report Finds," *Legal Times*, July 29, 2008, http://www.law.com/jsp/nylj/PubArticleNY.jsp?id=1202423334346.

6. Eric Lichtblau, "Report Assails Political Hiring in Justice Dept.," *New York Times*, June 25, 2008, http://www.nytimes.com/2008/06/25/washington/25justice.html.

7. David C. Iglesias, "Why I Was Fired," *New York Times*, March 21, 2007, http://www.nytimes.com/2007/03/21/opinion/21iglesias.html.

8. Jason Horowitz, "Prosecutor Makes a Meal of N.J. Senate Race," *New York Observer*, October 15, 2006, http://www.observer.com/node/39582.

9. Scott Horton, "U.S. Attorney in Wisconsin in the Hotseat," *Harper's*, April 6, 2007, http://www.harpers.org/archive/2007/04/horton-in-the-hotseat.

10. Donald C. Shields and John F. Cragan, "The Political Profiling of Elected Democratic Officials: When Rhetorical Vision Participation Runs Amok," ePluribus Media, February 18, 2007, http://www.epluribusmedia.org/columns/2007/20070212_political_profiling.html.

11. David B. Rivkin Jr. and Lee A. Casey, "No More Special Counsels," op-ed, *Washington Post*, October 29, 2005, http://www.washingtonpost.com/wp-dyn/content/article/2005/10/28/AR2005102801771_pf.html.

12. Charlie Savage, "Civil Rights Hiring Shifted in Bush Era: Conservative Leanings Stressed," *Boston Globe*, July 23, 2006, http://www.boston.com/news/nation/articles/2006/07/23/civil_rights_hiring_shifted_in_bush_era.

13. Nancy V. Baker, *Conflicting Loyalties: Law and Politics in the Attorney General's Office, 1789–1990* (Lawrence: University Press of Kansas, 1992).

14. William R. Yeomans, "An Uncivil Division," *Legal Affairs*, September–October 2005, http://www.legalaffairs.org/issues/September-October-2005/argument_yeomans_sepoct05.msp.

15. "Changing Tides: Exploring the Current State of Civil Rights Enforcement within the Department of Justice," Hearing before the Subcommittee on the Constitution, Civil Rights, and Civil Liberties, House Committee on the Judiciary, 110th Congress, 1st session, March 22, 2007, http://www.gpo.gov/fdsys/pkg/CHRG-110hhrg11034177/html/CHRG-110hhrg11034177.htm.

16. U.S. Department of Justice, "Investigation of Allegations of Politicized Hiring."

17. Richard B. Schmitt, "Sexuality Bias Seen at Justice Department," *Los Angeles Times*, July 29, 2008, http://articles.latimes.com/2008/jul/29/nation/na-justice29.

8. SHAKE UP OUR MEDIA

1. Edward R. Murrow, 1958, available at the Radio-Television News Directors Association, http://www.rtnda.org/pages/media_items/edward-r.-murrow-speech998.php.

2. Thomas Jefferson to Edward Carrington, 1787, in Andrew Lipscomb and Albert Bergh, ed., *The Writing of Thomas Jefferson, Memorial Edition*, vol. 6 (Washington, D.C.: Thomas Jefferson Memorial Association of the United States, 1903–4), p. 57.

3. James Goodale, "News Media and the Law," *New York Law Journal*, December 7, 1977, http://www.jamesgoodale.net/images/07.doc.

4. Douglass K. Daniel, "Study: False Statements Preceded War," Associated Press, January 22, 2008, cited at http://www.globalpolicy.org/security/issues/iraq/media/2008/0122falsestate.htm.

5. Rich Noyes, "When Watchdogs Snore: How ABC, CBS, and NBC Ignored Fannie and Freddie," NewsBusters, September 25, 2008, http://news busters.org/blogs/rich-noyes/2008/09/25/when-watchdogs-snore-how-abc-cbs-nbc-ignored-fannie-freddie.

6. Frank Ahrens, "Washington Post Co. Earnings Plummet in Third Quarter," *Washington Post*, October 31, 2008, http://www.washingtonpost.com/wp-dyn/content/article/2008/10/31/AR2008103101021_pf.html.

7. "The Changing Newsroom: Gains and Losses in Today's Papers," Pew Research Center, July 21, 2008, http://pewresearch.org/pubs/904/changing-newsroom.

8. "MSNBC Cleaves to Clinton Neckline Coverage Controversy," Media Matters for America, July 31, 2007, http://mediamatters.org/items/200708010003.

9. Clark Hoyt, "Urgent Issues, Buried in the Mud," *New York Times*, October 11, 2008, http://www.nytimes.com/2008/10/12/opinion/12pubed.html ?_r=1&pagewanted=2&n=Top/Opinion/Editorials%20and%20Op-Ed/Op-Ed/Contributors&oref=slogin.

10. Sherry Ricchiardi, "How the Media Abandoned Iraq: How America's Mainstream Media Has Let the Country's Third Longest War in History Slip Off the Radar Screen," *American Journalism Review*, June 4, 2008, http://www.globalpolicy.org/security/issues/iraq/media/2008/0604abandoned.htm.

11. "Big Events Eclipse the Issues," Project for Excellence in Journalism, Pew Research Center, http://journalism.org/node/12653.

12. James Rainey, "How Mayhill Fowler Got Online Scoops on Obama and Bill Clinton," *Los Angeles Times*, June 7, 2008, http://www.latimes.com/news/politics/la-na-fowler7-2008jun07,0,7012425.story.

13. Lee Hamilton, "Why We Need an Informed Citizenry," Center on Congress, Indiana University, http://www.centeroncongress.org/radio_commentaries/why_we_need_an_informed_citizenry.php.

14. Ricchiardi, "How the Media Abandoned Iraq."

15. "55% Say Media Bias Bigger Problem than Campaign Cash," Rasmussen Reports, August 11, 2008, http://www.rasmussenreports.com/public_content/politics/election_20082/2008_presidential_election/55_say_media_bias_bigger_problem_than_campaign_cash.

16. "Canvassing Campaign Media: An Analysis of Time, Tone and Topics," Project for Excellence in Journalism, Pew Research Center, October 22, 2008, http://pewresearch.org/pubs/1001/campaign-media.

17. If It's Sunday, It's Conservative: An Analysis of the Sunday Talk Show Guests on ABC, CBS, and NBC, 1997–2005," Media Matters for America, February 14, 2006, http://cloudfront.mediamatters.org/static/pdf/MMFA_Sunday_Show_Report.pdf.

18. "Is the Fairness Doctrine Fair Game?" Project for Excellence in Journalism, Pew Research Center, July 18, 2007, http://journalism.org/node/6571.

19. Ben H. Bagdikian, *The New Media Monopoly* (Boston: Beacon Press, 2004), p. 27.

20. Media Reform Information Center, November 11, 2008, http://www.corporations.org/media.

21. Robert W. McChesney and John Nichols, "Who'll Unplug Big Media? Stay Tuned," *Nation*, May 29, 2008, http://www.thenation.com/doc/20080616/mcchesney.

22. Lawrence K. Grossman, "Wanted: A New Breed of Media CEOs with Old-Fashioned Values (Television)," *Columbia Journalism Review*, January/February 2002, reprinted at *Entrepreneur*, http://www.entrepreneur.com/trade-journals/article/82776385.html.

23. Noam Cohen, "Blogger, Sans Pajamas, Rakes Muck and a Prize," *New York Times*, February 25, 2008, http://www.nytimes.com/2008/02/25/business/media/25marshall.html.

24. Pat Flannery, "Blogs Changing Political Discourse," Advertiser, May 25, 2006, http://theadvertiser.gns.gannettonline.com/apps/pbcs.dll/article?AID=/20060525/TECH01/605250301/1001/tech.

25. "Code of Ethics," Society of Professional Journalists, http://www.spj.org/ethicscode.asp.

26. Brad Stone, "A Call for Manners in the World of Nasty Blogs," *New York Times*, April 9, 2007, http://www.nytimes.com/2007/04/09/technology/09blog.html.

27. "A Bloggers' Code of Ethics," CyberJournalist.net, http://www.cyber journalist.net/news/000215.php.

28. Richard Perez-Pena, "Online Watchdog Sniffs for Media Bias," *New York Times*, October 15, 2008, http://www.nytimes.com/2008/10/16/arts/television/16spin.html?ref=arts.

9. WAKE UP, AMERICA

1. "Factoids," Saguaro Seminar: Civic Engagement in America, John F. Kennedy School of Government, Harvard University, http://www.hks.harvard.edu/saguaro/factoids.htm.

2. "Turnout in the World—Country by Country Performance," Institute for Democracy and Electoral Assistance, March 7, 2005, http://www.idea.int/vt/survey/voter_turnout_pop2.cfm.

3. "High Marks for the Campaign, a High Bar for Obama: Republicans Want More Conservative Direction for GOP," Pew Research Center, November 13, 2008, http://people-press.org/report/471/high-bar-for-obama.

4. Karlo Barrios Marcelo, "Media Use Among Young People in 2006," Center for Information and Research on Civic Learning and Engagement, December 2007, http://civicyouth.org/PopUps/FactSheets/FS07_Media Use.pdf.

5. "Volunteering in the United States," Corporation for National and Community Service, http://www.volunteeringinamerica.gov/viewprofile.cfm ?chartType1=1&chartType2=6&chartType3=3&chartType4=5&chartType5=2 &chartType6=4&&inline=inline.

6. "Army's Recruiting Lowest in Years," Associated Press, September 30, 2005, published at http://www.military.com/NewsContent/0,13319,77951,00. html.

7. Kimberly Hefling, "Army to Expand Recruiting Incentives," Associated Press, August 9, 2007, published at http://www.usatoday.com/news/topstories/2007–08–09–2117218834_x.htm.

8. Susanne M. Schafer, "Top Army Recruiter Weighs Fat Camp for Recruits," Associated Press, January 12, 2009, published at http://www.cnsnews.com/public/content/article.aspx?RsrcID=41812.

9. Laura House, "Amid Downturn, an Uptick in Doing Good," *New York*, December 14, 2008, http://nymag.com/news/intelligencer/52926/.

10. Micah L. Sifry and Andrew Rasiej, "Obama's Chief Tech Duties," Politico, December 11, 2008, http://www.politico.com/news/stories/1208/16445.html.

11. National Peace Corps Association, August 7, 2008, http://www.rpcv .org/pages/sitepage.cfm?id=1210.

12. National Commission on Terrorist Attacks upon the United States, *The 9/11 Commission Report: Final Report of the National Commission on Terrorist Attacks upon the United States* (New York: W. W. Norton, 2004), p. 18.

13. Richard Stengel, "A Time to Serve," *Time*, August 30, 2007, http://www .time.com/time/specials/2007/article/0,28804,1657256_1657317,00.html.

10. THE INCUBATORS

1. Jeffrey Schmalz, "New York Officials Shifting Blame in Struggle to Combat Corruption," *New York Times*, August 19, 1987, http://query.nytimes .com/gst/fullpage.html?res=9B0DE7DD1339F93AA2575BC0A961948260& scp=16&sq=new%20york%20state%20corruption&st=cse.

2. Ciara Torres-Spelliscy, "NYS 2008, Waiting for Campaign Finance Reform," Brennan Center for Justice, New York University School of Law, February 4, 2008, http://www.brennancenter.org/content/resource/nys_2008_ waiting_for_campaign_finance_reform.

3. "Californians and the Initiative Process," Public Policy Institute of California, November 2008, http://www.ppic.org/main/publication.asp?i=265.

4. "Under the Tarnish, Still Golden," *Economist*, April 2, 2009, http://www .economist.com/world/unitedstates/PrinterFriendly.cfm?story_id=13414116.

5. Scott P. Plotkin, "Welcome to California, the State of Dysfunction," *California Schools*, March 31, 2009, http://www.csba.org/NewsAndMedia/Publica tions/CASchoolsMagazine/2009/Spring/Departments/ScottSpring2009.aspx.

6. Jennifer Steinhauer, "Pinch of Reality Threatens the California Dream," *New York Times*, July 21, 2009, http://www.nytimes.com/2009/07/22/us/22calif .html?_r=1&hp.

7. Alexis de Tocqueville, *Democracy in America*, ed. Bruce Frohnen and trans. Henry Reeve (Washington, D.C.: Gateway Editions, 2002), p. 126.

8. Elizabeth Bryan, "Open the Books on Government Spending," Commonwealth Foundation, September 4, 2008, http://www.commonwealthfoun dation.org/node/963/print.

9. "State, Federal and Local Efforts to Increase Transparency in Government Spending," Americans for Tax Reform, August 29, 2008, http://www.fiscal accountability.org/userfiles/trnsp-memo.pdf.

10. State of Arizona, Openness and Savings Strategies, http://az.gov/oss.

11. State of Virginia, Virginia Ideas Forum, http://www.ideas.virginia.gov.

12. Paul J. Cosgrave, "Answers About 311, Part 2," *New York Times*, City

Room, September 11, 2008, http://cityroom.blogs.nytimes.com/2008/09/11/answers-about-311-part-2.

13. Michael Leahy, "A Look Back, and Up," *Washington Post*, June 17, 2007, http://www.washingtonpost.com/wp-dyn/content/article/2007/06/16/AR2007061601331.html.

14. "Governor Rell Signs Final Major Ethics Bill," press release, State of Connecticut Executive Chambers, June 18, 2008, http://www.ct.gov/governorrell/cwp/view.asp?A=3293&Q=417474.

15. Kristin Sullivan, "Pension Revocation Laws in Other States," Connecticut Office of Legislative Research, February 22, 2005, http://www.cga.ct.gov/2005/rpt/2005-R<->0190.htm.

16. "Members of Congress Increasingly Use Revolving Door to Launch Lucrative Lobbying Careers," press release, Public Citizen, July 5, 2007, http://www.citizen.org/pressroom/release.cfm?ID=1999.

17. Peggy Kerns, "Revolving Door Laws," National Conference of State Legislatures, November 2008, http://www.ncsl.org/programs/ethics/legisbrief-revolving.htm.

18. Ibid.

19. Ibid.

20. Nick Carey, "Fighting Corruption Is Hard Going in New Orleans," Reuters, August 13, 2008, http://features.us.reuters.com/cover/news/S1429240.html.

21. "Disclosure Ranking," Center for Public Integrity, April 17, 2006, updated January 2008, http://projects.publicintegrity.org/oi/db.aspx?act=rank.

22. "Governor Jindal Applauds BGA Ethics Ranking of LA as No. 5 in Nation, Up from No. 46, and Improving," press release, Office of Governor Bobby Jindal, October 27, 2008, http://gov.louisiana.gov/index.cfm?md=newsroom&tmp=detail&articleID=704.

23. "Governor Jindal Announces Accomplishments of Ethics Reform Special Session," press release, Office of Governor Bobby Jindal, February 26, 2008, http://gov.louisiana.gov/index.cfm?md=newsroom&tmp=detail&articleID=76.

24. Civic Literacy Initiative of Kentucky, http://civics.ky.gov/students.

25. Civic Literacy Initiative of Kentucky, http://civics.ky.gov/about.

26. Will Friedman, Alison Kadlec, and Lara Birnback, "Transforming Public Life: A Decade of Citizen Engagement in Bridgeport, CT," Public Agenda, Case Studies in Public Engagement, November 1, 2007, http://www.publicagenda.org/files/pdf/cape_bridgeport.pdf.

CONCLUSION: DEMOCRACY, REBORN

1. Thomas L. Friedman, "The Great Unraveling," *New York Times*, December 16, 2008, http://www.nytimes.com/2008/12/17/opinion/17friedman.html?scp=1&sq=%22Thomas%20Friedman%22%20%22Great%20Unraveling%22&st=cse.

2. Chris Patten, *What Next? Surviving the Twenty-first Century* (London: Allen Lane, 2008), p. 405.

3. "The Federal Budget," Concord Coalition, http://www.concordcoalition.org/learn/federal-budget.

4. "America Will Soon Owe More Than Its Citizens Are Worth," press release, Peter G. Peterson Foundation, December 15, 2008, http://www.pgpf.org/newsroom/press/owe/.

5. George F. Will, "Dr. Leavitt's Scary Diagnosis," *Washington Post*, January 1, 2009, http://www.washingtonpost.com/wp-dyn/content/article/2008/12/31/AR2008123102778.html.

6. Patten, *What Next?*, p. 405.

ACKNOWLEDGMENTS

For me, this book represents more than just an effort to write about changes that need to be made in the American political system. Rather, it is a culmination that represents a conclusion of more than thirty years of high-level involvement with and observation of the American political system. And it involves a series of ideas, thoughts, concepts, and recommendations that I have been mulling over and reviewing in my mind for the better part of ten or fifteen years. So, in a certain sense, I couldn't be more pleased or proud to write this book.

That being said, this work is immeasurably better because of the work of numerous people who have strived to improve my ideas, clarify my thinking, and better my prose.

First, I would like to thank Carly Cooperman, who organized a large and diverse group of researchers who helped me to flesh out much of what is herein. I would also like to thank Dan Gerstein and Ben Yarrow for their trenchant review of the manuscript. Their comments, suggestions, thoughts, and recommendations have made this book incalculably better. Eve Kessler acted as the conscience for this book, questioning, criticizing, reviewing, and gently and sometimes even not so gently forcing me to revise deeply held sentiments. Doug Garr similarly reviewed and revised much of my thinking as the book went forward and deserves an extraordinary amount of credit as well. While numerous researchers contributed to this book, Lisa Stahl, Stacy Aab, and Karen Ahn played a particularly large role in consistently providing substantive information on many of the topics discussed.

Finally, I would like to thank Robin Dennis, my editor, whose impact can be seen on every page of the book. Robin acted as a sounding board, an adviser, and a facilitator and I am profoundly grateful to her for her judgment, her vision, and her unflagging support in making this a much better book than it otherwise would have been.

In the end, of course, the work is my own and needs to be judged on its merits. One of the most unexpected and happiest parts of this process has been working with so many intelligent, thoughtful, and even idealistic people.

INDEX

ABOUT THE AUTHOR

DOUGLAS E. SCHOEN has been a Democratic Party adviser for the past thirty years. A founding partner of Penn, Schoen, and Berland, he was former president Bill Clinton's strategic consultant during the 1996 reelection campaign and has advised New York City mayor Michael Bloomberg, Indiana governor Evan Bayh, and former British prime minister Tony Blair. The author or coauthor of six books, including *Declaring Independence*, he lives in New York City.